Global Business

Global Business

An Economic, Social, and Environmental Perspective

Nader H. Asgary

Bentley University

Dina Frutos-Bencze

Saint Anselm College

Massood V. Samii

Southern New Hampshire University

Hossein Varamini

Elizabethtown College

INFORMATION AGE PUBLISHING, INC.
Charlotte, NC • www.infoagepub.com

Library of Congress Cataloging-in-Publication Data

A CIP record for this book is available from the Library of Congress
http://www.loc.gov

ISBN: 978-1-64113-803-1 (Paperback)
       978-1-64113-804-8 (Hardcover)
       978-1-64113-805-5 (ebook)

Contents

SECTION I

GLOBAL AND ECONOMIC ENVIRONMENTS

SECTION II

POLITICAL, CULTURAL, AND ETHICAL ENVIRONMENTS

SECTION III

FIRM-LEVEL MANAGEMENT

SECTION IV

CURRENT ISSUES IN GLOBAL BUSINESS

Introduction

In the past four decades, significant economic, political, and cultural chang-es have made international business more exciting, complex, and challeng-ing. The revolution in technology and communications has reduced the barriers among countries, firms, and citizens of the world. These changes have created opportunities for great expansions in international business and flattened the playing field for small and medium size companies by allowing them easier access to global markets. The continuous emergence of new economies and commercial markets, especially the development of the economies of China, Eastern Europe, India, Russia, Brazil, and many others have created opportunities for international business activities, but have also created potentially formidable challenges. While the globaliza-tion trend has created a much larger middle class world-wide, it has also contributed to a few populist movements and nationalist tendencies in some countries. Non-Governmental Organizations (NGOs) and global institutions have progressed in highlighting and addressing issues such as poverty, the environment, human rights, migration and corruption. Three main critical issues, environmental changes, poverty and human dignity, and ethics and corporate social responsibility are at the forefront of the challenges that need serious attention.

   Global Business: An Economic, Social, and Environmental Perspective is the second edition of the book titled *Foundations of International Business* pub-lished by Information Age in 2015. We have approached the second edi-tion from a forward looking perspective by incorporating economic, social, and environmental issues, which have strong links to stakeholders and are

Global Business, pages vii–xiii
Copyright © 2019 by Information Age Publishing
All rights of reproduction in any form reserved.

guided by the triple bottom-line (TBL) concept. A TBL approach emphasizes the importance of Profit, People, and Planet, or PPP.

The Triple Bottom Line concept is highlighted throughout each chapter. Successful Multinational Enterprises (MNEs) are increasingly linking the company's profit maximization goal (the economic or **P**rofit maximization components) to the social well-being of the community and corporate social responsibility initiatives of the firm (the social or **P**eople components), as well as the environmental consideration of scarce resources, climate change and sustainability (the environmental or **P**lanet component). This approach enables readers to assess global business opportunities and risks in a comprehensive and integral manner. We also have made important modifications in terms of content organization of this book, as described below.

Target Audience

The second edition of *Global Business: An Economic, Social, and Environmental Perspective* is a valuable stand-alone international business textbook for undergraduate and MBA courses such as international business, global strategy, and strategic management because it is more applied and less technical than some other textbooks.

In addition, the book is beneficial to anyone seeking to understand the basics of the international business environment. More than ever before, business strategists, managers and entrepreneurs need to incorporate all internal and external factors in the global business and consider the social and environmental consequences of their decisions. Therefore, we believe this book will be especially welcomed by faculty and students because of its succinctness, the updated reading lists, cases, and project recommendations. The topics presented in this new condensed way allow practitioners, scholars, and students of international business to have a broad understanding of the most relevant issues in a changing global environment.

Organization

This book is organized into four main sections: I. Global and Economic Environments; II. Political, Cultural, and Ethical Environments; III. Firm-Level Management; and IV. Current Issues in Global Business. Figure I.1 summarizes the four sections of the book and the central theme, the Triple Bottom Line concept.

Each chapter provides a theoretical background, real-world examples, applications, and implications of the concepts discussed. The structure of each chapter includes learning objectives, an opening case with questions,

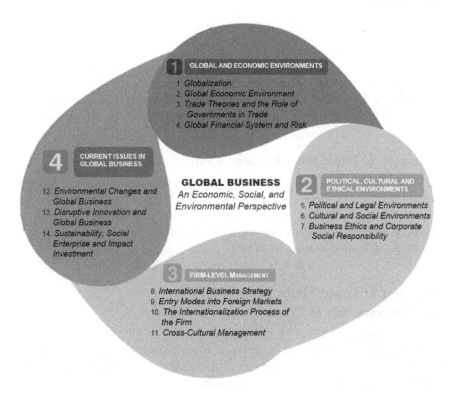

Figure I.1 Organization of the book.

debate issues, spotlight cases, a closing case with questions, chapter's key terms, additional questions and activities, and suggestions for further reading. While discussing essential theoretical and applied aspects of global business in a forward looking perspective, our aim has been to keep the book relatively short and user friendly to provide flexibility for faculty to add their own supplementary material.

Supplemental Materials for Instructors

The authors also provide PowerPoint slides and a test bank of short-answer questions for every chapter.

Section I—Global and Economic Environments

This section is includes four chapters that describe the concepts of globalization, trade theories, and the economic and financial environments.

Chapter 1: Globalization

This chapter discusses the determinants, consequences and trends of globalization. Globalization is one of the most widely used words in recent years, however, it is not a new concept. In addition, the key issues related to globalization are discussed, and arguments in favor and against the growth of interdependencies among the nations in recent decades are provided.

Chapter 2: The Global Economic Environment

This chapter discusses the key macroeconomic indicators and market characteristic of various regions of the world. It is crucial for managers or anyone doing business abroad to understand the implications of different economic systems and key macroeconomic indicators to determine which countries are attractive for business.

Chapter 3: Trade Theories and the Role of Governments in Trade

This chapter describes the benefits of trade through the exploration of the main theories of why nations trade. It also covers how governments restrict or promote trade. International trade impacts a country's economic growth, employment, and inflations rates.

Chapter 4: The Global Financial System and Risk

This chapter discusses the structure of the global financial system. The major institutions and workings of the international financial market are described. In addition, the functioning of currency markets as well as the factors that impact exchange rates are discussed. Finally, the challenges that the global financial system faces are analyzed.

Section II—Political, Cultural, and Ethical Environments

This section is composed of three chapters that deal with the institutional context in which global businesses is conducted.

Chapter 5: Political and Legal Environments

This chapter describes various political and legal systems and their impact on trade and business. These systems not only set regulatory standards, award subsidies and grants, impose taxes, quotas, and tariffs, they also create free trade agreements, common markets, and other political and economic unions. These activities impact capital flows and, by extension, the business world.

Chapter 6: Cultural and Social Environments

This chapter discusses socio-cultural aspects relevant to global businesses. The key characteristic of global business is the need to interact with people across national boundaries. A businessperson must understand foreign cultures to adjust to the local environment, avoid embarrassing mistakes, and improve the likelihood of success.

Chapter 7: Business Ethics and Corporate Social Responsibility

This chapter defines the concepts of business ethics, and the present history and applications of corporate social responsibility (CSR). The demand for businesses to conduct their business ethically and to be socially responsible has increased due to evolving communications, technological advancement as well as the expectations of the market participants. Besides bringing economic value to shareholders, modern companies are expected to support and advance the interests of their stakeholders.

Section III—Firm-Level Management

This section is composed of four chapters that present fundamental issues related to a firm's strategy, modes of entering into foreign markets, the internationalization process to create value for the multinational enterprise, and cross-cultural management.

Chapter 8: International Business Strategy

This chapter explains the process of strategic planning. Applications of the tripod model are also discussed. Strategy formulation is a complex process that requires building a vision for the future of the organization, evaluating the firm's core competence, determining its strength and weaknesses, as well as identifying the external environment in terms of opportunities and threats.

Chapter 9: Entry Modes into Foreign Markets

This chapter explains important factors in selecting entry modes and key aspects in their management. It details the circumstances in which each entry mode into a foreign market is most appropriate and the advantages and disadvantages that each provides. The choice of which entry mode to use in entering international markets should match a company's international strategy.

Chapter 10: The Internationalization Process of the Firm

This chapter describes the internationalization process as well as how value creation has been enhanced by internationalization. Companies internationalize their operations for different reasons. Such efforts provide a great potential for creating more value for the company. The continuous development of emerging markets has created not only great opportunities for international business activities, but also created stronger competitors from other countries.

Chapter 11: Cross-Cultural Management

This chapter discusses the effects of cultural and social environments on global business and present fundamental issues for successfully managing cross-culturally with a global mindset. In addition, the important determinants of cultures are discussed, and alternative strategies to effectively manage cultural differences are highlighted.

Section IV—Current Issues in Global Business

This section is composed of three chapters that present current issues in international business such as environmental change, technological aspects of global business, and sustainability and social enterprise.

Chapter 12: Environmental Changes and Global Business

This chapter focuses on various issues related to environmental changes, environmental degradation, and climate change. The primary key issues that could affect today's MNEs are global warming, depletion of natural resources, and high population levels. Given the growing importance of these challenges, global business has to incorporate their impact on operations and take proactive, and appropriate action.

Chapter 13: Disruptive Innovation and Global Business

This chapter discusses the concept of disruptive innovation and information and communication technologies (ICT). The emergence of ICT has increased transparency, decreased the cost of information flow across boundaries, and increased the volume and speed of information flow. Their impact on businesses is examined.

Chapter 14: Sustainability, Social Enterprise, and Impact Investment

This chapter discusses sustainable development, the concept of social enterprise, and impact investing. The Global Reporting Initiative (GRI) framework, and Social Return on Investment (SROI) concepts and their impact on businesses are also discussed. Finally, the role of technology in reducing waste and improving the efficiency of resources allocation is covered.

Acknowledgments

Dedicated to our families.

We would like to express our gratitude to Victoria Edwards, Anastassiya Sayenko, Shari Kain, and Wendy Sheaffer from Elizabethtown College for their significant contributions to the design and editing of the second edition of this book. The contributions of Brennan Delory, Devon Curtis, and Emily Malsch of Bentley University are also greatly appreciated. Dr. Pard Teekasap and Aida Garcia contributed to the first edition of this book, and we want to acknowledge them. We would also like to thank our administrative staff for their support during this process. Above all, we would like to acknowledge the contributions of our students who have made many constructive comments and suggestions to the various chapter drafts.

Finally, we would also like to thank our families for supporting us during the writing and editing process of the book. Dr. Asgary is grateful to his family and especially his wife, Jila, for their unconditional support and encouragement. Dr. Samii would like to thank his wife Farideh Namazi Samii for support and encouragement throughout the process. She was instrumental and a motivational force for him in this project in particular and generally for his career. Dr. Varamini thanks his family and especially his wife, Maryam, for their support and encouragement.

1

GLOBAL AND ECONOMIC ENVIRONMENTS

1. Globalization
2. Global Economic Environment
3. Trade Theories and the Role of Governments in Trade
4. Global Financial System and Risk

4

CURRENT ISSUES IN GLOBAL BUSINESS

12. Environmental Changes and Global Business
13. Disruptive Innovation and Global Business
14. Sustainability, Social Enterprise, and Impact Investment

3

FIRM-LEVEL MANAGEMENT

8. International Business Strategy
9. Entry Modes Into Foreign Markets
10. The Internationalization Process of the Firm
11. Cross-Cultural Management

2

POLITICAL, CULTURAL, AND ETHICAL ENVIRONMENTS

5. Political and Legal Environments
6. Cultural and Social Environments
7. Business Ethics and Corporate Social Responsibility

CHAPTER 1

Globalization

LEARNING OBJECTIVES

- Explain the concept of **globalization**, its driving factors, and implications.
- Understand the advantages and disadvantages of globalization for host and home countries.
- Become acquainted with the global political and economic structures and organizations involved in globalization.
- Evaluate the link between globalization and **Base of the Pyramid** challenges and opportunities.

Opening Case

Globalized Production and the Boeing 787 Dreamliner

Oct. 26, 2011—Aviation enthusiasts paid as much as $34,000 to board the Boeing 787 Dreamliner's first commercial flight, between Tokyo-Narita and Hong Kong. The aircraft, pictured in Figure 1.1, shows imported materials from

Global Business, pages 3–21
Copyright © 2019 by Information Age Publishing
All rights of reproduction in any form reserved.

countries such as South Korea, Sweden, and Italy to the United States for final assembly in Seattle, Washington. The Dreamliner demonstrates the level of integrated production feasible in our increasingly globalized world. However, it also offers a warning about the inherent risks and complexities. For example,

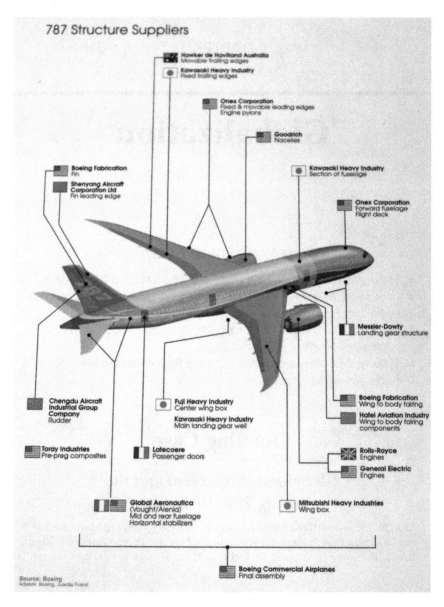

Figure 1.1 Overview of the Boeing 787's Components and Sourcing. *Source:* https://www.flickr.com/photos/niallkennedy/111073286

international and domestic supply changes delayed Boeing's first deliveries by six months. Despite additional delays to address various software problems and safety concerns, the model was continually plagued by hydraulic failures, engine problems, and cracking wings after its commercial launch. Industry insiders cited worldwide sourcing as the foundation of these issues. However, globalization made the creation of the Boeing 787 Dreamliner possible.

1. *Apart from the Boeing 787 Dreamliner, there are countless other globally-sourced products demonstrating international businesses' impact on our everyday lives. What are some examples? What countries are involved in the production and consumption of these goods?*

1.0   Introduction

Globalization is one of the most widely used words in recent years, but it is not a new concept. This chapter, explores globalization historically and conceptually, identifies its driving factors, and discusses its implications.

Most people view the increase in trade in recent decades as a sign of globalization, but trade among nations is nothing new. One can consider the agreement between Alexander the Great and Chandragupta Maurya in C.325 BCE at as the first step in establishing trade among the Mediterranean, Persia, India and Central Asia. Some scholars, such as Thomas Friedman, focus on early signs of globalization in 1492, when Columbus travelled west and the age of European seaborne empires began.[1]

The history of globalization can also be traced to Adam Smith, Karl Marx and Friedrich Engels. Their writings recognize science, technology and capitalism as the forces of globalization. A more recent work by Manuel Castells (2010), *The Rise of the Network Society*, defines the global economy as one "with the capacity to work as a unit in real time on a planetary scale".

Friedman divides the history of globalization into three separate eras in his book *The World is Flat*. Military forces drove global integration during the first era, or Globalization 1.0, from 1492 to 1800. Globalization 2.0 continued from 1800 to 2000, when multinationals drove globalization. According to Friedman, the first two eras were driven primarily by Europeans and Americans, whereas non-western individuals have primarily led Globalization 3.0, which goes from 2000 to the present day.

So, what is globalization? The renowned economist and Noble Prize winner Joseph Stiglitz defined globalization as follows:[2]

Globalization is the closer integration of the countries and peoples of the world... brought about by the enormous reduction of costs of transportation and communication, and the breaking down of artificial barriers to the flows of goods, services, capital, knowledge, and people across borders.

Globalization encompasses many things: the international flow of ideas and knowledge, the sharing of cultures, global civil society, and global environmental movement. (Stiglitz, 2007)

Dani Rodrik, also a renowned political economist, stated that the natural benchmark of globalization is to consider a world in which the markets for goods, services, and factors of production are perfectly integrated. Given the uneven distribution of economic opportunities and conditions within and across countries, he concludes that we are far from being fully integrated (Rodrik, 2008).

The **KOF Index** issued by the KOF Swiss Economic Institute (from the German name Konjunkturforschungsstelle) seeks to measure globalization economically, socially, and politically (see Figure 1.2). Countries with a high KOF index score, such as Canada, exhibit higher level of globalization than those with low scores, such as Sudan.

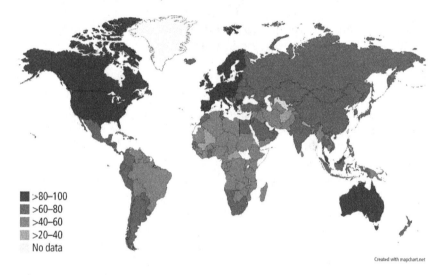

Created with mapchart.net

Figure 1.2 KOF Index of Globalization in 2016.[3]

1.1 Driving Factors Behind Globalization

In addition to understanding globalization conceptually and historically, it is important to understand the phenomenon's catalysts and implications. This section discusses in detail the following driving factors:

1. Communications and Transportation Technology
2. Trade Liberalizations

Several macro driving factors have helped the globalization process. Developments in **communications** and **transportation technology** have helped to reduce overall costs and improve communications. The Internet, teleconferencing, e-mail systems, and texting are examples of technological innovations in communications. These innovations enable us to know about products or services created in other regions and facilitate the exploration of new markets much faster than a few decades ago. The widespread use of uniform metal containers to ship goods, rather than loading a ship's hull with individual wooden crates, illustrates the advances made in transportation technology. Containerization reduced the per-ton loading cost of shipments, increased the number of items shipped simultaneously, and decreased theft, which, in turn, reduced insurance costs.

Another driving factor of globalization is **trade liberalization**. Many countries have reduced their barriers to trade and investment in order to access foreign markets and benefit from globalization. Many perceive economic liberalization as beneficial in the long run because it enables the introduction of new products and services to the market at lower prices, thereby increasing domestic competition. To attract private investment, a large number of developing countries have also made policy changes and other serious attempts toward **privatization**. Their efforts have helped expand global investment and the flow of funds across borders. **Foreign Direct Investment** (FDI) has increased in the form of **greenfield investment**, **mergers**, and **acquisitions**. These concepts are described in later chapters.

1.2   Major Implications of Globalization

1. Integrated performance standards for multinational enterprises
2. Cultural, social, and political changes
3. Economic opportunities and challenges
4. Reduction and elimination of barriers to movement of resources

The liberalization of the global financial system has led to further integration and convergence of financial performance standards for **multinational enterprises** (MNEs). For instance, many multinationals raise part of their capital by selling stocks or bonds in other countries. Another outcome of global financial integration has been the need to rethink corporate governance across borders.

The rapid and dynamic transformation of the economic landscape across the globe has had a significant impact on cultural, social, and political matters within and among countries. Globalization, which started with the concept of efficient allocation of economic resources by reducing and eliminating barriers to trade and investment, has led to various economic opportunities and created some challenges for business, governments, and people.

The reduction and elimination of **barriers to movement** of capital, goods, services, and, in some instances, labor (e.g., in the European Union) have provided opportunities for businesses to establish themselves throughout the world. **Regional Trade Agreements** (RTAs) are a means of reducing or eliminating barriers to movement. The number of trade agreements in force has increased significantly from 1950 to 2010, as evinced in Figure 1.3. These agreements enable MNEs to take advantage of lower input costs and expand their consumer markets.

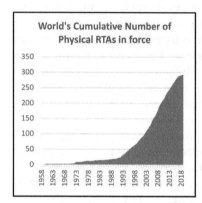
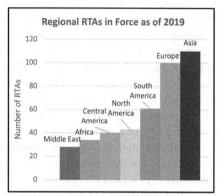

Figure 1.3 Cumulative RTAs (1958-2019) and Regional RTAs in force. *Source:* Adapted from data at http://rtais.wto.org/ui/PublicMaintainRTAHome.aspx

1.3 Major Components of Globalization

1.3.1 Globalization of Production

Corporations aim to maximize shareholder value through increased profits and efficiency. To this end, they search for locations where they can minimize the **cost of production** (labor, raw materials, capital, land, etc.) while maintaining an acceptable level of quality. Since a corporation is unlikely to find a single location that minimizes the costs of all of inputs, different phases of production commonly occur in different countries.

For example, although a product is designed in one country, its raw materials and intermediary goods may be purchased from several countries, assembled elsewhere, and sold in yet other nations. Corporations such as Boeing, General Motors (GM), and General Electric (GE) are good examples of companies that take advantage of national differences in the cost and quality of inputs by dispersing their production facilities in a number of different countries. An additional example is the McDonald's

SPOTLIGHT
Francis Fukuyama and Samuel P. Huntington on Westernization

In 1989, Francis Fukuyama published "The End of History?" as the Cold War drew to a close. He wrote, "we may be witnessing not just the end of the Cold War, or the passing of a particular period of postwar history, but the end of history as such: that is, the end point of mankind's ideological evolution and the universalization of Western liberal democracy as the final form of human government" and "the triumph of the West, of the Western idea, is evident first of all in the total exhaustion of viable systematic alternatives to Western liberalism" (Fukuyama, 1989).

By contrast, Samuel P. Huntington's article, "The Clash of Civilizations," rejects the notion that the world would become increasingly connected and homogenous. Instead, he reasoned the world's broadest cultural groups, or "civilizations," would seek to distinguish themselves more sharply and, as a result, come into conflict with one another.

Huntington identifies eight major "civilizations"—Western, Confucian, Japanese, Islamic, Hindu, Slavic-Orthodox, Latin American, and African—and claims conflict will occur between these civilizations on the basis of cultural differences. He predicts that the most intense conflict will occur in "fault lines" and "torn states." These regions do not have a single dominant culture but identify as two or more of the eight civilizations. Huntington cites Turkey as an example (Huntington, 1993).

Though more than twenty years have passed since their original publication, the articles written by Fukuyama and Huntington continue to influence contemporary debate.

Corporation, which routinely purchases different ingredients for its sandwiches (bread, sesame seeds, cheese, beef patties, etc.) from different countries for its restaurants in over one hundred countries.

Major Advantages of Globalized Production
- Lower Cost Labor for Production and Services
  - Examples
    - Low labor costs in China or Bangladesh;
    - Indian call centers
- Technical Expertise
  - Examples.
    - Indian physicians reading U.S. x-rays;
    - Global consulting firms (i.e., Deloitte)

1.3.2 Globalization of Markets

Rather than customizing their products and services to a small group of buyers, many global companies have used **economies of scale** to produce standardized products for global customers. This strategy allows them to charge a lower price and deliver more reliable products.

The resulting emergence of global markets for standardized consumer products, such as steel, chemicals, computers, semiconductors, pharmaceuticals, and telecommunications has had a significant impact on the growth of globalization.

Debate—Globalization

Economic growth and overall global prosperity have been noticeable in the last two decades. Notwithstanding the debate, the process has been moving forward and, by all indications, will continue in the foreseeable future.

However, the impact of globalization on the economies of host countries and home countries is one of the most debated and controversial issues regarding international economics and international business.

Pro	Con
International trade and investment have been instrumental in the economic growth of host countries where investment is flowing from home countries.	There have been considerable drawbacks both economically and socio-culturally for the host countries.

The list below summarizes the pros and cons of globalization based on the host and home country relationship.

Pros

- *Economic Growth.* Incentivizes economic growth of developing economies (host countries). Therefore, it will improve purchasing power of developing economies.
- *Higher Employment.* Creates employment through export and foreign direct investment in both developing and developed economies (host and home countries).
- *Cheaper Products.* Provides lower cost products for developed economies (home countries).
- *Innovation.* Globalization is also believed to stimulate innovation.

- *Global Marketplace.* Globalization leads MNEs to consider distant countries as places for producing or for looking for suppliers. The process is leading to the creation of one global marketplace.

Cons

- *Employment Loss.* The movement of jobs overseas may result in loss of employment in developed countries, and consequently prevent wage and salary increases. On the other hand, employment losses can also occur in developing countries when MNEs seek particular skills and increase domestic competition.
- *Competitive Pressure.* In developing countries the concern is that large multinationals may lead to increase competitive pressure on the local companies that are smaller and do not have enough resources to compete. For instance, in developing countries it would be difficult for smaller national retail stores to compete with Wal-Mart.
- *Loss of Sovereignty.* The existence of international trade agreements diminishes a country's sovereignty and freedom from external control by curtailing the ability to act in their own best interest. Small countries are particularly concerned that their dependence on a larger country for supplies and sales will make them vulnerable to the demands of a country they might oppose.
- *MNE Political Interference.* Large international companies may be so powerful that they can dictate the terms of their operations by getting involved in local politics.
- *Convergence.* Globalization brings convergence of work methods, social structures and even language, which might threaten local socio-cultural characteristics and traditions.
- *Environmental Risk.* Many developing countries do not have strict environmental laws and enforcement mechanisms. Therefore, the concern is that multinationals would move the polluting industries into the countries that either don't have environmental regulations or that are not enforcing those laws.
- *Growing Income Inequality.* While developing countries benefit from economic growth, the benefits are not distributed evenly. The global trend is that rich people are becoming richer and poor people are becoming poorer. In other words, the gap between rich and poor is widening

1.4   States and Sovereignty

The role that governments and institutions of civil societies play is essential for the development of a country.

States remain the primary actors for handling social and political externalities created by globalization. Powerful states use a range of foreign policy substitutes to advance their preferences into their desired outcomes. Non-state actors can still influence outcomes on the margins, but their interactions with the states are more nuanced than the globalization literature suggests. Globalization undercuts **state sovereignty**, weakening governments' ability to effectively regulate their domestic affairs (Drezner, 2001).

The political dimension of globalization is an important issue that can be viewed from two different perspectives:

1. The impact and the role of multinationals on the political process of host and home countries
2. The issue of the influence of the political structure of the country on the global business structure

In this context, **corruption** in international business activities has received considerable attention in recent years. The political system and environment of a country affect all the companies and their ways of doing business. The **political impact** is higher for international companies, since their presence in several countries means they are subjected to different political systems. It has been demonstrated that only international companies that accept and try to adapt to different political systems are the ones that succeed. On the other hand, many multinationals have an income that far exceeds the **gross national income** (GNI) of some of the developing countries in which they operate (see Figure 1.4). These concepts are expanded upon in later chapters, but it is important to note that an MNE could influence the internal political-economic process of the countries in which they operate.

For example, the Nigerian police provided Royal Dutch Shell with security in exchange for monetary and logistical support in the 1990s. However, their authority was often used to suppress groups protesting Shell's presence in the region (Center for Constitutional Rights, 2009).[4] Thus, developing nations may be wary of MNE interference in their domestic political affairs.

1.5 The Role of Global Institutions

Globalization has transformed the role of governments in two ways.

1. The traditional role of all players has been strained.
2. The capacity of governments and their non-governmental partners to deliver high quality public services has been challenged (Kettl, 2000).

Country/Corporation	Revenue (US$, bns)
1 United States	3,251
2 China	2,426
3 Germany	1,515
4 Japan	1,439
5 France	1,253
6 United Kingdom	1,101
7 Italy	876
8 Brazil	631
9 Canada	585
10 Walmart	482
11 Spain	474
12 Australia	426
13 Netherlands	337
14 State Grid	330
15 China National Petroleum	299
16 Sinopec Group	294
17 Korea, South	291
18 Royal Dutch Shell	272
19 Mexico	260
20 Sweden	251
21 Exxon Mobil	246
22 Volkswagen	237
23 Toyota Motor	237
24 India	236
25 Apple	234
26 Belgium	227
27 BP	226
28 Switzerland	222
29 Norway	220

Figure 1.4 Comparison of country and MNE revenue.

To accommodate for governments' inability to provide public services, global institutions and non-governmental organizations have become increasingly important.

Lin and Nugent defined an **institution** as a set of humanly devised behavioral rules that govern and shape the interaction of human beings by partially helping them to form expectations of what other people will do (Lin & Nugent, 1995). An institution provides several elements: formal and informal rules of behavior, means of enforcing rules, conflict resolution and supporting market transactions. Rodrik states that institutions can create or destroy incentives for individuals to engage in trade, invest in human and physical capital, and encourage innovation. Thus, institutions have always played an essential role in governmental regulation and business operations; however, their role has become more relevant since the advent of globalization. Technological developments have allowed for faster and easier transportation, communication, and trade between nations, and also led to the development of relevant institutions (WTO, 2004).

However, when local services are not provided, citizens tend to reject the idea of globalization. In developed nations, resistance to globalization often targets supranational organizations. For example, when Britain was determining whether or not to leave the European Union in 2016, "TAKE Control" was the main slogan of the "Vote Leave," a campaign asserting that participation in the European Union interfered with Britain's autonomy[5] (Economist, 2016). Scholars such as Dani Rodrik and Joseph Stiglitz argue that in order to be more internationalized, voters and citizens need to start thinking globally rather than locally (Rodrik, 2008).

1.6   Non-State Actors

Globalization has also led to the empowerment of **non-state actors**, such as:

- Multinational enterprises (MNEs)
- Non-governmental organizations (NGOs)
- Transnational activist networks

Increasing pressure and the desire of citizens of developing countries to attain the quality and living standards of developed nations, supported by globalization forces, have caused a major transformation in most developing governments. There are cases in which institutions and other non-state actors have filled the governance void. In **developed countries**, institutions and private organizations are integrated into society, while in **developing countries** they are still evolving.

The role of nationally representative and globally responsive governments is crucial in addressing today's discourse in the global arena. Also modifying the current management of international organizations such as the **International Monetary Fund** (IMF) and the **World Bank** are essential for sustainable development in a globalized world. The type of globalization that should be embraced is the one that can economically empower

SPOTLIGHT
NGOs

To explore NGOs by country and activity, visit the World Association of Non-Governmental Organizations (WANGO) online directory:
http://www.wango.org/resources.aspx?section=ngodir

the greatest number of people and is also socially and environmentally responsible.

As a result, many governments have to consider the influence and power of non-state actors in decision-making. Globalization has caused national governments to think and act globally. However, there are those who argue that this process has undermined the ability of some governments to continue to act as they used to.

The impact of non-state actors can be seen across the developing and developed world. **The National Intelligence Council** (NIC-Eurasia) Group categorizes the political structure of nations as weak, modernizing, and developed/post-industrial (NIC, 2014). Nations can be categorized according to the impact of non-state actors in three general categories:

- Developing
- Transitional
- Developed

In general, non-state actors have had more freedom in developing and in developed nations than in transitional ones. Many developing nations tend to be former colonies where governments struggle to provide order (i.e., Afghanistan, Somalia, Lebanon, Congo, and others). In this group, different non-state actors may seriously challenge the central government and may be a substitute for governments in providing services. For example, in some African countries, the **World Health Organization** (WHO) has played an important role in alleviating HIV and Ebola pandemics, with different levels of success in different countries.

Transitional states are sovereign nations that are in transition from a **centrally planned economy** to a **market economy**. In countries where the national government was strongly involved in managing the affairs of the nation such involvement has now been diminished. These countries view foreign non-state actors as a nuisance to national sovereignty and may attempt to influence and regulate their operation. For example, a number of countries have attempted to oppose pressure from human rights organizations. Another example is the pressure to provide **intellectual property rights** protections.

In developed countries where institutional structures are well developed, the non-state actors tend to focus on challenging violations of ethical standards by governments and multinational corporations. For example, the recent movement **Occupy Wall Street** is against abuses of unregulated financial markets.

1.7   Challenges of Our Generation

These are some of the timely questions that need to be addressed.

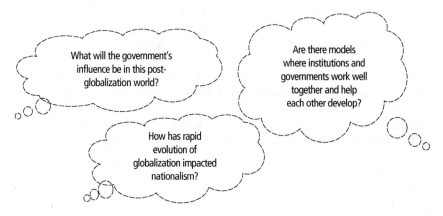

The current state of the world shows significant **economic disparity** among citizens worldwide. Additionally, the degree of **citizen participation** in formulating political systems varies dramatically among countries. There are many democratic systems of government in the world and the number of democratic governments since World War I has increased. There are many non-democratic governments with limited citizen participation and there-fore, viable economic, political, and social institutions have not developed. Sustainable globalization requires addressing existing economic and political disparities. Jeffrey Sachs's main message is to improve human well-being in a socially and environmentally conducive manner (Sachs, 2006). He states:

> "…to be able to advance the Enlightenment vision of Jefferson, Smith, Kant, and Condorcet, our generation's work can be defined in the Enlightenment terms:
> - To help foster **political systems** that promote human well-being based on the consent of the governed
> - To help foster **economic systems** that spread the benefits of science, tech-nology to everyone in the world.
> - To help foster **international cooperation** in order to secure a perpetual peace.
> - To help promote science and technology in human rationality to improve the human condition." (Sachs, 2006)

1.8   The Base of the Pyramid Concept

The **Base of the Pyramid** (BoP) concept was introduced by C. K. Prahalad (see Figure 1.5). The main argument is that the BoP consists of approximately 5 bil-lion people with an income of less than $2 per day, which constitutes a market that cannot and should not be overlooked (Prahalad, 2009).

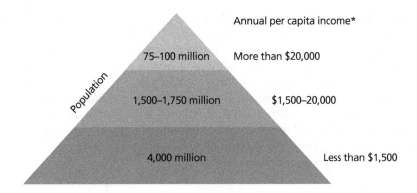

Figure 1.5 Base of the Pyramid (BoP) concept.
* *Source:* UN Development Report

The Base of the Pyramid has the following characteristics (London & Hart, 2010):

1. Heterogeneous across multiple dimensions.
2. Includes the portion of the world's population with the least amount of income.
3. Local enterprises are generally well integrated with the formal capitalist economy.
4. Constitutes the majority of humanity.
5. Exists primarily in the informal economy.

This base can be both a market for products as well as a source of inexpensive **input factors**. The BoP does not have access to world class products or services, nor to the world market. It does not have experience in marketing, modern business processes and management, or financial resources either. In other words, the global knowledge of the BoP is limited. However, at the same time, the BoP provides both opportunities and challenges for MNEs in terms of value creation. BoP not only provides the MNEs with low cost labor, but it also creates a potential market for MNEs' products. Investment and job creation will lead to increases in **per capita income** of the BoP that in turn will lead to increases in their purchasing power and consumption. While initially it is possible to make a fortune from the BoP, the opportunity increases drastically and exponentially over time.

1.9 Conclusion

In this chapter, the concept of globalization, globalization trends and the political-economic implications were discussed. Topics such as the evolution of globalization, key drivers of globalization, and the role of major global institutions on globalization were identified. Globalization started centuries ago but it has been gaining speed in recent decades due to lower barriers and technological advancements. Some countries have tried to slow down the impact of globalization with different degrees of success. However, the view toward globalization depends on its impact on individuals, communities and countries. While hundreds of millions of people all over the world have benefited from the consequences of globalization by gaining jobs and access to more opportunities, millions of others have experienced job losses, cultural invasions, and more pollution.

Triple Bottom Line (TBL) Connection

Mars is a family-owned company, headquartered in Virginia. But don't let that fool you—it is also the third-largest company in the U.S. and it is a multinational enterprise with 400 offices and manufacturing sites in 73 countries, including China, Madagascar, and Saudi Arabia. Each worksite displays the company's "Five Principles"—quality, responsibility, mutuality, efficiency, and freedom.

Mars recognizes that profitability and sustainability go hand-in-hand. To combat global threats like climate change and resource scarcity, Mars developed a "Sustainable in a Generation Plan," which echoes the Triple Bottom Line's emphasis on people, profit, and planet in its three tenets: Healthy Planet, Thriving People, and Nourishing Wellbeing.

To learn more, visit:

http://fortune.com/2013/01/17/mars-incorporated-a-pretty-sweet-place -to-work/

http://www.mars.com/global/sustainable-in-a-generation/our-approach -to-sustainability

Chapter Review

Key Terms

- Globalization
- Trade Liberalization
- Privatization
- State sovereignty
- Developed Countries
- Developing Countries

- Transitioning Countries
- Non-Governmental Organizations
- Multinational Enterprises
- Economies of Scale
- Cost of Production
- Base of the Pyramid

Questions & Assignments

Questions

1. You are the talented owner of a small business that makes and sells custom clothing. Three years ago, you expanded your business by creating a website, which allowed you to communicate with new suppliers, distributors, and customers. Your brand is becoming increasingly popular, and you often receive offers from foreign suppliers and distributors who want to help you go global.

   What are some of the economic, political, and social implications of globalization? Describe the potential positive and negative effects on your business, as well as the home and host countries. How would you handle change if you were a large company like H&M? Illustrate with examples.

Assignment

1. Consider your personal strengths, interests, and aspirations, then read the following article from Business Insider. Given the choice, which MNE would you like to work for? Why?

   Rogers, A. (2011). The 25 best multinational companies to work for. *Business Insider.* http://www.businessinsider.com/the-25-best-multinational-companies-2011-10

Notes

1. For a more complete view of the history of globalization, see "A Quick Guide to the World History of Globalization": www.sas.upenn.edu/~dludden/global1.htm.
2. See *Making Globalization Work* (2007) by Joseph E. Stiglitz, published by W.W. Norton and Company.
3. Gygli, Savina, Florian Haelg, Niklas Potrafke and Jan-Egbert Sturm (2019): The KOF Globalisation Index—Revisited, *Review of International Organizations*, https://doi.org/10.1007/s11558-019-09344-2

4. For a complete view if this issue, see https://ccrjustice.org/home/press-center/press-releases/settlement-reached-human-rights-cases-against-royal-dutchshell
5. See the full article "The Real Danger of Brexit," February 27, 2016, *The Economist.*

Suggested Reading

Barkacs, L., & Barkacs, C. (2014). Fair trade in a Wal-Mart world: What does globalization portend for the triple bottom line? *Chicago Kent-Journal of International and Comparative Law.* http://scholarship.kentlaw.iit.edu/cgi/viewcontent.cgi?article=1128&context=ckjicl

Collins, M. (2015). The pros and cons of globalization. *Forbes.* https://www.forbes.com/sites/mikecollins/2015/05/06/the-pros-and-cons-of-globalization/" \l "331a740ccce0

Evans, M. (2018, April 22). U.S. Hospital Firms, Hungry to Expand, Look to China. *Wall Street Journal.* https://www.wsj.com/articles/overseas-markets-beckon-u-s-hospital-firms-hungry-to-expand-1524394800?mod=searchresults&page=1&pos=18

Ghemawat, P. (2017). Globalization in the Age of Trump. *Harvard Business Review.* https://hbr.org/2017/07/globalization-in-the-age-of-trump

References

Castells, Manuel (2010). The Rise of the Network Society, Volume 1, Second Edition, Wiley-Blackwell.

Drezner, D. W. (2001). Globalization and policy convergence. *International Studies Review, 3*(1), 53–78.

Fukuyama, F. (1989). The end of history? *The national interest*(16), 3-18.

Huntington, S. P. (1993). The clash of civilizations? *Culture and Politics* (pp. 99–118): Springer.

Kettl, D. F. (2000). The transformation of governance: Globalization, devolution, and the role of government. *Public Administration Review, 60*(6), 488–497.

Lin, J. Y., & Nugent, J. B. (1995). Institutions and Economic Development. In J. Behrman & T. N. Srinivasan (Eds.), *Handbook of Development Economics* (Vol. 3A). New York, NY: Elsevier Science.

London, T., & Hart, S. L. (2010). *Next generation business strategies for the base of the pyramid: New approaches for building mutual value.* FT Press.

NIC. (2014). Eurasia. *National Intelligence Council.* Retrieved from http://www.dni.gov/index.php/about/organization/national-intelligence-council-nic-publications

Prahalad, C. K. (2009). *The fortune at the bottom of the pyramid, revised and updated 5th anniversary edition: Eradicating poverty through profits.* FT Press.

Rodrik, D. (2008). *One economics, many recipes: globalization, institutions, and economic growth.* Princeton University Press.

Sachs, J. (2006). *The end of poverty: economic possibilities for our time.* New York, NY: Penguin Press.

WTO. (2004). Governance and Institutions. *World Trade Report.* Retrieved from http://www.wto.org/english/res_e/booksp_e/anrep_e/wtr04_2d_e.pdf

CHAPTER 2

The Global Economic Environment

Global Business, pages 23–41
Copyright © 2019 by Information Age Publishing
All rights of reproduction in any form reserved.

Opening Case

Electricity in the Developing World— A Light-Bulb Moment

Electricity powers growth, boosts education, and improves lives. Yet about 1.1bn mostly rural dwellers in Asia and Africa remain stuck in the dark. They have no electric light, rely on kerosene and diesel for power, and struggle to irrigate their crops. The good news is that people can be connected to clean, reliable power faster than ever before. To realize the potential, governments need to rethink the role of utilities. Typically, countries connect citizens with vast grid-extension programs. Big grids make perfect sense for populous places. They can inexpensively supply power generated far away to millions and, as they incorporate more wind and solar energy, they are becoming greener. In remote places, however, the economic case for grids becomes hard to make. Many utilities are short of cash, if not bankrupt. The cost of taking power to those least able to afford it adds to their debts. It took 20 years for China and Thailand to improve electrification rates from about 30–40% to 85–90%. Reaching the remaining sliver took 20 more years; China managed it only in 2015.

Mini-grids, which can operate independently from national grids are a way for private companies to offer services more quickly and reliably than state-

Figure 2.1 Electricity in developing countries. *Photo:* Tehmul Ghyara, https://openphoto.net/volumes/tehmul/20050919/opl_IMG_0452.JPG

owned incumbents. Mini-grids are banks of batteries often charged by solar arrays. Unlike "rooftop" solar systems, which are increasingly common in parts of Africa but provide little juice, mini-grids provide round-the-clock electricity capable of powering machinery, irrigation systems and freezers, as well as lighting. Although they are expensive, mini-grids are likely to become cheaper as they grow more common. In the interim, providers are using specialists in rural development and microfinance to teach people how to set up businesses that benefit from a lot of power. They find that if people learn how to make money from electricity, they willingly pay for it.

Adapted from: *The Economist*, June 12, 2018 print edition, under the headline "Light-bulb Moment."

1. *Often government officials do not want to decentralize the power supply for fear of losing political control. How to incentivize governments to embrace the mini-grid model? Discuss various options.*

2. *What economic issues does the opening case highlight? Why are those issues relevant for MNEs?*

2.0 Introduction

All countries differ in terms of levels of economic development, performance, and potential. Therefore, it is crucial for managers or anyone doing business in other countries to understand the implications of different economic systems and key macroeconomic indicators to determine which countries are attractive for business. This knowledge is applied for conducting a systematic economic analysis, which helps in the decision-making processes of where to establish new operations, or whether or not to continue business operations in a foreign country.

Multinational enterprises (MNEs) have also had an important role in shaping the economic environment of many countries because they are intermediaries in transferring products through trade and foreign direct investment (FDI). A better understanding of the process of economic transition and development will help managers reach decisions that benefit not only their firms, but potentially also the countries in which those firms operate.

2.1 Types of Economic Systems

A country's growth potential can be assessed by analyzing both its current economic system, as well as the transition process by which it may be moving from one type of system to another. An **economic system** is the set of structures and processes that guide a country about allocating its resources (capital, labor, and natural resources), and conducting its business activities. There are three broad types of economic systems.

2.1.1 Market Economy

In a **market economy** the individuals, rather than the government, make the majority of economic decisions. This definition suggests that most of the land, factories, and other economic resources are privately owned by individuals or businesses. The goods and services that a country produces, and the quantity in which they are produced, are not planned by anyone. Major economic decisions are made by the market according to the laws of supply and demand which provide price flexibility. How much of each good is to be produced depends on their relative price ratios and the cost of production, which takes into account the wage structure within each particular industry. Investment allocation in a market economy depends on the rate of return on investment and the profit within each industry.

Even though in this system a country's government does not intervene in its economic activities, the role of the government is to encourage free and fair competition between private producers. This function is usually accomplished through the enforcement of antitrust laws, the preservation of property rights, and by providing a stable fiscal and monetary environment as well as political stability. All these factors help companies forecast and mitigate any risks associated with future investments in market economies.

2.1.2 Command Economy

In **command economies** (also called centrally planned economies), the government has ownership and control of the factors of production. In the past, most communist political systems exhibited a command economy where the planning authorities made major economic decisions. They also determined the products, the quantities and the prices at which the products were sold. There are now far fewer communist countries than three decades ago. Politically, China remains a hardline communist country, however, the economic system has transitioned to be more like a market economy. In the early 1990s, several countries began to dismantle their command economies in favor of market-based economies due to political change and because a centrally-planned system failed to produce quality products efficiently. Government ownership limited the incentives to maximize benefits from resources, which lowered economic growth, living standards, and innovation.

2.1.3 Mixed Economy

In a **mixed economy** some elements of market economies and command economies are present. Economic decisions are largely market-driven and ownership is largely private, but the government nonetheless intervenes mainly in the economic sectors important to national security and long-term stability. Oftentimes, mixed economies provide generous welfare systems to support the unemployed, provide health care for all, and facilitate citizens' access to low cost or free education. The extent and nature of such intervention may take the form of government ownership of certain factors of production, the granting of subsidies, the heavy taxation of certain economic activities, and/or the redistribution of income and wealth. From this perspective, countries in the European Union (EU) are considered mixed economies, even though they have extensively privatized their economic sectors and thus function as market economies.

Each economic system has some drawbacks. Market economies go through cycles of expansion and contraction called **business cycles**. The social cost of a business cycle in terms of financial losses for firms and human suffering during a contraction period is considerable (e.g., the U.S. real estate bubble and the global financial crisis in 2007-2008). Therefore, in a market economy, policies and regulations that prevent abuse of economic power are necessary. Financial safety nets that protect individual citizens in contracting economic cycles are essential. An unregulated market economy may lead to the concentration of assets and economic power in the hands of a small group that could abuse this power. In addition, there is the potential for moral hazard so that some may abuse their economic position and continuously exploit others for profit (Krugman & Wells, 2012).

In a command economy, **resource allocation** is usually sub-optimal since the decision makers have no way of knowing whether their decision was the best one. In the absence of a price mechanism, making the optimal decision among many different choices would be difficult if not impossible. Finally, limitations on private ownership stifle entrepreneurship and innovation.

2.2   Political Economy

There is a connection between political ideology and economic systems. In most cases, political authoritarianism goes hand in hand with command economies. On the other hand, market economies are most often found in democratic countries. While this phenomenon is the norm, there are cases where a totalitarian political system has a highly market driven economy as in the case of China. Also, many of the Persian Gulf countries such as the United Arab Emirates (UAE), Qatar, and Bahrain have market economies, but the political system is a totalitarian one.

2.3   Economic System Transition

The process of transition from a command to a market-based economy was not limited to the breakup of the Soviet Union into several independent countries in the late1980s and early 1990s. China, the most populated centrally-planned economy, also started a transition toward a market economy in the late 70s. Countries such as Brazil and India did not have a communist political system, but had a strong government control of the economy, particularly through import substitution policies and restrictive foreign investment policies. These countries also began an economic change toward a market-based system in the past two decades.

2.4   The Dynamics of Economic Transitions

In order to make a successful transition from a command economy to a market-based economy, many conditions must be present. According to the International Monetary Fund (IMF) the following four characteristics are critical for a successful economic system transition:

Liberalization. Most prices need to be determined by supply and demand, trade and investment barriers need to be lowered. Currency convertibility has to be allowed.

Macroeconomic Stabilization. Primarily inflation has to be under control. This goal requires discipline over the government budget, the growth of money and credit (e.g., discipline in fiscal and monetary policy), and progress toward a sustainable balance of payments.

Privatization. Government-owned resources need to be transferred to private individuals and/or entities. A key factor is that private enterprises must compete in open markets for materials, labor, and capital; thus, they succeed or fail on their own merits.

Legal & Institutional Reforms. The rule of law must be established. Appropriate competition policies must be introduced. Financial institutions, including stock markets and a banking system must be created. Intellectual property rights and antitrust legislation needs to be implemented and enforced.[1]

Debate—Privatization

Pros	Cons
• **Incentives.** Private firms have profit incentives to innovate	• **Ineffective.** Private firms may be ineffective at providing welfare, e.g., high cost of U.S. healthcare

Pros	Cons
• **Merit.** Private firms will employ the best available talent, while the government may select talent based on political motives	• **Monopolies.** Private monopolies may charge high prices, e.g., trains
• **Delegation.** Privatization allows the government to focus on its essential functions	• **Priorities.** Private firms may ignore external costs, while the government can put social well-being first.

2.5 Economic Development

The concept of **economic development** is not easy to define. In general, economic development is the process by which a country improves the economic, political, and social well-being of its people. Since economic development is a measure for assessing the economic well-being of the people in one country as compared with that of the people of another country, it is useful to place countries into groups to try to better understand the economic and social outcomes of a particular foreign country. However, it is a challenge to have a standard classification of countries as the following sections explains.

2.6 International Organizations That Facilitate International Progress

2.6.1 World Bank

The **World Bank** is a **developmental agency**. Its founding was a part of the **Bretton Woods Agreement**, named after the conference's location in Bretton Woods, New Hampshire in 1944. There, representatives of 44 countries including the United States, France, and Great Britain met to establish the foundation of the post-war global financial system. Two institutions were set up to assure the success of the agreement; these were the International Monetary Fund (IMF) and the **International Bank for Reconstruction and Development** (IBRD), later known as the World Bank.

The IBRD sought to stimulate economic recovery in Europe. As Europeans paid back their loans with interest, the bank's hard currency reserve increased, and its focus turned to helping emerging economies by providing them with project-based financing. The World Bank now raises capital at a very low interest rate, thanks to its **AAA rating**.[2]

2.6.2 International Monetary Fund (IMF)

Like the World Bank, the **International Monetary Fund** (IMF) was established in the Bretton Woods Agreement, following World War II.

The IMF's mandate was, and still is, the management of the global financial and economic system through the creation of **liquidity** and management of the **exchange rate system**. Because the post-war global financial system required all countries to maintain a fixed rate against an **anchor currency** (in other words, it was a **fixed exchange rate régime**), the IMF's primary function was managing the international exchange rate.

The IMF has been credited for addressing several global financial challenges including the Asian Financial Crisis in 1997 and the Global Financial Crisis of 2008–2010 by preventing the collapse of the international financial system.

2.6.3 United Nations (UN)

Delegates from fifty countries founded the **United Nations** (UN) following World War II, and more than 190 countries are now members. The organization seeks to address a variety of international issues, including peace, security, climate change, sustainable development, and human rights. It also acts as a forum in which members can express their views. A detailed description of the United Nations' founding, structure, and roles appears in a later chapter.

2.7 Country Classifications

There are several country classifications based on different economic indicators. For example, the World Bank classifies countries as developed and developing, but the International Monetary Fund (IMF) has different categories. Table 2.1 shows four country classification systems of selected international organizations.

2.7.1 World Bank Classifications

The World Bank classifies countries into four categories based on the **Gross National Income** (GNI) per capita in current US Dollars. Low- and middle-income economies are usually referred to as **developing economies**, and the upper-middle and the high-income are referred to as **developed countries**.[3]

TABLE 2.1   Country Classification Systems in Selected International Organizations

World Bank GNI per capita, as of 2017	IMF per capita income, export diversification, degree of integration into the global finan- cial system	UNCTAD country aggregate indicators	UNDP HDI
High-income economies: $12,056 or more	Advanced Economies	Developed Economies	Very High Human Development
Upper middle-income economies: $3,896 to $12,055	Emerging Markets	Economies in Transition	High Human Development
Lower middle-income economies: $996 to $3,895	Developing Economies	Developing Economies	Medium Human Development
Low-income economies: of $995 or less		Least Developed Countries (LDCs)	Low Human Development

2.7.2   IMF Classifications

The IMF classifies the world into **advanced economies, emerging markets,** and **developing economies**. The main criteria used for this classification are per capita income levels, export diversification, and the degree of integration into the global financial system. However, the IMF indicates that these are not the only factors considered in deciding the classification of countries and their classification has evolved over time.[4]

2.7.3   The United Nations Conference on Trade and Development (UNCTAD)

The UNCTAD classifies all countries of the world into three broad categories: developed economies, economies in transition, and developing economies. More recently, a fourth category called **Least Developed Countries** (LDCs) was added. The composition of these groupings is intended to reflect the basic economic country conditions.[5]

2.7.4   The United Nations Development Program (UNDP)

The UNDP's country classification system is based on the **Human Development Index** (HDI) which is a composite index of life expectancy, education,

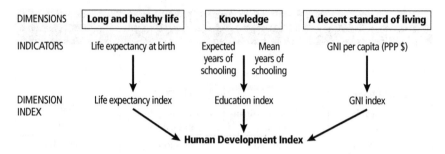

Figure 2.2 Human Development Index dimensions.

and per capita income indicators, which are used to rank countries into four tiers of human development. The HDI was created to emphasize that people and their capabilities should be the ultimate criteria for assessing the development of a country, not economic growth alone.[6] Figure 2.2 illustrates the HDI dimensions.

2.8 Economic Analysis

There is no universal scheme with which to assess the performance and potential of a country's economy. Not only it is difficult to specify a definitive set of economic indicators, but often it is difficult to understand the systematic relationship of one economic indicator to another. However, by reducing the economic environment to its fundamental components, it is possible to begin to understand how they shape the market and how they subsequently interact with one another. In practice, managers begin an economic analysis by looking and understanding some of the economic indicators listed below.

2.8.1 National Production

Gross Domestic Product (GDP) measures the value of goods and services generated by both domestic and foreign-owned firms within a nation's borders in a given period, usually a year.

Gross National Income (GNI) measures the income generated both by total domestic production plus the international production activities of national firms, e.g., it is the market value of all final goods and services newly produced by a country's domestically-owned firms, plus the net flows of factor income (e.g., rents, profits, and labor income) in a given year.

Gross National Product (GNP) is the value of all final goods and services produced within a country in a given year, plus the income earned by its citizens abroad, minus income earned by foreigners. Managers improve the usefulness of GDP, GNI and GNP by adjusting it for the population of a country, its growth rate, the local cost of living, and economic sustainability.

Per Capita Conversion. GNI per capita is the value of all goods and services produced in the economy divided by the population, which then reflects the average income of a country's citizens.

Rate of Change. GNI, GNP and GDP are a snapshot of one year's economic output, and do not indicate whether an economy is growing. Generally, the GNI growth rate provides a broad indicator of economic potential; if GNI grows at a higher (or lower) rate than the population, standards of living are said to be rising (or falling).

Purchasing Power Parity. Exchange rates define the number of units of one currency that are required to purchase one unit of another currency, but exchange rates do not incorporate differences in the cost of living. Purchasing Power Parity (PPP) represents the number of units of a country's currency required to buy the same amount of goods and services in the domestic market that one unit of income would buy in another country. PPP is estimated by calculating the value of a universal "basket" of goods that can be purchased with one unit of a country's currency Purchasing Power Parity. This concept allows managers to compare the wealth of a country.

2.8.2 The Degree of Human Development Using the Human Development Index

Some criticize the use of purely monetary indicators and call for evaluating a country's degree of economic development by using the UNDP"s Human Development Index (HDI) as an indicator of current and future economic activity. HDI demonstrates that high national income alone does not guarantee human progress, as there is often disparity between wealth and HDI. This measure is based on three main factors: Per capita income, years of schooling and life expectancy. As mentioned earlier, countries are often categorized based on their HDI value. Table 2.2 provides the index intervals for each category, which are also reflected in Figure 2.3.

TABLE 2.2 Human Development Index Categories of Development	
Category	**Index Interval**
Very High Human Development	0.800 to 1.000
High Human Development	0.700 to 0.799
Medium Human Development	0.550 to 0.699
Low Human Development	Less than 0.550

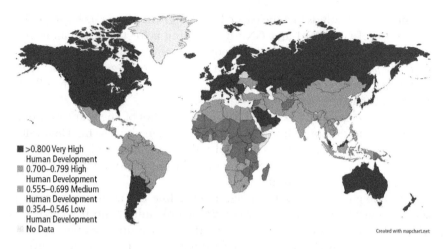

Created with mapchart.net

Figure 2.3 Human Development Index intervals mapping for 2017.

2.8.3   The Economic Freedom Index

This measure, published by the Heritage Foundation, approximates the extent to which a government intervenes in the areas of free choice, free enterprise, and free prices for reasons that go beyond basic national needs. Factors of the index include: trade policy, the fiscal burden of the government, the extent and nature of government intervention in the economy, monetary policy, capital flows and investment, banking and financial activities, wage and price levels, property rights, other government regulation, and informal market activities. Countries ranking highest on this index tend to enjoy both the highest standards of living as well as the greatest degree of political freedom. Figure 2.4 maps the most recent rankings. Check the link to the Economic Freedom Index: https://www.heritage.org/index/.

2.8.4   Other Indicators

Managers often study many second-order indicators of economic performance and potential. **Inflation** is the pervasive and sustained rise in the aggregate level of prices as measured by a cost of living index. Rising prices make it more difficult for consumers to buy products unless their incomes rise at the same or faster pace. Historically chronic inflation erodes confidence in a country's currency. Among other things, high inflation results in governments' setting higher interest rates, installing wage and price controls, imposing protectionist trade policies, and currency controls. The Consumer

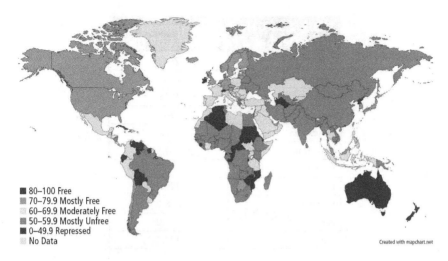

Figure 2.4 Economic Freedom Index mapping for 2019.

Price Index (CPI) is the official measure of inflation in the U.S. and the Harmonized Index of Consumer Prices (HICP) is the EU's measure.

The **Unemployment Rate** represents the number of unemployed workers divided by the total civilian labor force in a given country. Given the wide differences in social policies and institutional frameworks, the meaning of the unemployment rate varies from one country to another.

Debt is the total sum of a government's financial obligations. It measures the state's borrowing from its population, foreign organizations, foreign governments, and international institutions. Internal debt results when a government spends more than it collects in revenues. The subsequent pressure to revise government policies often leads to economic uncertainty. External debt results when a government borrows money from foreign lenders. Growing debt can often be an early warning for tax increases, reduced growth, and rising inflation. Table 2.3 lists the countries with the highest national debt as a percent of their GDP. Based on 2018 estimates, the United States' debt to GDP ratio is 108, making it the 17th country with the highest ratio in this category. In contract, Canada ranks as the 35th with the ratio of only 86.6.

Income distribution describes what share of a country's income goes to various segments of the population. The **Gini index** measures the extent to which the distribution of income (or, in some cases, consumption expenditure) among individuals or households within an economy deviates from a perfectly equal distribution. Uneven income distribution occurs in virtually every country with the U.S. having the largest inequality compared to other industrialized nations (see Table 2.4). A Gini index of 0 represents perfect equality, while an index of 100 implies perfect inequality.

TABLE 2.3 General Government Gross Debt as a Percent of GDP (IMF)	
Country	2018
Japan	236.0
Greece	191.3
Sudan	176.5
Venezuela	162.0
Lebanon	157.3
Italy	129.7
Eritrea	129.4
Barbados	128.7
Yemen	128.2
Cabo Verde	124.7

TABLE 2.4 Examples of GINI Coefficients, 2016 (World Bank)	
2016 GINI Index World Bank Estimate	
Ukraine	25.0
Moldova	26.3
Kyrgyz Republic	26.8
Belarus	27.0
Bangladesh	32.4
Georgia	36.5
United States	41.5
Turkey	41.9
Mexico	43.4
Colombia	50.8

The **balance of payments (BOP)**, officially known as the Statement of International Transactions reports the total of all money flowing into a country less all money flowing out of that country to any other country during a given period. The two primary accounts are the **current account**, which tracks all trade activity in merchandise and services, and the **capital account**, which tracks both loans given to foreigners and loans received by citizens. A trade surplus indicates that the value of exports exceeds the value of imports, a trade deficit indicates that the value of imports exceeds the value of exports. Managers use the BOP to assess a country's economic stability. By measuring a country's transactions with the rest of the world, the BOP estimates a country's financial stability.

SPOTLIGHT

Colombia Remains One of the Most Unequal Countries

Despite global economic growth, the unequal distribution of income in Colombia has increased in the last few decades. Such a negative trend can be explained by several factors. First, new economic behavior centered around innovation excludes certain population groups. Secondly, Colombia's tax reform of 2017 reduced the number of taxes paid by businesses to only income tax, while increasing the taxes paid by citizens. The value-added tax (VAT) on basic products such as cooking oil, pasta, and cleaning products have increased from 16% to 19%. Finally, wrong economic diagnoses which lead to poor policy decisions are at fault. Changes in the areas described above will likely determine the movements in economic inequality in the next few years.

Based on
http://unperiodico.unal.edu.co/pages/detail/despite-economic-growth
-colombia-continues-to-be-one-of-the-most-unequal-countries-in-the
-world/

2.8.5 Green Measures

A growing concern for the ecological welfare of the world has caused a call for newer measures of national wellness. Social and ecological costs can result in distortions when only economic factors are measured. For instance, some economic activities by Multinational Enterprises (MNEs) could create environmental damage or may cause too much loud noises in some neighborhoods. On the other hand, operations of MNEs may reduce poverty and crime in other communities by creating employment opportunities for young people. Presently, there is no consensus on how to adjust GDP for green concerns, but a variety of options are discussed in later chapters.

2.9 Economic Risk

In the context of international business, **economic risk** is often described as the probability that an investment abroad will be affected by **macroeconomic conditions** (inflation, exchange rates, government regulation, and even political stability), in the foreign location. In other words, economic risk refers to the risk that a venture will be economically unsustainable and less profitable, due to changes in economic trends, which may negatively impact the venture. Economic risk is one of the reasons international business ventures carry higher risk as compared to domestic investing. On the other hand, economic risk can also provide additional opportunities for investors.

There are many types of economic risk that businesses should identify and manage. A few of the common types of economic risk in foreign locations are the following:

- *Interest Rates.* Changes can lead to reduced profits.
- *Wages.* When minimum wage increases, the cost of production increases.
- *Market Prices.* A country's economy greatly influences market prices. When market prices decrease but production costs stay the same, profitability can be significantly reduced.
- *Import/Export Duty.* An increase of import/export duties (taxes) can decrease profitability.

Businesses need to proactively identify and monitor all these economic conditions to develop and support a robust economic risk management strategy.

2.10 Conclusion

All countries differ in terms of levels of economic development, performance, and potential. Therefore, it is crucial for managers or anyone doing business in foreign countries to understand the implications of different economic systems and their transition over time, as well as key macroeconomic indicators of each country. Economic analyses must be performed to assess the extent to which a country may or may not be suitable for business operations.

TBL Connection
The Case of Sierra Leone

With the human development index of only 0.419 the West African nation of Sierra Leone is one of the world's poorest countries. Decades of economic decline and 11 years of armed conflict which ended in 2002 had a significant negative impact on it. According to the UNDP, about 60% of Sierra Leoneans live below the national poverty line, and the adult literacy rate reaches only 41%. Today, significant unemployment rates among youth, gender inequality, and vulnerability of the population to natural disasters remain some of the major challenges the nation faces.

Despite the issues described above, as well as shortage in skilled labor and poor infrastructure, some foreign companies choose to invest in

Sierra Leone. China remains the most significant investor, followed by Belgium, Germany, and the United States. Chinese investors are currently financing the construction of a new airport, a hospital, a hydroelectric dam, a rubber production facility, and some other projects. In 2016, they also targeted sectors such as mining and transportation. The government of Sierra Leone is working to attract other investors by offering various economic incentives including tax exemptions.

1. What impact may FDI have on people of Sierra Leone? Provide examples.

2. How can businesses and individuals investing in Sierra Leone promote well-being of locals?

Chapter Review

Key Terms

- Market economy
- Command Economy
- Mixed Economy
- Economic Development
- GDP (per capita)
- GNI
- GNP
- HDI
- Economic Freedom Index
- Balance of Payments
- Current Account
- Capital Account
- Debt
- Unemployment Rate
- GINI Index
- Income distribution
- Economic Risk

Questions & Assignments

Questions

1. Managers often study many second-order indicators of economic performance and potential, including inflation, unemployment,

debt, income distribution, poverty, and the balance of payments, which of these indicators may be more relevant to the assessment of an industrialized economy as compared to the assessment of an emerging economy? Explain your rationale.

Assignments

1. Select a developed economy such as Japan, the United Kingdom, France, or Germany, and select one of the BRICs (Brazil, Russia, India, and China). Compare the key elements of those two economic systems. Be sure to discuss the interaction between politics and economics in the two countries.

2. There are many reputable sources of economic data. International organizations such as the World Bank, the United Nations and the IMF, to name a few, have databases that are constantly updated from which anyone can download data for free. Check out some of these databases and try to find the indicators listed below for one of the following country pairs: Chile/Argentina, Thailand/Vietnam, or Nigeria/Kenya.
   a. GDP
   b. GNI per capita
   c. GDP growth
   d. Population
   e. Unemployment rate

3. What trends do you see for each indicator in the country pair of your choice? Which country (from the country pair) would be more attractive for establishing operations in the manufacturing/services/technology sectors? If you were interested in finding out which country is more concerned about the environment, which indicators would you look for? List them and explain what information they provide.

United Nations Conference on Trade and Development Statistics (UNCTADStat)
   http://unctadstat.unctad.org/wds/ReportFolders/reportFolders.aspx?sCS_ChosenLang=en
UNDP HDI Data
   http://www.hdr.undp.org/en/data
World Bank Database
   http://databank.worldbank.org/data/home.aspx
IMF's World Economic Outlook Database
   http://www.imf.org/external/pubs/ft/weo/2018/01/weodata/index.aspx
GlobalEdge (Michigan State University-AIB)
   https://globaledge.msu.edu/

Notes

1. IMF. (2000). Transition Economies: An IMF Perspective on Progress and Prospects—An IMF Issues Brief. *Issues Briefs*. Retrieved from http://www.imf.org/external/np/exr/ib/2000/110300.htm#I
2. World Bank Group. (2014). Retrieved from http://www.worldbank.org/
3. WorldBank.org. (2018). *New country classifications by income level: 2017–2018*. In T. W. B. D. Team (Ed.), (July 5, 2018 ed.). http://blogs.worldbank.org/opendata/energy/new-country-classifications-income-level-2017-2018
4. International Monetary Fund. (2018). *World Economic Outlook Database* (Vol. 2018). https://www.imf.org/external/pubs/ft/weo/2018/01/weodata/index.aspx
5. United Nations Conference on Trade and Development. (2018). *Country Classficications*. http://unctadstat.unctad.org/EN/Classifications.html
6. United Nations Development Programme. (2018). *Human Development Index* (HDI). http://hdr.undp.org/en/content/human-development-index-hdi

Suggested Reading

IMF's World Economic Outlook Report
    https://www.imf.org/en/Publications/WEO/Issues/2018/03/20/world-economic-outlook-april-2018
UNCTAD's World Investment Report
    http://unctad.org/en/pages/PublicationWebflyer.aspx?publicationid=2130
John Elkington (1994). Towards the sustainable corporation: Win-win-win business strategies for sustainable development. *California Management Review 36*(2), 90–100.
Andrew Savitz, *The Triple Bottom Line* (San Francisco, CA: Jossey-Bass, 2006).

References

Krugman, P., & Wells, R. (2012). *Macroeconomics* (3rd ed.). New York, NY: Worth Publishers.

CHAPTER 3

Trade Theories and the Role of Governments in Trade

LEARNING OBJECTIVES

- Understand the basic **theories of international trade** and explain how free trade improves global efficiency
- Identify factors affecting national **trade patterns** and explain why production factors, especially labor and capital, move internationally
- Describe the national **competitive advantage** theory and the **Porter Diamond**.
- Explain why governments sometimes intervene in trade and describe the instruments that governments use to restrict or promote trade
- Describe the potential and actual effects of **governmental intervention** on free trade

Global Business, pages 43–70
Copyright © 2019 by Information Age Publishing
All rights of reproduction in any form reserved.

Opening Case

Escalating Trade Tensions in 2018

Throughout his 2016 presidential campaign, Donald Trump consistently favored proposals to renegotiate trade agreements. He often criticized the North American Free Trade Agreement (NAFTA) and withdrew the United States from the Trans-Pacific Partnership (TPP) soon after becoming president. It is believed that such policies will put the United States first and ensure fair bilateral trade.

In March 2018, the United States imposed a 25% tariff on steel and a 10% tariff on aluminum on all countries. Initially, the EU, Mexico, Canada, Australia, Argentina, Brazil, and South Korea were exempt. When the tariff was finally imposed on the EU, Canada, and Mexico, it triggered immediate retaliation from other countries. President Trump justified the protectionist policy as national defense, arguing that steel and aluminum industries are vital for the security of the United States. While steel workers applauded the development, Defense Secretary Jim Mattis questioned the argument, highlighting that 3% of domestic production would be sufficient to meet military demand.

The trade tensions continued when the United States complained to the WTO about weak Chinese protection of intellectual property rights. Around the same time, China responded to steel and aluminum protectionist actions

Figure 3.1 Trade tensions. *Source:* https://www.flickr.com/photos/strausser/73380166/

by imposing tariffs on $3 billion American goods. In July 2018, the United States announced a $50 billion tariff on Chinese goods, with a threat to impose additional tariffs in case of Chinese retaliation. When the tariffs went into effect in July and August, China retaliated with reciprocal tariffs. As of September, the latest round of tensions resulted in a 10% tariff on $200 billion worth of Chinese goods. The list of targeted products includes everything from vegetables to chemical elements and conduction materials.

While some economists have supported Trump's policy, many others argue that it will hurt American businesses, farmers and consumers in the long run. Many American companies, including Walmart, Gap, Coca-Cola, and General Motors, have announced they may raise prices as a result of higher input costs. China's economy will also be impacted. According to J.P. Morgan, China can lose as many as 3 million jobs if it does not have any countermeasures for the latest round of tariffs.

Based on

https://www.cnbc.com/2018/09/27/us-tariffs-could-hit-tech-and-autos-manufacturing-in-china.html

https://www.bloomberg.com/news/articles/2018-07-06/the-trade-war-is-on-timeline-of-how-we-got-here-and-what-s-next

http://www.chicagotribune.com/business/ct-biz-trump-eu-steel-aluminum-tariffs-20180531-story.html

1. *What positive and negative impact might Donald Trump's trade restrictions have on the U.S. economy? What signal does the policy send to allies of the United States?*

3.0 Introduction

Trade between countries is one of the oldest business activities. Over time, international trade theorists have developed several frameworks for policy analysis and evaluation of the impact of trade on the participants. This chapter describes the benefits of trade through the exploration of the main theories of why nations trade. International trade influences a country's economic growth, employment, and inflations rates. In general, importing countries obtain products at lower costs than the equivalent ones produced domestically, and exporting countries tend to benefit from the job creation and revenues generated from the growth of their exporting industries. In addition, multinational enterprises (MNEs) usually benefit from the profit margin generated by export-import activities. Figure 3.2 shows the value in billion USD of exports in goods and services for the world, high-income countries, low and middle-income countries, and LDCs.

The figure illustrates that since the 1990s the world's trade has increased significantly. The increase is attributed to the globalization of economies and

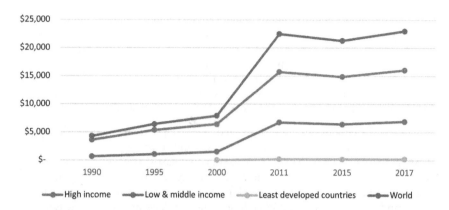

Figure 3.2 Exports of goods and services in billion US$ (*Source:* World Bank, 2018).

the lowering of trade barriers. A great deal of the increase in trade is due to increasing exports from Asian countries. The share of Asian exports in the world increased from approximately 24% in 1983 to more than 33% in 2018, with the exports of goods alone accounting for 36.3% of worldwide exports. The share of U.S. and European exports both declined in this period.

International trade has evolved to be truly global. For example, after the former Soviet Union collapsed, countries such as the Czech Republic, Poland, Slovakia, Romania, and Hungary, among many others in Eastern Europe and Central Asia started actively participating in international trade. Many other countries in Latin America and Africa that initially adhered to an economic policy of import substitution as the foundation of their economic development policy followed a similar path. Other countries such as China, India, and Brazil that had focused on internal self-sufficiency in the past, also rely more heavily on the international flow of goods and services now.

3.1 Trade Theories

There is no doubt that international trade has historically been a significant aspect of business. Several classical trade theories explain why nations find it advantageous to engage in international trade. Trade theories help managers and government policymakers focus on several critical questions:

- Why do countries trade with each other?
- Where should they produce and sell their products?
- How do they decide what products to export or import?
- What factors create competitive advantages in a certain product for a country?
- Do countries move from having a competitive advantage in one product to another over time?

3.1.1 Theory of Absolute Advantage

1. Countries maximize their economic well-being by specializing;
   a. they export goods they can produce more cheaply than other nations, and
   b. they import goods that are expensive to produce locally.
2. Variations in each nation's natural advantage(s) determine their specialization
3. Free trade enhances global efficiency. Tariffs & quotas inhibit global efficiency.

Adam Smith developed the **Theory of Absolute Advantage** in 1776. His theory proposed that the wealth of a nation consisted of the goods and services available to its citizens. His theory of absolute advantage holds that a country can maximize its own economic well-being by specializing in the production of those goods and services that it can produce more efficiently than any other nation and enhance global efficiency through its participation in (unrestricted) free trade. He argued that countries should specialize in the production of the goods they can produce at lower costs (on an absolute basis) in terms of resources used and export some of those products to other countries. At the same time, countries should import products that would be costlier to produce (Rassekh, 2015).

In addition, this theory states that if countries specialize in particular industries, the productivity would increase, which in turn would lead to higher amounts of trade and better economic conditions for the countries involved. Variations in **natural advantages** among countries help explain where particular products can be produced most efficiently. **Acquired advantages** refer to those advantages developed in either production or process technology. Adam Smith reasoned that international trade should not be burdened by tariffs and quotas, but should flow according to **market forces**.

3.1.2 Theory of Comparative Advantage

1. Expands on Smith's Theory of Absolute Advantage:
   a. Each country has a scarce amount of resources, such as labor & capital.
   b. Producing goods *other than those it can produce most efficiently* wastes resources.
   c. "Opportunity cost" is profit lost when *not* producing the most resource-efficient good.

David Ricardo developed the **Theory of Comparative Advantage** in 1817 as an extension of Smith's Theory of Absolute Advantage. Ricardo's theory explains why there are benefits from trade between two countries, even when one of the countries has absolute advantage in the production of all goods (e.g., a country produces all products more efficiently than another country). In other words, there would still be gains from trade if a country specialized in the production of those things it can produce most efficiently, even if other countries can produce those same things even more efficiently.

This theory is built on the concept of **opportunity cost,** which means that each country has a certain amount of productive resources such as labor, capital, and natural resources that should be used in the production of goods that can be produced most efficiently relative to its trading partners. Production of any other goods would use resources that could have been used more efficiently and therefore there is an opportunity cost in using those resources.

The issue of efficiency can be further articulated by the concept of **economies of scale**. There are countries that are relatively small in size and therefore cannot achieve economies of scale in their production without international trade and export. These countries can achieve economies of scale and reduce cost of production through specialization. For example, South Korea and Sweden are too small in terms of population to support a large auto industry. Each country has two car manufacturing companies that rely mainly on car exports.

3.1.3   Assumptions & Limitations

The theories of absolute and comparative advantage hold that specialization will maximize output and that countries will be better off by trading the output from their own specialization for the output from other countries' specialization. However, both theories make certain assumptions that may not always be valid. Both theories assume the following:

1. Resources are fully employed;
2. There are no transportation costs;
3. Resources have full mobility.

These assumptions do not reflect reality. In addition, the theories assume that the main objective of individuals and countries is to pursue economic efficiency, which is not always the case, and the theories do not take into account that the relative conditions that surround a country's particular advantage or disadvantage are *dynamic* (constantly changing). Thus, an assumption that future advantages will remain constant is unrealistic. Finally, both theories use the example of two countries and two commodities, or products, to demonstrate trade gains. The analysis becomes more complex when 200 countries trading thousands of products are considered.

3.1.4 Dynamic Comparative Advantage

Many countries have attempted to change their comparative advantage from labor to technology and knowledge intensive industry. The technology and knowledge intensive industries have higher **value added**, which is defined as the incremental input in terms of labor, capital, and resources and leads to higher per capita incomes.

For example, in the 1960s Japan was a country with cheap labor, but by the mid-1980s its comparative advantage had shifted to the technology intensive industry sector and their per capita income increased to the same level as the per capita income of the United States and Western European countries. Another example is South Korea, which also managed to transform its economy from labor abundant to a technology rich one and began exporting advanced manufacturing products such as computers, telecommunication equipment, and automobiles. These countries developed their comparative advantage by building their research and development capabilities, investing in education, improving management, and by developing knowledge intensive industries (Bhagwati, Panagariya, & Srinivasan, 1998; Daniels, Radebaugh, & Sullivan, 2014).

3.1.5 Factor Proportions (Factor Endowment) Theory

1. Different countries have different endowments with various factors of production:
    a. products using resources the country has abundantly are produced/exported;
    b. products using resources the country does not have are imported.
2. Various products use different factors of production, with different intensity.
3. Variations (particularly in labor) have led to international specialization by task.

The question of what determines the comparative advantage of a country was further explored by **Eli Heckscher** and **Bertil Ohlin** in the Heckscher–Ohlin (H–O) theory of international trade. The **Factor Proportions** (or **Factor Endowment**) **Theory** proposed by H–O argues that various countries have different endowments of various factors of production. At the same time, various products use different factors of production with different intensity (Heckscher & Ohlin, 1991).

Based on this theory, a country would be exporting products that use intensively the abundant factor of production they have. In turn, a country would import products that use factors of production not available or less abundant within the country. Thus, the theory focuses on the productivity of the production process.

Nonetheless, production factors are not homogenous, and variations (particularly in labor) have led to **international specialization by task**; e.g., countries with less skilled and lower paid workers tend to export products that embody a higher intensity of labor.

Factor proportions analysis becomes more complicated when the same product can be produced by different methods, such as different mixes of labor and capital. The optimum location will depend on comparisons of the production costs. Although larger nations tend to depend more on longer production runs, companies may locate long-run production facilities in small countries if export barriers to other markets are relatively low. In addition, firms tend to locate longer-run production facilities in just a few countries. However, when long runs are less important, there is a greater tendency to scatter production units around the world in a way that will minimize the transportation cost associated with exports.

For example, India and China would export **labor-intensive** products because of their large labor pools, while Western European countries would export products that are **capital intensive**. Germany produces and exports automobiles and other highly technical products to the rest of the world. Countries with abundant labor resources can export labor-intensive products such as textiles. However, their situation in the long run is different from the countries with abundant capital resources. Countries with labor cost advantage can export labor-intensive products that create more demand for labor. Since the population of a country is limited, a high demand for labor will drive up the costs of labor and make it less competitive for labor-intensive products. Therefore, the labor cost advantage is only a short-term advantage. However, countries with **capital advantage** can enjoy a long-term growth because they will have low cost of capital and will be competitive in capital-intensive products. Therefore, these countries can continue to export capital-intensive products. Unlike labor-intensive products, exports of capital-intensive products will increase the capital supply due to the inflow of capital from export. Therefore, countries with capital advantages will have more capital supply from exporting capital-intensive products.

3.1.6   Product Life Cycle Theory

1. A product's sales begin domestically.
2. Production and sales tend to move abroad as the product matures.

Developed by **Raymond Vernon**, the **Product Life Cycle**, or PLC, theory suggests that when a product is first developed, its inputs come from the country where the product idea originated. As the demand for product grows around the globe, the company begins to export and eventually turns to producing the product abroad in an effort to remain competitive. In some cases, the product becomes an import in the country of invention. Figure 3.3 illustrates the typical stages of a product life cycle (Vernon, 1966).

Introduction Stage. The product is new in the home country. The firm attempts to familiarize itself with the market and chooses to keep the production local.

Growth Stage. The demand for product increases the sales, which drives down production costs and increases profits. Oftentimes, the sales expand overseas; the firm begins to export.

Maturity Stage. The product is well known around the globe. By that time, there are several major competitors in the market. As profit margins decrease, the business begins exploring an option of producing the product at a cheaper price overseas. The rationale behind such a strategy is to eliminate transportation costs for products sold in foreign markets and possibly to move all production abroad and import the product to its country of origin.

Decline Stage. As the product enters this stage in both domestic and foreign markets, the company can attempt to either differentiate it or deal with the consequences of a declining business.

One popular example of a product that closely followed the cycle described above is the personal computer. Other examples include copy machines, DVD players and most other electronics. The Product Life Cycle theory, however, is not applicable to all goods and services. Today, some corporations choose to produce the product abroad at much earlier stages.

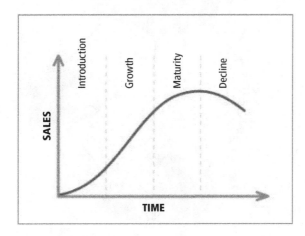

Figure 3.3 Stages of a product life cycle.

3.1.7 Porter's National Competitive Advantage Theory

1. Global competitiveness in a certain industry depends on its capacity to innovate & upgrade
2. This capacity is determined by the industry's resources, the demand for its products, conditions in related industries, and the competitiveness of firms within the industry.

Like the PLC theory, **Porter's Diamond of National Advantage** (see Figure 3.4) also helps to explain how countries develop, maintain, and possibly lose their competitive advantages over time. **Michael Porter's** theory states that a country's competitiveness in an industry depends on the capacity of the industry to innovate and upgrade. This theory attempts to explain why some nations are more competitive in certain industries by theorizing that national competitive advantage is embedded in the following four determinants (Porter, 1990).

Factor Conditions. These are the **basic** (labor, natural resources, climate, surface features) and **advanced factors** (workforce's skills, quality of the technological infrastructure) as well as **resource availability** (inputs, capital, technology) a country has that contribute to the competitiveness in particular industries.

Demand Conditions. Sophisticated buyers in the home market are important to national competitive advantage in a product area because it drives

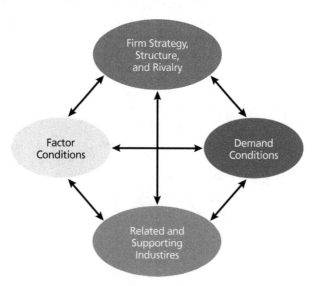

Figure 3.4 Porter's Diamond of National Advantage diagram.

companies to modify existing products to include new design features and develop new products and technologies.

Related and Supporting Industries. **Supporting industries** provide inputs, forming clusters of related activities in the same region that reinforce productivity and competitiveness.

Firm Strategy, Structure, and Rivalry. The creation and persistence of national competitive advantage requires leading-edge product and process technologies and business strategies. The more intense the struggle to survive among domestic companies, the greater is their competitiveness, which helps them to compete against imports and against companies that might develop a production presence in the home market.

All four determinants are interlinked and generally need to be favorable if a given national industry is going to attain global competitiveness. In the U.S. automobile industry, the four Porter's Diamond factors may account for the success of companies such as GM and Ford.

3.1.8 Limitations of the Diamond of National Advantage Theory

Porter's theory holds promise but has not been subjected to research using actual data on each of the factors involved and national competitiveness. The existence of the four favorable conditions may represent necessary, but insufficient conditions for the development of a particular national industry.

3.2 Free Trade

An important concept that relates to international flow of goods and services is **free trade**. It implies that countries should neither artificially limit imports nor artificially promote exports. Free trade also implies **specialization**.

The first pillar of the current global trading system is the belief that:

1. An open and free trade system is better than a system of managed trade with government involvement, and
2. Free trade will lead to a shift in the resources of a nation to the products that can be produced relatively more efficiently as compared to other countries and thus export those products.

In turn, products that cannot be produced efficiently relative to their trading partners will be imported. This argument is the basis for the theory of comparative advantage (Appleyard, Field, & Cobb, 2010).

The basic assumption of this theory is that *individuals* are best positioned to make decisions about the choices for product consumption. Therefore, any government intervention in international trade through tariff and non-tariff barriers affects the price structure and influences consumer choices. That is, bureaucratic decision makers, who may or may not represent the optimal choice of citizens, influence the system.

Free trade will lead to an increase in global production and consumption. Since the standard of living improves with an increase in consumption, free trade leads to improvement in the global standard of living, creates new entrepreneurial opportunities, expands the choice of goods and services, and creates jobs.

Even though the goal of most countries is free trade, structurally, various groups within each country can potentially ask the government for protection from free trade, which can make trade negotiations difficult. Considering the number of countries in the world and their own interests, it would be virtually impossible to negotiate an acceptable and comprehensive trade regime for all parties. Therefore, the observed trend has been the development of **regional trading blocs**. Negotiations among participants in the trading blocs have become the norm. For example, in the case of the European Union, the degree of integration has expanded beyond the usual economic trade and investment to include political integration. Even within trading blocs, however, the issue of fairness remains a topic of debate, as illustrated in the opening case. Excessive reliance on imports from other countries might be beneficial for businesses, but may also hurt workers in an importing country.

3.3   Government Interventions in Trade

Despite the growth of global trade over the past few decades, governments still intervene in order to attain economic, social, and/or political objectives. Officials enact those trade policies they feel best protect their countries, their citizens, some industries, promote other sectors, and perhaps increase their own political longevity. Proposals for **trade regulation reform** often spark fierce debate among competing parties or stakeholders. Governmental intervention in the trade process may be either economic or noneconomic in nature.

3.3.1   Economic Arguments for Government Intervention

In principle, no country permits totally unregulated flow of goods and services across its borders. Likewise, governments may choose to enable the global competitiveness of their own domestic firms. **Protectionism** refers to those government restrictions and incentives that are specifically designed to help a county's domestic firms compete with foreign competitors at home and abroad.

3.3.2 Protecting "Infant Industries"

The **infant-industry argument** holds that a government should temporarily shield emerging industries in which the country may ultimately possess a comparative advantage from international competition until the firms are able to compete effectively in world markets. Protection can be removed after firms gain the knowledge to become innovative, and become efficient and competitive.

Two basic problems associated with this argument are the assumptions that governments can in fact identify those industries that have a high probability of success and the firms within those industries that should receive government assistance. Protection can cause domestic firms to grow complacent toward innovation, limit their competitiveness, and increase consumer prices.

3.3.3 Balance-of-Trade Adjustments

The **trade account** (the current account) is a major part of the **balance of payments** for most countries. If balance-of-payments difficulties persist, a government may restrict imports and/or encourage exports in order to balance its trade account. Governments can **depreciate** or **devalue** their currency in order to make their products cheaper in relation to foreign products. Alternatively, fiscal and monetary policy can be adjusted to lower price increases as compared to prices in other countries.

3.3.4 Restrictions as a Bargaining Tool

Import restrictions may be levied as a means to try to persuade other countries to lower their import barriers. The danger, however, is that each country will, in turn, retaliate by escalating its own restrictions. To successfully use restrictions as a bargaining tool requires that they be believable and important to the targeted parties.

3.3.5 Price-Control Objectives

Countries may withhold products from international markets in an effort to raise world prices and thus improve export earnings and/or favor domestic customers. The Organization of Petroleum Exporting Companies

(OPEC) has controlled the supply of oil in order to affect prices. Another method of price control is through pricing exports below cost, or below their home-country prices or below their "**fair market value**," which is known as **dumping**. Most countries prohibit imports of "dumped" products, but enforcement usually occurs only if the product disrupts domestic production. In 2006, for example, India accused China of dumping silk and satin into the Indian market. While Indian producers alone cannot satisfy domestic demand for the products, they also cannot compete with Chinese prices.

SPOTLIGHT
Protectionism is not a Modern Issue

- Protectionism has been used as a tool throughout history.
- The ancient Greeks imposed 5% duties at all ports of their empire.
- Prior to the development of free market principles by Adam Smith and David Ricardo, the Navigation Act forced foreign products to come ashore from British ships. Records from the 12th century refer to import taxes.
- The Wall Street Crash of 1929 led to Smoot–Hawley tariffs. Some economists argue that retaliation to those tariffs might have deepened the Great Depression.
- In 2018, the United States withdrew from TPP, imposed steel and aluminum tariffs on most countries, including its allies, and put in place a tariff targeting more than $200 billion worth of Chinese products.

Based on
https://www.theguardian.com/business/2018/aug/13/is-free-trade-always-the-answer
https://www.tes.com/lessons/qavCi43fmJBtlw/trade-in-ancient-greece; https://www.britannica.com/event/Navigation-Acts;
https://www.freedomworks.org/content/new-smoot-hawley-protectionism-bad-american-businesses-workers-and-consumers
https://www.bloomberg.com/news/articles/2018-01-29/the-state-of-trump-trade

National Photo Company [Public domain], via Wikimedia Commons, https://upload.wikimedia.org/wikipedia/commons/d/dc/Smoot_and_Hawley_standing_together%2C_April_11%2C_1929.jpg
World Economic Forum Turkey 2008, https://commons.wikimedia.org/wiki/File:Flickr_-_World_Economic_Forum_-_World_Economic_Forum_Turkey_2008_(2).jpg

3.3.6 Political Motives

Governments may also choose to intervene in the trade process for non-economic reasons.

3.3.7 Job Protection

Persistent unemployment pushes many groups to call for protectionism. Displaced workers often do not find jobs that provide comparable compensation. By limiting imports, local jobs are retained as firms and consumers are forced to purchase domestically produced goods and services. However, unless the protectionist country is relatively small, such measures usually do little to limit unemployment and often result in a decline in export-related jobs. Further, such measures are likely to lead to retaliation unless either the protectionist or the affected country is relatively small. Thus, governments must carefully balance the costs of higher prices with the costs of unemployment and the displaced production that would result from free trade when enacting such measures.

3.3.8 Preserve National Security

Groups concerned about security use national defense arguments to prevent exporting, even to friendly countries, of strategic goods that might fall

SPOTLIGHT
U.S. Tariffs on Chinese Imports

As of July 2018, Trump administration's tariffs on China targeted mostly industrial goods like aircraft engines and gas compressors. Apple's iPhone, which is assembled in China, might be affected in the future. When an iPhone arrives in the United States, it is recorded as an import at a cost of $240, which is added to the massive U.S.–China bilateral trade deficit. Trade deficits in the modern economy, however, are not always what they seem. One estimate suggests that for iPhone 7, only 3.6% of the factory cost total of $237.45 was earned by China. In practice, the rest was earned by Japan, Taiwan, South Korea, and the United States, which all contribute to production of the phone.

Based on

Dedrick, Jason, Greg Linden and Kenneth L. Kraemer. "Supply Chain Economics— A closer look at the global supply chain of the iPhone raises questions about U.S. tariffs on China." *US News* (July 6, 2018). https://www.usnews.com/news/best-countries/articles/2018-07-06/would-trumps-tariffs-on-chinese-goods-affect-the-iphone into the hands of potential enemies or that might be in short supply domestically. Trade controls on non-defense goods may also be used as a foreign policy weapon to try to prevent another country from meetings its political objectives. Industries essential to national security receive government-sponsored protection for both imports and exports. Many countries fiercely protect their agricultural sector for national security reasons because a nation that imports its food supplies could face starvation in times of war. The first move by President Trump to impose tariffs on imported steel was established using the national security argument.

3.3.9 Maintain or Extend Spheres of Influence

Governments of the largest nations may become involved in trade to gain influence over smaller nations. For example, in 1962, the United States banned all trade and investment with Cuba in the hope of exerting political influence against its communist leaders. To maintain their spheres of influence, governments may give aid and credits to encourage imports from countries that join a political alliance or vote a preferred way within international bodies. Further, trade restrictions may coerce governments to take certain political actions or punish firms whose governments do not comply.

Debate—Should Government Impose Trade Sanctions

Pros

- *Effectiveness.* Often, punitive actions such as removing diplomatic recognition, boycotting events, or eliminating foreign aid or loans may be ineffective without the addition of trade sanctions.
- *No Military Force.* Trade sanctions allow a country to demonstrate its power and achieve political goals without the use of military force.
- *Ideological Consistency.* A country should not engage in trade with countries it does not support politically. *Example:* In 1960s, an embargo against Cuba was established to reduce the threat of its connection to communist regimes.

Cons

- *Sanctions hurt Citizens.* If sanctions are successful at weakening the targeted countries' economies, the costs are borne not by government officials, but by innocent people. Trade sanctions might hurt consumers who relied on cheap foreign imports. *Example:* U.S. sanctions on Iran following the termination of the Iran Nuclear Deal in 2018 negatively affected Iranians' purchasing power for important imported goods, such as medication.

- *Downward Spiral.* Sanctions might inspire negative sentiments against the imposing nation, worsening political tensions.

3.3.10 Cultural Motives

Exposure to people and products of other countries slowly alters cultures. Unwanted cultural influence causes great distress and can force governments to block imports. Many countries have laws that protect their media programming for cultural imperialism. For example, many foreign media entertainment is dubbed into the country's language instead of simply being subtitled. Often, the United States is seen as a threat to national cultures because of its global strength in consumer goods, entertainment, and media.

3.4   Role of International Organizations to Promote Trade

In 1944, representatives of 44 nations gathered in Bretton Woods, New Hampshire to discuss solutions for solving key economic and political issues facing the world after the Great Depression of the 1930s and World War II. They agreed to create the United Nations to promote peace and security and established the World Bank and the International Monetary Funds to coordinate economic growth and increase trade among members. One of the agreements under the Bretton Woods Agreement was the creation of the first multilateral free trade agreement, known as the **General Agreement of Trade and Tariff** (GATT), which went into effect in 1948. The main goal was significant reduction in tariffs and other trade restrictions among members. As a result of the GATT, the average tariff rate went down significantly, as members met from time to time in different rounds of negotiations to discuss trade issues and agree to further tariff reductions.

Despite its success in reducing trade restrictions, the GATT was criticized for two reasons: one was the lack of enforcement mechanisms when members were violating the agreement, and the second was the lack of standards to address the growing disputes for intellectual property rights issues. The **World Trade Organization** (WTO) was established in 1995 in Geneva, Switzerland as a replacement for the GATT, but also to include a more systematic enforcement mechanism and to address the intellectual property rights issues. In 2016, it had 164 members.[1]

WTO defines its mission as:

> The WTO provides a forum for negotiating agreements aimed at reducing obstacles to international trade and ensuring a level playing field for all, thus contributing to economic growth and development. The WTO also provides a legal and institutional framework for the implementation and monitoring of these agreements, as well as for settling disputes arising from their interpretation and application.[2]

WTO has played a significant role in recent decades in addressing trade disputes among members through its Dispute Settlement Body. Since its inception in 1995, WTO has received more than 500 cases of trade disputes and has offered over 350 rulings on these disputes.

3.5   Instruments of Trade Restriction

The choice of instruments to influence the international trade process is crucial because each type of control may incite different responses from both domestic and foreign groups. While some instruments directly limit the amount that can be traded, others indirectly affect the amount traded by influencing prices.

3.5.1   Tariffs

A **tariff**, or duty is a tax applied either on exported or imported goods. **Export tariffs** are levied by the country of origin on exported products; a **transit tariff** is levied by a country through which goods pass en route to their final destination; **import tariffs** are levied by the country of destination on imported products. Import tariffs are considered the simplest way to collect the tax, since a product cannot enter the country unless this tax is paid. Therefore, they can serve as a major source of revenue in developing countries. A tariff increases the price of a product, and, at the higher price, the quantity demanded will be less. Import tariffs raise the price of imported goods by placing a tax on them that is not placed on domestic goods, thereby giving domestically produced goods a relative price advantage. While tariffs may help specific segments of the economy in the short-term, it is a benefit at the expense of the consumers who end up paying higher prices.

- *Specific Tariff.* A fixed fee per unit of import. Effectively, it is a fee paid for every good imported and it is unchanging and unique, which means it does not change depending of the value of the good. *Example:* Paying an additional $5 dollar per barrel of oil imported.

- *Ad valorem Tariff.* A percentage of the value of the import. This type of tariff is usually more problematic to implement since it can vary constantly depending on changes in value of the imported good. *Example:* Paying an additional 10% for an imported car.
- *Compound tariff.* Calculated partly as a percentage of the stated price of an imported product, and partly as a specific fee for each unit.

3.5.2 Non-Tariff Barriers

Non-tariff barriers (NTBs) represent administrative regulations, policies, and procedures that directly or indirectly impede international trade. When the quantity of imports is limited, the resulting shift in the supply curve means that the equilibrium price will then be higher for domestic consumers.

- *Quotas* are restrictions on the amount (measured in units or weight) of a good that can enter or leave a country during a certain period. This type of trade intervention affects the international supply in a direct way as compared with the effects of tariffs. Import quotas restrict and directly determine the amount of products that are going to be imported to the country. Governments administer quota systems by granting quota licenses to other countries' companies or governments (import quotas) and domestic producers (export quotas).
  - **Import quotas**, just like import tariffs protect domestic producers by placing a limit on the amount of goods entering the country. This form of trade restriction helps domestic producers maintain market shares and prices by retraining competition in the short-term.
  - **Export quotas** are applied when countries wish to maintain supplies in the home market. This tool is more common for countries that export natural resources that are needed in the domestic market. A **voluntary export restraint** (VER) is a unique version of export quota that a nation imposes on its exports, usually at the request of an importing nation. If domestic producers do not curtail production, consumers benefit from lower prices due to a greater supply. Export quotas hurt consumers in the importing nation because of reduced selection and higher prices.
- *Tariff-quota.* A lower tariff rate for a certain quantity of imports and a higher rate for quantities that exceed the quota (e.g., agricultural trade).

SPOTLIGHT
China Imposes Temporary Anti-Dumping Measures on Japan, South Korea

In July of 2018, China's Ministry of Commerce announced that it would impose temporary anti-dumping measures on nitrile rubber from South Korea and Japan. The Chinese ministry will collect deposits ranging between 12% and 37.3% on imports from South Korea and deposits ranging from 18.1% and 56.4% on imports from Japan. Several major Japanese and South Korean exporters are expected to be impacted by the move.

Based on

https://www.reuters.com/article/china-antidumping-rubber/china-imposes-
temporary-anti-dumping-measures-on-japan-s-korea-nitrile-rubber-
idUSB9N1U401P

1. *If a country believes that another country is "dumping" products in their territory, what is the process to resolve the issue? Investigate and explain.*

- *Local Content Requirements.* Local content requirement laws are intended to favor the purchase of domestically sourced products over imported products. These laws may help protect domestic producers from the price advantage of companies based in other, low-wage countries. Developing countries use them to boost industrialization. In some cases, local content requirements might even apply to the employment of country's nationals. *Example:* Angola's Petroleum Activities Law of 2004 sets the local workforce target at 70%, and oil companies are required to submit an annual "Angolanization" plan to the Ministry of Petroleum.
- *Administrative Delays.* Intentional administrative or bureaucratic delays are designed to impair the rapid flow of imports into a country. They create uncertainty and increase the cost of carrying inventory. Competitive pressures, however, can motivate countries to improve inefficient administrative systems. Japan is known for utilizing administrative delays as an instrument of trade restriction. *Example:* At one point, Netherlands exported tulip bulbs to most countries around the world except for Japan. The customs inspectors insisted on checking every tulip bulb, creating delays and damaging the product (Hill, 2016).
- *Standards and Labels.* The professed purpose of standards is to protect the safety or health of the domestic population. However, countries may also devise classification, labeling, and testing standards

that facilitate the sale of domestic products but obstruct the sale of foreign-sourced products. *Example:* The European Union has rather strict labeling requirements; some of the mandatory labels include recycling and energy efficiency labels. While they were not necessarily created with the goal of decreasing imports, they might prevent some foreign companies from entering the market.

- *Currency Controls.* Currency controls are restrictions on the convertibility of a currency into other currencies. Governments could reduce imports of certain products, say automobiles or luxury appliances, by stipulating an exchange rate that is unfavorable to potential importers. They may also give a low exchange rate to importers of necessary imports such as medicines or food items. In addition, governments can give some exporters favorable rates to encourage exports of items such as machinery or farm products.
- *Embargoes.* An embargo is a complete ban on trade (imports and exports) in one or more products with a particular country. It is the most restrictive non-tariff trade barrier and often has political goals. Embargoes can be decreed by individual nations or by supranational organizations such as the United Nations (UN). *Example:* Following the Islamic Revolution of 1979 and the resulting hostage crisis involving American diplomats, the United States imposed and asset freeze and trade embargo on Iran.

3.5.3   Instruments of Trade Promotion

- *Subsidies.* Subsidies are direct or indirect financial assistance in the form of cash payments, low-interest loans, tax breaks, product price supports, or some other form of support from governments to their domestic firms to help them fend off international competitors. One of the most popular forms of government subsidy can be seen in the agriculture industry. The drawback of subsidies is that they can encourage inefficiency and complacency. Because governments pay for subsidies with tax income, it can be considered that subsidies benefit companies but harm consumers. Although subsidies provide short-term relief, the idea that subsidies are helpful in the long term is questionable. Table 3.1 illustrates the allocation of subsidies for the agricultural and industrial sectors by selected WTO members.
- *Export Financing and Special Government Agencies.* Governments promote exports by helping companies finance their export activities through loans or loan guarantees. Two agencies help U.S. companies to obtain export financing: **Export-Import Bank** (https://

TABLE 3.1 Sectoral Allocation of Subsidies of Selected WTO Members (yearly average 1999–2000)[3]

	Agriculture (%)	Industry (%)
Australia	30	51
European Communities	42	8
EU (15)	1	19
Japan	78	22
United States	60	8

www.exim.gov/) and the **Overseas Private Investment Corporation** (OPIC, https://www.opic.gov/). Governments have special agencies responsible for promoting exports. Such agencies organize trips for trade officials and businesspeople to visit other countries and open trade offices in other countries. *Example:* Many of the States in the U.S. have trade representatives in different regions of the world to conduct market research and help companies in their respective States sell their products and services overseas.

- *Free Trade Zones.* These are designated geographic regions in which merchandise is allowed to pass through with lower customs duties (taxes) or fewer customs procedures. A common purpose of such zones is final product assembly. *Example:* Mexico's maquiladora zones import materials from the United States without duties, process them, and re-export them to the United States, which charges duties only on the value added in Mexico.

3.6   The Role of Trade Blocs and Regional Economic Integration

Trade blocs refer to intergovernmental agreements to reduce, or even eliminate, trade barriers among member nations. Such agreements could be as simple as removing tariffs on products among trading partners to eliminating restrictions on movements of all resources (see Figure 3.5). The range or different levels of agreement are listed below.

- *Bilateral Trade Agreements.* A country may select to form a trade agreement with one other country at a time rather than with a group of countries. *Examples:* (a) President Trump has noted a few times his preference to negotiate a bilateral trade agreement with Mexico and another agreement with Canada rather than keeping a

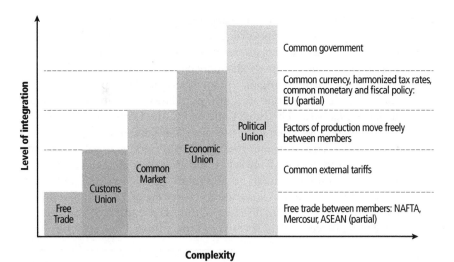

Figure 3.5 Levels of economic integration.

multilateral agreement with both countries. (b) Costa Rica's agreement with China and an agreement with Canada.

- *Free Trade Area.* Most of the trade barriers in goods and services are removed for member countries. *Examples:* (a) The European Free Trade Association (EFTA) composed of Norway, Iceland, Switzerland and Liechtenstein is one of the oldest free trade areas. (b) The North American Free Trade Agreement (NAFTA) among the U.S., Canada and Mexico.

- *Custom Union.* This arrangement is one-step beyond the free trade area. It not only removes the trade barriers among the member countries but also establishes a uniform external trade policy for non-members. *Example:* The Andean Community is an agreement among Bolivia, Ecuador, and Peru where they have reduced trade barriers toward each other, but they agreed on a similar trade policy for non-members.

- *Common Market.* This type of trade arrangement goes a step beyond the custom union level. It allows free movement of resources such as labor and capital among members. However, it is very challenging for members of a common market to agree on details of their monetary, fiscal, and employment policies. *Examples:* (a) The European Common Community (ECC) was one of the best examples of a Common Market arrangement before it moved to form the EU. (b) Argentina, Brazil, Paraguay and Uruguay, have removed many trade barriers and hope to form a Common Market.

- *Economic Union.* In addition to accepting the characteristics of the common market, members of an economic union adopt the same currency, tax policy, and similar monetary and fiscal policies. Forming an economic union is extremely challenging because of the difficulty of harmonizing all the member countries' policies given their differing economic strength, population, culture, and domestic issues. *Example:* The Euro Zone within the European Union.
- *Political Union.* Member countries have the same federal government, legislature, supreme court, and other political, social and economic arrangements. They act as one country and must agree on their foreign policy toward non-members. *Examples:* (a) The United States, and (b) The EU has tried to move toward becoming a political union, but given the diversity of the EU members, it may take a long time, if ever, for the EU to effectively form a political union.

TBL Connection
Fair Trade

While many trade agreements include labor provisions, to date, there has only been one instance of a labor issue being pursued through a dispute settlement process of a trade agreement. In 2010, the U.S. government started a case against Guatemala. The final decision was announced only in 2017. The panel found violations of Guatemalan labor laws, but it was decided that they do not affect the country's competitive advantage and should not be covered by the trade agreement.

In international business, the "fair trade" approach aims to help producers in developing nations to have better working and trading conditions and promote sustainability. Fair trade is a social movement that advocates for the payment of higher prices to local producers as well as higher social and environmental standards from multinational enterprises. The fair trade movement focuses in particular on exports from developing countries to developed countries, such as handicrafts and agricultural products like coffee and cocoa. In 2008, the Fairtrade Labeling Organizations International (FLO) estimated that over 7.5 million producers and their families were benefiting from fair trade funded infrastructure, technical assistance, and community development projects. Products certified with FLO International's fair trade certification amounted to approximately $4.98 billion (€3.4) worldwide, a 22% year-to-year increase (FTI, 2014). While the fair trade certification represents a tiny fraction of world trade in physical merchandise, some fair trade products account for 20-50% of all sales in their product categories in individual countries (WTO, 2010).

Fair trade's increasing popularity has drawn criticism from both ends of the political spectrum. The Adam Smith Institute sees fair trade as a type of subsidy or marketing ploy that impedes growth (Munger, 2014). Segments of the left, such as French author Christian Jacquiau, criticize fair trade for not adequately challenging the current trading system (Hamel, 2006). Despite some criticism of the movement, many international companies including Starbucks and Ben & Jerry's have adopted fair trade in their business operations.

Based on

https://www.scmp.com/business/article/2164417/can-international-trade-agreements-help-introduce-labour-reforms

1. *Why do some international corporations choose to adopt the fair-trade approach?*

3.7   Conclusion

Trade theories are useful for understanding patterns of trade, and for understanding competitive and comparative advantages a country can develop. Basic knowledge of the instruments of trade is beneficial for any future business manager in order to determine how to deal with trade restrictions if they arise. If a trend towards protectionism continues, firms may choose to move operations to a different country, concentrating on market niches that attract less international competition, adopting internal innovations that lead to greater efficiency or superior products, or trying to get government protection.

Chapter Review

Key Terms

- Absolute Advantage
- Comparative Advantage
- Factor Proportions
- Product Life Cycle
- Porter's Diamond of National Advantage
- Free Trade
- Fair Trade
- Infant Industry

- Tariffs: Specific, Ad Valorem, Quotas
- Non-Tariff Barriers
- Dumping

Questions & Assignments

Questions

1. Can a country simultaneously have a comparative advantage and an absolute advantage in the production of a given product? Explain

2. What role does geography play in the theories described in the chapter, in terms of decisions concerning international trade? Explain.

3. Would it make sense for the best physician in town, who also happens to be the most talented medical secretary, to handle all of the administrative duties of an office?

4. Given the uncertainty in today's world, many wonder if it is necessary or even desirable to have national economies linked so closely together. Discuss what a country can do to protect itself from the impact of negative global economic events. Discuss whether the impact of global recession on transitional economies is the same as the impact on developed countries. If not, in what ways are they different and why?

Assignments

1. The theories of absolute and comparative advantage and the product life cycle contribute to the explanation of the international trade process. Select two to three different types of products and discuss the likelihood that (a) an innovating country, (b) a rapidly developing country, and (c) an emerging country would enjoy an absolute advantage, a comparative advantage, or no particular advantage as each of the products moves through the four stages of the product life cycle. Ensure that students cite examples and explain their reasoning.

2. Porter's Diamond theory deals with the competitive advantages of nations. Select two to five countries and lead the class in a comparative analysis of the four points of Porter's Diamond. Conclude the discussion by exploring the associated competitive advantages that may accrue to foreign firms that choose to operate in each of those countries.

3. Find a list of all the products and industries affected by the recent tariffs imposed on China. To which products/industries can you

apply the national security rationale? Read this article to answer the question.

> Bryan, Bob. "Trump just slapped tariffs on $34 billion worth of Chinese goods—here's the full list of products that will get hit." *Business Insider.* (June 6, 2018). https://www.businessinsider.com/trump-china-tariff-full-list-of-goods-products-2018-6

Notes

1. WTO. (2014). *Understanding the World Trade Organization—members.* Retrieved from http://www.wto.org/english/thewto_e/whatis_e/tif_e/org6_e.htm
2. WTO. (2018). *What is the WTO? About the WTO—A statement by former Director-General Pascal Lamy.* Retrieved from http://www.wto.org/english/thewto_e/whatis_e/wto_dg_stat_e.htm
3. WTO. (2010). *International Trade Statistics 2010.* Retrieved from http://www.wto.org/english/res_e/statis_e/its2010_e/its10_toc_e.htm

Suggested Reading

WTO's Principles

> https://www.wto.org/english/thewto_e/whatis_e/tif_e/fact2_e.htm

John Steele Gordon, "The United States of Free Trade"

> https://www.wsj.com/articles/the-united-states-of-free-trade-1537566912

References

Appleyard, Field, & Cobb. (2010). *International Economics* (7th ed.). New York, NY: McGraw-Hill.

Bhagwati, J. N., Panagariya, A., & Srinivasan, T. N. (1998). *Lectures on international trade.* MIT press.

Daniels, J. D., Radebaugh, L. H., & Sullivan, D. P. (2014). *International Business: Environments and Operations* (15th ed.). Upper Saddle River, NJ 07458: Pearson.

FTI. (2014). Fairtrade International. Retrieved from http://www.fairtrade.net/

Hamel, I. (2006). Fair trade firm accused of foul play–SWI swissinfo.ch. Retrieved from http://www.swissinfo.ch/eng/fair-trade-firm-accused-of-foul-play/5351232

Heckscher, E. F., & Ohlin, B. G. (1991). *Heckscher-Ohlin trade theory.* The MIT Press.

Munger, M. (2014). Forget Fairtrade Fortnight, let the market work « Adam Smith Institute. Retrieved from http://www.adamsmith.org/blog/tax-spending/forget-fairtrade-fortnight-let-the-market-work/

Porter, M. E. (1990). The Competitive Advantage of Nations. *Harvard Business Review, 68*(2).

Rassekh, F. (2015). Comparative Advantage in Smith's" Wealth of Nations" and Ricardo's" Principles": a Brief History of its Early Development. *History of Economic Ideas, 23*(1), 59-76.

Vernon, R. (1966). International investment and international trade in the product cycle. *The Quarterly Journal of Economics,* 190-207.

WTO. (2010). International Trade Statistics 2010. Retrieved from http://www.wto. org/english/res_e/statis_e/its2010_e/its10_toc_e.htm

CHAPTER 4

The Global Financial
System and Risk

LEARNING OBJECTIVES

- Understand the relationship between various **global financial institu-tions** and markets
- Discuss the **fixed** and the **floating exchange rate** systems
- Understand various **exchange rate models** to determine the currency rate between currencies
- Learn about **International Parity Conditions** for exchange rates

Opening Case

Bitcoin

Historically, each country's central bank has managed inflation, economic growth, and the overall economic health by manipulating the amount of cur-rency, or money supply. Monetary authorities decrease supply when there is inflationary pressure and increase supply during economic slow-downs. How-

DAILY PERCENT CHANGE IN PRICE OF BITCOIN, GOLD AND S&P 500

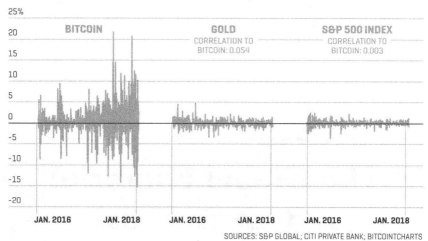

Figure 4.1 Volatility of Bitcon relative to gold and the S&P 500 Index. *Source:* http://fortune.com/2018/01/30/bitcoin-gold-cryptocurrency-citi/

ever, increasing supply too quickly may result in excessive inflation. In international exchange markets, domestic monetary policy may even impact the value of foreign currencies.

By contrast, cryptocurrencies operate independently of government regulation. Obtaining cryptocurrency, or "mining," requires only a capable computer, internet access, and software to access the user network. The amount of mineable coin is limited. Scarcity, rather than a central bank, determines the value of these digital currencies, which are exchangeable for products, services, and monetary assets. Supporters praise cryptocurrency for its relatively unrestricted nature, privacy, speed, and low cost.

Bitcoin, introduced by Satoshi Nakamoto in 2009, is the most-well known cryptocurrency. According to the Cambridge Judge Business School, it boasted 261,710 daily transactions during the fourth quarter of 2016. However, its price is extremely volatile. In 2013, the per-coin price rose from $13.30 to $770, and by January 2018, it had increased to $13,412. To maintain the per-coin price without manipulating the coin supply, most Bitcoin transactions are denominated in fractions of a single coin.

Certain countries have announced their intent to develop a national cryptocurrency. This hybrid could achieve the best of both worlds: state sponsorship reduces volatility, and scarcity-based valuation resists inflationary pressure. (McGlynn, 2014) The Bank of England hypothesizes that a state-backed cryptocurrency could permanently raise GDP by three percent by stabilizing the business cycle, maximizing tax revenue, and reducing real interest rates and monetary transaction costs. (Saville, 2017) China, Venezuela, and Iran may also seek to evade U.S. sanctions, which limit their international activities and inhibit foreign investment.

Based on

http://fortune.com/2018/01/30/bitcoin-gold-cryptocurrency-citi/

https://www.statista.com/statistics/730838/number-of-daily-cryptocurrency-transactionsby-type/.

https://seekingalpha.com/article/4130151-state-sponsored-cryptocurrencies-revisited

McGlynn, D. (2014). Digital Currency. *CQ Researcher, 24*(34), 793–816.

1. *How might the success of Bitcoin and other cryptocurrencies impact the future of international business transactions?*

4.0   Introduction

This chapter discusses the structure of the global financial environment. The major institutions and workings of the international financial market are described. In addition, the functioning of currency markets, and the factors that impact exchange rates are discussed. Finally, the challenges that the global financial system faces are analyzed.

The **Global Financial System** (GFS) can be divided into two components: global financial institutions and global financial markets. **Global financial institutions** include the International Monetary Fund (IMF), regional financial institutions, the World Bank, and regional development banks. The main function of these institutions is to help in the economic development of their members and to stabilize the financial and economic environment. The **global financial market** consists of foreign exchange markets, international equity markets, and international debt markets. These markets extend beyond geographic boundaries for investment and financing by bringing lenders and investors together irrespective of the geographic location.

Global financial institutions such as the World Bank and the International Monetary Fund oversee the global economy from micro and macro perspectives and initiate and support policies that stabilize and grow the world economy. There are **regional financial institutions** such as the European Central Bank that focuses on specific regions with the same aim. The main focus of the global financial markets is the operation of the foreign exchange market, the international equity market, international debt market, and other financial instruments. The **foreign exchange market** deals with currency exchange transactions of various countries. Its mission is to bring together buyers and sellers of a currency. These buyers and sellers are Multinational Enterprises (MNEs), speculators, banks, private citizens, tourists, government agencies and any other participants who may need access to foreign currencies.

The dynamic pattern of the GFS has been continuously improved in terms of the efficiency of global financial operations. This improvement has been instrumental for consistent global economic growth. However, simultaneously, this trend has resulted in the transfer of risk across geographic boundaries. In other words, the systemic risk of the financial market has become globalized, and it affects MNEs' operations.

4.1   Global Financial Institutions

Global financial institutions such as the World Bank and the International Monetary Fund were set up after World War II as part of the **Bretton Woods Agreement** to manage and stabilize the global financial system. Regional financial institutions such as the European Central Bank, and the Asian Development Bank focus on their respective regions. In addition, there are international banks that operate around the world with headquarters in specific countries. The main function of international banks is to provide value to their shareholders by providing high rate of returns and by diversifying risk. Finally, there are **private international investment funds** that seek the highest short-term rate of return and invest in the global equity markets including emerging market economies. In this section, each of these global institutions is discussed in detail.

4.1.1   Historical Context

Under the **Bretton Woods system** (1944-1973), the foundation of the currency market was a **fixed exchange rate regime**. In that system, all currencies were fixed (or pegged) against the U.S. dollar with exchange rates permitted to move a maximum of 2.25% around the fixed rate. The dollar was fixed against the price of gold, which was set at $35 per ounce. The major advantage of the fixed exchange rate system was that there was currency stability and speculation was discouraged. In the fixed exchange rate system, currencies that were not pegged at the correct level against dollar would experience a balance of payment deficit or surplus. When a country had a deficit, it was necessary to draw on the hard currency reserves of the country to cover the deficit. If the balance of payment deficit persisted, the country had to borrow hard currency in the international market to cover the deficit. In the extreme case of a persistent deficit, the country would seek permission to devalue its currency.

The **Jamaica agreement** of 1976 established the current foreign exchange system, a **floating rate system** under which global financial markets determine exchange rates. Adjustments toward equilibrium in the floating system take place continuously within small increments. There is no need for governments to intervene in the market by drawing on hard currency reserves, or to make fiscal or monetary policy adjustment based on external balances. The **G20 countries**, a major global economic power, meet regularly to discuss the exchange rates among major countries, coordinate their policies and make sure that the global currency market remains relatively stable. While countries do not normally interfere with the functioning of the market, during times of high turbulence, they attempt to stabilize the market through intervention. Major currencies such as Japanese Yen, the Euro, the Canadian dollar and the British Pound are "free floating" against dollar.

Although the global currency market is viewed as a system of flexible exchange rates, there are a number of countries that have their currency fixed (or **pegged**) to the U.S. dollar. Therefore, the value of these currencies moves up and down with the U.S. dollar against other major currencies.

The Chinese Renminbi. The most important, and to some degree controversial, pegged currency is the Chinese Renminbi (RMB or Chinese Yuan) parity with the U.S. dollar. This type of arrangement is particularly controversial since China has had a large trade surplus with the United States and does not allow the market forces to determine the value of its currency. One way to reduce a trade imbalance is by increasing the value of the currency of the country with a trade surplus against the currency of the country with a trade deficit. However, in the case of the Chinese Yuan, which has a fairly fixed value against dollar, it is not possible to use the exchange rate as an instrument of adjustment. This issue has created a dispute between the United States and China. While China has increased the value of the RMB against the dollar a number of times, the United States maintains that the currency is still undervalued and further adjustment is necessary. According to critics, if China allows its currency to fluctuate more freely, the RMB's value will go up relative to the USD and other major currencies, resulting in less exports from China and a lower trade surplus relative to its trading partners.

Debate—Exchange Rate Systems

Free Float

Pros
- *Efficient Market Valuation.* Exchange rates reflect currencies' true value, relative to other currencies and economic factors. They are also self-correcting and rapidly adjust to new information or conditions.
- *Less Government Intervention.* Although central banks occasionally intervene in hybrid "managed float" systems, they do so less often than in a fixed exchange rate system. This benefits the market,

which can adjust uninhibitedly and therefore more efficiently, as well as the government, which does not have to expend resources managing the market.

- *Relative Isolation from Foreign Shocks.* Because the currencies' values are not directly tied to one another, if one currency depreciates or appreciates, other currencies will not necessarily follow suit.

Cons

- *Constant Fluctuation.* For the exchange rates to reflect the currencies' true value in a constantly changing world, exchange rates must constantly change, or adjust. This increased volatility and unpredictability increases the amount of resources MNEs must devote to (a) forecasting future exchange rates and (b) hedging against the risks of fluctuation.
- *Exacerbated Problems.* Underlying economic problems, such as inflation or instability, may intensify, especially in developing nations.

Fixed ("Pegged")

Pros

- *Stability.* Rates set by governing bodies do not change daily. This stable financial environment allows investors, such as MNEs, to confidently plan strategic ventures and set prices. Thus, fixed currencies enable developing countries to attract foreign investment and increase demand for the currency.
- *Constrained Government Policy.* Fixed exchange systems require governments to have enough foreign currency to accommodate for citizens' requests to exchange the local currency for its equivalence in foreign currency. Thus, they cannot pursue extreme macroeconomic policies that would deplete the reserves.

Cons

- *Foreign Reserve Costs.* Maintaining foreign reserves is costly.
- *Intervention by Monetary Authorities.* An arbitrarily chosen exchange rate may not be the "optimal" rate. Monetary authorities cannot presume to know the equilibrium exchange rate better than the market.
- *Lagging Adjustment.* The economy may be unable to rapidly respond to economic shocks due to the fixed nature of the exchange rate.
- *Long Run Instability.* Pegs are difficult to maintain in the long run and may lead to financial crises. A pegged currency's value fluctuates in tandem with the currency to which it is tied. The domestic interest rate must also match the foreign rate. Thus, increases in the foreign

currency value or interest rate may reduce the pegged economies' competitiveness. At heightened exchange rates, the nation's foreign reserves may not accommodate for the demand to exchange the local (pegged) currency for its equivalence in foreign currency.

- *Overlooks Underlying Structural Problems.* Countries with pegs are often associated with having unsophisticated capital markets and weak regulating institutions. Pegging the currency alone is not sufficient to correct these basal issues.
- *Incompatible with Domestic Economic Targets.* A fixed exchange rate may not be compatible with the government's targets for growth, inflation, and unemployment. For example, a fixed exchange rate may expose domestic industries to increased competition from imported goods, which may unfavorably affect the nation's balance of trade.

4.1.2 The International Monetary Fund

History. The **International Monetary Fund** (IMF) was established after World War II as part of the Bretton Woods agreement. The agreement was named after the town of Bretton Woods in New Hampshire, USA. At the conference, representatives from 44 nations including the United States, France, and Britain met and established the foundation of a post war global financial system. Two institutions were set up to assure the success of the agreement; these were the IMF and the International Bank for Reconstruction and Development (IBRD), later known as the World Bank.

Initial Mandate. The IMF's mandate is the management of the global financial and economic system through (a) the creation of liquidity, (b) management of the exchange rate system, and (c) provide short-term loans to countries with a balance of payment deficit.

Initially, the management of the international exchange rate was the main focus of the IMF, because the structure of global financial system was initially based on a fixed exchange rate régime. Under the fixed exchange rate system, the IMF provided loans to countries that had short term balance of payment deficits and permitted devaluation for those with a structural deficit. However, the fixed exchange rate system eventually collapsed when the U.S. faced an external deficit and it unilaterally floated the dollar against gold in 1973.

Current Role. In the current system, the IMF reviews and recommends economic policy to member countries. It does not directly manage countries' exchange rates.

Another role of the IMF is to provide balance of payment support to member countries. If a country needs to borrow from the IMF to support their balance of payments, the IMF insists that the country initiates a structural adjustment of the economy prior to lending funds.

The **structural adjustment requirement** of the IMF in many cases is viewed as an excessive imposition on the borrowing country. The structural adjustment requirement has raised issues regarding the structural global financial system and has called for readjustment. This topic is discussed in the latter part of this chapter, but the IMF believes structural adjustment is necessary to create healthy and sustainable economic growth for both the country and the global economy.

While the function of the IMF has somewhat changed over time, particularly after the breakdown of the fixed exchange rate system, the underlying function of managing the global financial system remains. The IMF defines its function as:

> The International Monetary Fund (IMF) is an organization of 189 countries, working to foster global monetary cooperation, secure financial stability, facilitate international trade, promote high employment and sustainable economic growth, and reduce poverty around the world. (IMF, 2019)

The IMF has been credited for addressing a number of global financial challenges including the Asian Financial crisis in 1997 and the global financial crisis of 2008–2010 by preventing the collapse of the international financial system.

SPOTLIGHT
The Asian Crisis and the Role of IMF

In the period between 1990 and 1997, Asian countries experienced rapid economic growth. The state of the region, however, began to change in the summer and fall of 1997. When investors began losing confidence in the Thai market and started pulling out their funds, a downward pressure was put on the baht which was pegged to the U.S. dollar at the time. On July 2, 1997, the baht was detached from the dollar and despite the efforts of Thailand's central bank to maintain currency's value, market pressure drove it down by more than 20%. The crisis was contagious and had a significant impact on values of currencies such as the the Malaysian ringgit, the Philippine peso, the Taiwan dollar, the Singapore dollar, the Indonesian rupiah, the Russian ruble, and other currencies.

The IMF organized rescue packages with structural reform requirements for several nations with the most severe financial troubles, including Thailand, Russia, and South Korea. The rescue package to Thailand alone amounted to $16 billion. According to the reform requirements, Thailand was supposed to shut down all banks experiencing issues due to risky lending policies, and South Korea had to restrict excessive borrowing of its conglomerates. The support of the IMF was not always welcome. Many critics questioned the effectiveness of the packages, and the Indonesian government chose to decline the package altogether.

1. *If the IMF had not provided the bailouts, what would the recovery have been like for countries in crisis?*

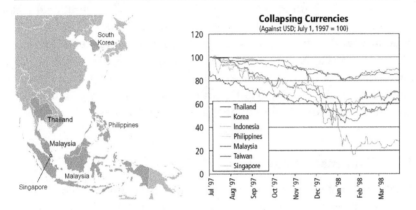

Figure 4.2 The Asian financial crisis. *Source:* https://commons.wikimedia.org/wiki/File:Asian_Financial_Crisis_EN.png; http://www.grips.ac.jp/teacher/oono/hp/lecture_F/lec11.htm

4.1.3 The World Bank

History. The World Bank was originally called the **International Bank for Reconstruction and Development** (IBRD). It was intially established as an institution to help the economic restructuring of Europe after World War II. In the beginning funds were provided by the United States to rebuild the infrastructure in Europe after the war. As Europeans paid back their loans with interest, the hard currency reserve of the World Bank increased.

Current Role. The focus then turned to helping emerging economies by providing them project-based financing. The World Bank can now raise capital in capital markets at a very low interest rate since it has the highest credit rating of AAA ("World Bank Group," 2014).

Organizational Structure. The World Bank is essentially a developmental agency. The bank has two major parts:

1. International Bank for Reconstruction and Development (IBRD). The IBRD gives loans at market rate interest (including risk premium) to its members for development projects. Projects that

are funded by the World Bank must meet both the **private rate of return** and the **social rate of return**. They must also be in line with the priorities of the bank.

2. International Development Agency (IDA). The IDA was established in 1960 and provides low interest loans (at subsidized rates) to lower income countries to help with their economic development.

The other institutions of the World Bank are the **International Financial Corporation** (IFC), the **Multilateral Guarantee Agency** (MIGA), and the **International Center for Settlement of Investments Dispute** (ICSID). The IFC's mission is to help the development of the private sectors in developing countries. The MIGA provides political risk insurance for investment in developing countries. The ICSID's primary function is to facilitate conciliation and arbitration of international investment disputes.

4.1.4   International Banks

International banks operate in many different countries. They not only facilitate investment but also play a key role in financing international trade and managing the flow of funds in international trade. Banks are the core of integration in the global financial system. Their functions include the following:

- Transfer of funds to private and public sectors
- Investment in various locations
- Helping raise capital from one country for another country
- Providing information to their clients of market opportunities.

International banks can be categorized as follows:

International commercial banks. These types of banks have overseas branches. They collect deposits and lend to individuals or businesses. International commercial banks also provide trade financing by issuing letters of credit. They have to follow the host country's rules and regulations.

Investment banks. They are a vehicle for bringing investors and those who require funds together for a fee. They help private sectors or even governments to raise capital by structuring loans and issuing **financial instruments**. Financial instruments include bonds (government bonds are called sovereign bonds), medium term instruments, and even short term commercial papers. They underwrite selling shares and bonds for investors. They also invest in overseas financial instruments.

International banks. International banks play a number of roles depending on their objectives and their mission. At the retail level, they collect deposits and lend locally. In many cases they are also involved in investment banking, and in such cases, they may not even accept deposits.

The business development aspect includes providing information on trade and investment opportunities and setting up deals for their customers. International banks also put together business deals for their customers across the globe. Most of the deals require financing that the bank can provide. Many international banks are globalized not only in terms of operations and services but also in terms of capital structure and even management. In this way, international banks are key facilitators of global economic operations such as international trade and financial integration.

Global Financial Crisis of 2008. The global financial crisis of 2008–2010 brought to light both the importance and shortfalls of the international banking system. In particular, it initiated the debate about creating a central body, or perhaps even an inter-government organization, to govern global financial institutions.

One such effort is based on the **Basel Accord** for banking supervision. A meeting of central bank officials from around the world in 1988 in Basel, Switzerland addressed capital requirements of international banks. This agreement became known as the Basel I Accord issued by the Basel Committee on Banking Supervision.

By early 2000, it became clear that Basel I was outdated and that a new set of initiatives was required. This shortcoming led to the next round of discussions in 2004 and an agreement that was called **Basel II** that raised the capital requirements of banks based on their different types of exposure, provided regulators with greater tools to address systemic risk, and promoted market discipline for risk management. In general, international banks face considerably higher risk in their overseas investments and operations. After the 2008-2010 financial crisis, **Basel III** was created to address the requirement for off balance sheet financing of banks and adequacy of capital requirement to match risk exposure (BIS, 2014).

4.1.5 Global Private Investment Funds

Private Investment (PI) funds or **hedge funds** are an aggregation of capital from a small number of major investors (usually less than hundred investors). They are managed by a professional investment organization. These funds are highly aggressive in their approach and seek the highest rate of return during a strong market and reduce loses quickly by exiting the markets during a downturn. Private Investment funds are subject to minimal regulation and they do not face the constraint standard investment organizations and mutual funds face.

The **global investment funds** invest in any company located anywhere in the world including their own country. **International funds** are similar to global funds, but international funds cannot invest in their home country. Investment in other countries must follow rules and regulations of the host country and in many cases even their home country.

4.2　Global Financial Markets

The main global financial markets are:

1. The foreign exchange market
2. The international equity market
3. The international debt market (including loans and bonds)

Global financial markets also include a market for complex financial instruments such as swaps, collateralized debt, futures, and options. In this section, only the three main markets are addressed.

4.2.1　Foreign Exchange Market

The **foreign exchange market**, in its broadest sense, deals with currency exchange transactions of various countries. The foreign exchange market brings together buyers and sellers of a currency.

There are a many reasons for currency exchange transactions. Examples include the export and import of goods and services among countries, overseas investments, payment of profit of foreign firms to their parent country, purchase of foreign equity, purchase of foreign bonds, and access to foreign currencies for traveling.

The main players in this market are international banks, foreign exchange traders and central banks of various countries. The most active foreign exchange markets around the globe are in London, New York, Zurich, Frankfurt, Paris, Shanghai, Seoul, Tokyo, and Sidney. Due to time differences, foreign exchange markets are open 24 hours each day.

In 2017, the ForEx market completed $5.016 trillion worth of transactions per day, according to the Bank of International Settlement. Out of that, $1,652 billion was in spot exchanges, $700 billion in forward exchanges, $2378 billion in swaps, and $254 billion in options and other transactions (BIS, 2017).

4.2.2 Spot Exchange Rate

The **spot exchange rate** is the rate at which one currency is exchanged for a unit of another currency, at that instant in time. A currency rate can either be a direct quotation or an indirect quotation against another currency. A **direct quotation** is the amount of home currency per unit of foreign currency. An **indirect quotation** is the reverse; it is amount of foreign currency per unit of home currency.

> *Example.* In case of the U.S. dollar, the direct quotation is the amount of dollar per unit of foreign currency. For example, 1.25 $/€ (dollar per Euro) is a direct quotation from the U.S. perspective, but a direct quotation in Europe would be 0.80 €/$ (Euro per dollar), which is 1 over 1.25. Again, a *direct* quotation is the amount of home currency per unit of foreign currency, and an *indirect* quotation is unit of foreign currency per one unit of home currency.

Transactions in the spot currency market are in the form of bid and offer (also called ask). A **bid** is the rate that currency traders buy the currency, and **offer** (or **ask**) is the rate that they sell the currency.

The difference between bid and offer is **spread**. The spread represents two different factors: (a) the transaction cost and (b) the risk factor. The lowest spread is when the transaction takes place in an international bank. The further away from major banks (e.g., at an airport), the higher the spread since both **transaction cost** (number of time transactions takes place until it is cleared at the major bank) and **risk** (time until transaction is settled at with major bank) increase.

Currency spot transactions occur when the currency exchange takes place at the *current* moment in time. In contrast, transactions in the forward market take place sometime in the *future*, but the rate is set at the *current* time. **Forward rates** are set based on the International Fisher Effect model, discussed later.

4.2.3 Exchange Rate Determination

There are different models to determine exchange rates between various countries. One set of models focuses on the relationship between the balance of trade and the exchange rate, and the competitiveness of the external sector in the world trading system. The second set of models focuses on the relationship between capital flows caused by interest rate differentials between the home country and the foreign countries, and the exchange rate. At the end, both trade and capital flows play a key role in determining exchange rates.

4.2.4 Supply and Demand for Currency

Currency trade takes place for a number of different reasons. Import and export transactions are the most obvious, but there are other reasons including investments in foreign equity markets, foreign direct investment, and even for speculation. Borrowing and lending further creates a need for the foreign exchange market.

The supply and demand approach states that the exchange rate of a country is determined by the supply and demand of goods (including financial) and services from that country. The following model, assumes there is no capital flow. Furthermore, the analysis is limited to two major trading partners: U.S. and Europe. The focus is supply and demand for Euros (€), the currency of most of the countries in the European Union (EU).

The currency market for the Euro and the U.S. dollar is presented in Figure 4.3. In that figure, the supply and demand for Euro are at equilibrium with exchange rate of 0.8$/€.

If the Euro becomes stronger against the dollar, at 1$/€, then U.S. goods become cheaper in Europe, and European goods more expensive in the United States. Thus, demand for European goods would drop in the United

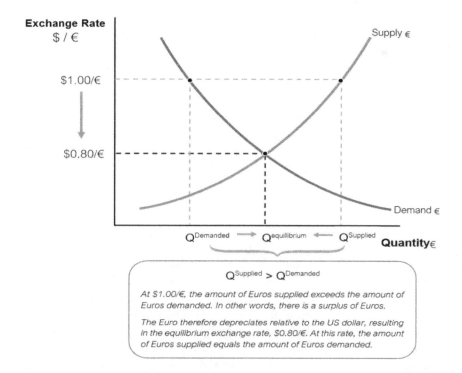

Figure 4.3 Exchange rate determination.

States, and demand for U.S. products would increase in Europe. There is a **balance of trade deficit** in Europe and a **surplus** in the United States.

The system then has to get to a balanced structure. Under the fixed system (before 1972), the governments of European countries would have to sell U.S. dollars and buy Euros to balance the trade deficit. In the current exchange rate system, balance is achieved by market forces. In other words, if there is demand for a currency, the price of the currency will be higher.

This pressure will lead the system toward an equilibrium rate of 0.8\$/€. The Euro has become weaker, and the dollar, stronger. The exchange rate is determined by the **purchasing power** of the home currency, relative to that of the foreign partner's currency.

What changes the purchasing power of one currency against another? The main factor that leads to change in the exchange rate between two countries is the competitiveness of the price of goods as a result of change in their prices, according to relative purchasing power parity. In sum, differences in inflation contribute to differences in countries' competitiveness, relative to one another.

4.2.5 Capital Flow

Capital flow between countries also impacts their exchange rate. The two models: the Fisher Effect and the International Fisher Effect explain the relation between capital movement among countries and the exchange rate.

- *The Fisher Effect Model* shows the relationship between the interest rate, inflation, and capital flow. When all the variables remain constant, any increase in the nominal interest rate will lead to a capital inflow.
- *The International Fisher Effect (IFE) model* focuses on the relation between interest rates and exchange rates. It argues that if the interest rate increases in a country, to avoid capital flow, the exchange rate must go down.

4.2.6 Complete Exchange Rate Model

Exchange rate forecasting is an art. While the main factors impacting future exchange rate were discussed in the previous section, there are other factors that impact future exchange rate. Factors such as political risk and excessive trade deficits cause major changes in the economic forecast, impacting the exchange rate.

- *Political Crisis.* In a period of political crisis, the exchange rate normally falls. Historically, the U.S. dollar was viewed as a safe refuge for international capital during the global crisis. However, the emergence of the Euro as a competitive currency could change the picture and it could also be used as safe store of value during international political crisis period.

- *Balance of Payment Deficit.* A large balance of payment deficit, as was explained previously, could lead to currency devaluation. It should be noted that while in a floating system this disequilibrium is corrected by exchange rate adjustments, in a managed exchange rate system, it requires government drawing on their foreign currency.

4.2.7   The Forward Market

As was mentioned earlier, there are a number of other currency markets known as **derivatives**. One such a market is the **forward currency market**.

The forward currency rate is a rate that is quoted by a bank or other financial institutions for a transaction in the future. The forward market is custom made, implying that the amount and the date of the transaction are negotiated between two parties ahead of time. The quotation in the forward market is in terms of bid and offer. The spread increases as the length of the contract into the future increases. For example, the spread for a six month forward contract is greater than the spread for one month.

The forward market is used to hedge currency risk. **Hedging** means eliminating or reducing the foreign exchange risk. In the case of a foreign currency *receivable*, a firm could sell the foreign currency in the forward market at a fixed rate eliminating the foreign exchange risk. In the case of *payables*, the firm can buy foreign currency at a forward rate and lock-in the rate ahead of time. In either case, the exchange rate risk is eliminated. The cost of hedging the currency risk in a forward market can be treated as business expense to eliminate risk, in the same way a firm buys insurance against risk.

One drawback of using the forward market is that if a transaction is fixed, and at maturity the exchange rate is in our favor, we must still honor the deal. In other words, while hedging in the forward market eliminates exchange rate risk, it also eliminates the potential of foreign exchange gain. But, leaving the foreign currency denominated receivables or payables unhedged in hopes of a foreign currency gain makes the firm in essence a **speculator** on the foreign exchange market. Since currency speculation is not a core competency of firms involved in international trade and investment, then it is highly recommended that firms eliminate the risk by covering their foreign exchange exposure. There are many tools available to MNEs to hedge their foreign exchange risk, but they are covered in International Financial Mangement courses.

4.2.8 The Global Equity Market

Most countries around the world have stock markets where stock of various companies are traded normally in their own currencies. These **equity markets** have blossomed after emerging economies changed toward a more open and free market.

The transition economies' stock markets, in particular, have expanded as a result of privatizating of state-owned companies. Developed economies have had their equity markets functioning for many decades and are well established. But the development of equity markets in emerging economies is a relatively new phenomenon.

One of the main characteristics of the equity markets is that they do not generally discriminate based on whether the fund is domestic or foreign investment. This openness of the equity markets has benefited both overseas investors that are looking for the highest rate of return and the domestic companies that are searching for liquidity.

Another benefit of international investment for investors is the ability to diversify their risk. The **risk diversification** is based on the principle that country specific risk varies among nations. By investing funds in various countries, the risk of investment is spread around and it is reduced. **The lower correlation between equity markets in which investment takes place, the greater is the risk diversification.**

Two main factors impact the risk of international portfolio investment.

- *Correlation of Various Equity Markets.* The more correlated the movement of the stock markets of two countries, the lower the benefits of risk diversification of investment between the two countries.
- *Currencies' Voltaility.* The more volatile the exchange rate between the two countries, the higher the risk of the portfolio in dollar terms, assuming that dollar is the home currency.

Increasingly, various stock markets across the globe are becoming integrated due to cross listing as well as general economic and business linkages across the globe.

Cross listing occurs when a firm lists its stock in a country other than the home country. Cross listing is particularly attractive for companies from small countries with limited capital base that are trying to raise funds in the United States. They offer their shares in U.S. dollars in the **New York Stock Exchange** (NYSE) in the form of **American Depository Receipts** (ADRs). ADRs are the price of stock (or a multiple of the price) in U.S. dollars. Therefore, if the stock price changes either in the home country or in the United States, or if the exchange rate changes, through **arbitrage** (buying in one market and selling simultaneously in the other market), the value of the stock becomes the same in all markets.[1]

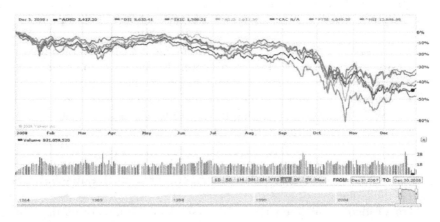

Figure 4.4 2008 global market crash. *Source:* https://seekingalpha.com/article/112780-global-stock-market-performance-in-2008

4.2.9 Currency Swaps

Currency swaps are financial instruments in which a certain amount of a foreign currency is exchanged at a spot exchange rate and at the same time a forward exchange transaction is set based on an agreement on specific terms of exchange without going through a market.

For example, two companies from different countries may enter into a currency swap, particularly if there is exchange rate control. They do that by exchanging home currencies for a foreign currency with a partner outside the market.

Currency swaps are done for a fixed period, and the rates are agreed between partners. After the period expires, they can revert back and settle their payments by once again exchanging currencies. Besides currency swaps, there are other types of swaps that are used by MNEs, usually with the help of a broker, to reduce the foreign exchange risk.

4.2.10 The Global Debt Market

The **global debt market** provides a variety of financing instruments with different options regarding maturity, payment structure, and currencies. The main sources of debt financing are international bank loans, syndicated loans, the international bond market, and the Euro market.

International banks have historically been a source of funds for local firms outside their country. Borrowing dollars outside the U.S. (called **Euro dollars**) has the benefit of obtaining a lower interest rate on a loan than a dollar loan in the United States. The lower cost of borrowing is because the Euro dollar market is unregulated and is a wholesale market.

Euro dollar credit is usually given to institutions or to the governments (call **sovereign credit**) by the banks in USD dollar terms. Normally, the credit is pegged to the **LIBOR** (London Interbank Offer Rate). The LIBOR is the short-term borrowing rate in London among major banks. It is used as the benchmark for lending and borrowing internationally. Normally borrowing rate is the LIBOR rate plus certain points. The points reflect the risk associated with that specific borrowing.

A **syndicated loan** is similar to a bank loan, but it includes a group of banks that partner in lending. The syndicated loan is particularly the case for large loans when a bank does not want to be highly exposed to such a loan. This type of loan is usually organized by a bank called the lead bank. In turn, the lead bank markets the loan to a small number of international banks. There is also a management bank. The management bank's function is to collect interest and to distribute it to member banks based on their participation. The management bank in essence acts as the representative of all the other banks participating in the financing of the credit.

4.3   Impact of the Global Financial System

The global financial system has provided a working structure that has led to a relatively high economic growth for a number of countries and specifically has helped to fuel the growth of many emerging economies. It has led to the movement of capital resources from countries with excessive capital with low marginal productivity to countries with limited capital and where marginal productivity of capital was high. Yet the system has its own critics and there are those who call for the reforming of Global Financial system (Stiglitz, 2007).

Criticism #1

"Due to the integration of the global system, the financial problems of each country will have global implications which are transferred to other countries." This "**contagion effect**" is particularly true for countries that are economically and financially strong. A financial problem in one these countries can be globalized and have such an impact that potentially could lead to the collapse of the global financial system. Stiglitz argues that a global financial crisis has become the norm rather than an occasional occurrence (J. Stiglitz, 2003).

In the last three decades, there have been numerous crises such as the Mexican peso crisis in 1995, the Asian financial crisis in1997, the Russian crisis in 1998, the Argentina financial crisis in 2002, the U.S. financial crisis in 2008, and most recently the Greek financial crisis in 2010. These are a few of well-known crises that have occurred and that have had a global impact. Each crisis had its unique causes, but their impact affected many different countries. The U.S. financial crisis in 2008 almost resulted in the collapse of the whole system.

Criticism #2

"The current system has led the flow of funds to go from emerging economies to developed countries including the United States" (J. E. Stiglitz, 2003). This second set of criticisms is based on the fairness of the structure of global financial system. One of the most outspoken critics of the system is Joseph Stiglitz, who has argued that a well-functioning system will shift funds from capital rich developed countries to poor countries. But even when there is capital flow to developing countries, it is not going to the countries most in need of global financial resources, such as Sub-Saharan Africa.

Counter Argument

"The problem is partially due to the governance and legal institutions in those countries." It is argued that improvements in the governance and legal systems to protect investment would lead to an increase in flow of capital resulting in higher economic growth and improvement in economic well-being of people, which in turn further increases the capital flow.

Criticism #3

"Capital flows across geographical boundaries, particularly in the equity market, have become highly short term and speculative." This problem, also known as

"**hot money**," has created an inherent destabilization of the global financial market. In other words, excessive capital flow creates an artificial liquidity that fuels a fast rate of economic growth. However, once there are signs of economic problems, then there is a quick capital outflow. Therefore the system has a built in destabilizing element (J. Bhagwati, 1998).

Counter Argument

"The system has managed to address each crisis and has sustained itself." If it was not for the current system, the world's economy would have collapsed. They also argue that while the system has not helped every country to move out of poverty, it has been instrumental in shifting many of the low income countries toward becoming middle income level. Supporters admit that there are some shortcomings particularly in regards to modern financial instruments, but any adjustment must be in the form of fine-tuning and not a complete change of the system.

4.3.2 Suggested Reform

Joseph Stieglitz, in his critique of the current global system, put forward a number of ideas for reforming the global financial system. One idea proposed by Stieglitz was a new global reserve system.

He also suggested that international financial institutions such as the IMF must become more democratic and more sensitive toward the needs of least developed countries. His suggestion is that the "global greenback" can be managed by the International Monetary Fund in a similar manner as the Special Drawing Rights (SDRs) if the IMF is reformed. Obviously, the concept of **global currency** faces strong opposition from the U.S. and has not emerged in any way as a practical option to the US dollar.

4.4 Parity Conditions

4.4.1 Absolute PPP

Under **Absolute PPP**, the price of a basket of goods in one currency should be the same as the price in another currency. The exchange rate between two currencies is equal to the price ratio of the products, $E = P_h / P_i$.

This simple approach assumes that there are only two countries and only two products or two identical baskets of goods.

Some economists compare the price of a Big Mac in various countries to determine whether a currency is overpriced or not. The Big Mac is a convenient product since it is sold in 120 countries. The theory is that the Big Mac should cost the same in each location.

The Big Mac costs about $3 in the United States, but its price is significantly lower than $3 in some countries such as India and Hong Kong, and much higher than $3 in Switzerland and Norway. So, the U.S. dollar has a higher purchasing power in India than in Switzerland.

This comparison does not take into consideration other factors that affect the price, such as the price of rent, insurance, profit margins, taxes or transportation costs that vary from country to country.

One of the more recent ways to compare prices of products across national boundaries is the use of the **Starbucks Index** that compares the price of a Tall Latte in different major cities (Figure 4.5). This index, just like the Big Mac Index, compares the purchasing power of different currencies, as measured by the price of a Tall Latte.

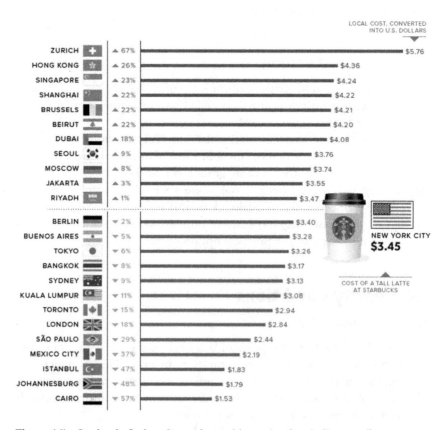

Figure 4.5 Starbucks Index. *Source:* https://www.visualcapitalist.com/latte-index-currencies/

For instance, the price of the Tall Latte in Figure 4.5 was equal to $5.76 in Zurich, which is about 76% more expensive than the price in NYC. However, the Tall Latte was sold for $1.53 in Cairo, 57% cheaper than its price in NYC. This type of comparison does not indicate that the overall prices in Zurich are more than 75% higher than in NYC, but implies that Zurich is a very expensive city whereas if you convert your $ to the Egyptian Pound, you could buy a lot more in Cairo than in NYC. In other words, the U.S. dollar has a high purchasing power in Egypt, India or Turkey while its purchasing power is fairly low in some other cities such as Zurich, Hong Kong or Singapore.

4.4.2 Relative PPP

Relative PPP argues that the exchange rate between two countries is a function of the inflation rate between the two countries. It is assumed that the exchange rate between the two countries is at equilibrium and that to remain at equilibrium the exchange rate change must be equal and opposite to the inflation rate differential between the two countries.

How accurately does PPP forecast value of exchange rate? Empirical studies have determined that in the long run and when the inflation rate differentials are high, PPP is a fairly good estimator of future exchange rate. However, it is not a good predictor for short term forecast or when the inflation rate differential is small.

This lack of support for PPP is because there are factors such as the role of government, tax treatments, expectations, and interest rates that impact the value of the future exchange rate that could be more significant than the inflation rate differential. Furthermore, inflation rates refelect prices of non-traded goods such as land and some services such as hair cut that cannot be imported from other countries if they are cheaper.

4.4.3 The Fisher Effect

This approach is based upon the principle that money will flow to the country where it will earn the highest return considering the interest rate and the inflation rate in the countries. The model claims that if two countries start at equilibrium and the objective is not to have capital flow between the countries, then the interest rate differential must be equal to the inflation rate differential between the two countries. In other words, the real interest rate has to be the same in order to prevent capital flow between two countries.

4.4.4 The International Fisher Effect

The **International Fisher Effect** (IFE) simplifies the Fisher Effect by considering the interest rates instead of a combination of the interest rates and the inflation rates. The International Fisher Effect argues that if the exchange rate change must be equal and opposite to that of the interest rate differential between two countries. For instance, if the nominal interest rate in Canada is 2% higher than the rate in the U.S., the IFE claims that the Canadian dollar will depreciate by the same 2%. This theory is based on the assumption that exchange rates and interest rates are free of government interventions and they move based on demand and supply.

4.5 Conclusion

Global trade and investment has brought the world closer and created an integrated system of economic interdependency between various countries. The main benefit has been a period of relative high economic growth, emergence, and transformation of a number of developing countries through this system, toward developed economies. Examples of this phenomenon include China, India, South Korea, and Brazil.

However, global trade and investment have also created a system of risk transfer, particularly from major economies to smaller ones. The system withstood pressure during the Asian financial crisis of 1997-1999, but the United States' economic and financial crises of 2008 affected trade partners and the greater the financial system alike. In sum, although we have a global financial and economic system, systemic risk has internationalized.

TBL Connection
International Finance Facility for Immunisation (IFFIm)

In 2003, the United Kingdom got inspired by the Millennium Development Goals set by members of the United Nations and proposed to create a facility that would tackle health and well-being issues around the globe. The following year the idea became a reality in a form of new financial instrument called the International Finance Facility for Immunisation (IFFIm). The facility issues investment-grade bonds in the global equity market to raise funds for Gavi, an organization that provides life-saving immunization in the poorest countries of the world. The risk of funding it is shared by Australia, France, Italy, the Netherlands, Norway, South Africa, Spain, Sweden, and the UK. The World Bank serves as its treasury manager.

The unique aspect of the financial instrument is that it combines people and profit pillars of the TBL by paying a competitive return to its investors around the globe and supporting a social issue. The bonds were purchased by retail and institutional investors in Japanese, Australian, Eurobond, and Islamic financial markets. Over the period between 2000 and 2016, Gavi vaccinated close to 640 million children. The disbursements were used for tetanus, measles-rubella, hepatitis-B, polio, and many other important vaccinations in 71 developing countries. In the Democratic Republic of Congo, for instance, Gavi partnered with Word Health Organization, UNICEF, and Bill & Melinda Gates Foundation to eradicate polio. The IFFim is just one of the examples of how public-private partnerships and financial engineering could be utilized to promote global development.

1. *What differentiates IFFIm from philanthropy? What is the benefit of issuing IFFIm bonds in equity markets around the globe? What are some of the potential issues associated with the instrument?*

Based on

https://www.iffim.org/

Chapter Review

Key Terms

- Global Financial System
- Global Financial Institutions
- Global Financial Markets
- Bretton Woods System
- Jamaica Agreement
- Fixed Exchange Rate
- Floating Exchange Rate
- International Monetary Fund (IMF)
- Private Investment Funds
- Foreign Exchange Market
- Currency swaps
- Spot Exchange Rate
- International Fisher Effect (IFE)
- Forward Market
- Global Debt Market
- Global Equity Market
- Purchasing Power Parity (PPP)

Questions & Assignments

Questions

1. Describe the difference between floating and fixed exchange rates. What are the implications of each exchange rate system for the MNEs?
2. How and why do MNEs use the forward market? Discuss the advantages and disadvantages of using it.
3. Consider Figure 4.4 from the 2008 Financial Crisis spotlight. Why did the indices of different equity markets across the globe move in the same direction?

Assignments

You are the CFO of a multinational perfume manufacturing company with the headquarters in Lyon, France. Your brand has been gaining recognition around the globe and the sales in the United States alone have gone up by 10% in the last quarter. Your team developed a forecast of $/€ exchange rate for the next 3 months. Given your team's forecast is accurate and you will have receivables in dollars in two months, will the exchange rate movement affect your company in a positive or a negative way?

Spot Rate	1 Month Later	2 Months Later	3 Months Later
1.13 $/€	1.14 $/€	1.15 $/€	1.15 $/€

Compare the World Bank to the International Monetary Fund. What is the role of each of the institutions? Select one of the institutions and develop a brief summary about one of its latest project.

Note

1. For further discussion of ADRs see Eiteman, Stonehill, and Moffett Multinational Business Finance, 10th edition Pages 328-331. Eitman David, S. A. (2004). Multinational Business Finance. Boston: Pearson Addison Welsley.

Suggested Reading

IMF. (2018). *Global Financial Stability Report*. Retrieved from https://www.imf.org/en/Publications/GFSR/Issues/2018/09/25/Global-Financial-Stability-Report-October-2018

Camarda, B. (n.d.) *How Currency Risk Impacts Business Earnings*. Retrieved from https://www.americanexpress.com/us/foreign-exchange/articles/currency-risks-impacting-international-businesses/

Breene, K. (2016). *What is the Future of Global Finance?* Retrieved from https://www
.weforum.org/agenda/2016/01/what-is-the-future-of-global-finance/

References

Bhagwati, J. N. (1998). The capital myth—The difference between trade in widgets
and dollars. *Foreign Affairs, 77,* 7–12.

BIS. (2014). *Basel Committee on Banking Supervision.* Retrieved from http://www.bis
.org/bcbs/BIS. (2017)

Fenner, R. (2008). *U.S. rating downgrade exacerbates currency misery for Elpida, Fuji
Heavy—Bloomberg.* Retrieved from http://mobile.bloomberg.com/news/2011
-08-08/u-s-downgrade-exacerbates-yen-misery-for-elpida-fuji-heavy

IMF. (2019). *IMF—International Monetary Fund home page.* Retrieved from http://www
.imf.org/external/index.htm

International Finance Facility for Immunisation. (n.d.). Retrieved from https://
www.iffim.org/

Macro, S. S. (2017, December 6). *State-sponsored cryptocurrencies revisited.* Retrieved from
https://seekingalpha.com/article/4130151-state-sponsored-cryptocurrencies
-revisited

Madura, J. (2003). *International financial management.* Mason, OH: Thomson/
South-Western.

McGlynn, D. (2014). *Digital currency.* Retrieved from https://library.cqpress.com/
cqresearcher/document.php?id=cqresrre2014092600

Number of daily cryptocurrency transactions by type 2016 | Statistic. (n.d.). Re-
trieved from https://www.statista.com/statistics/730838/number-of-daily
-cryptocurrency-transactionsby-type/.

Singh, A. (2008, December 31). *Global stock market performance in 2008.* Retrieved from
https://seekingalpha.com/article/112780-global-stock-market-performance
-in-2008

Stiglitz, J. E. (2003). Dealing with debt. *Harvard International Review, 25*(1), 54–60.

Stiglitz, J. E. (2003). *Globalization and its Discontents.* New York, NY: Norton.

Stiglitz, J. E. (2007). *Making globalization work.* New York, NY: Norton.

Wieczner, J. (2018). *Why bitcoin may not be digital gold after all.* Retrieved from http://
fortune.com/2018/01/30/bitcoin-gold-cryptocurrency-citi/

World Bank Group. (2014). Retrieved from http://www.worldbank.org/

CHAPTER 5

Political and Legal Environments

LEARNING OBJECTIVES

- Describe the major **political systems** and their relation to a country's **economic** and **legal systems**.
- Understand the role of prominent **supranational organizations** in international business.
- Identify sources of **legal differences**, **ethical ambiguity**, and **political risk** in global business. Also explain **mitigation** methods, such as institutional mediation.
- Discuss the implications of **new political trends** on global business.

Opening Case

"Asset Seizure"—General Motors in Venezuela

In the spring of 2017, U.S.-based company General Motors (GM) announced it would halt operations in Valencia, Venezuela after foreign officials seized

Global Business, pages 101–117
Copyright © 2019 by Information Age Publishing
All rights of reproduction in any form reserved.

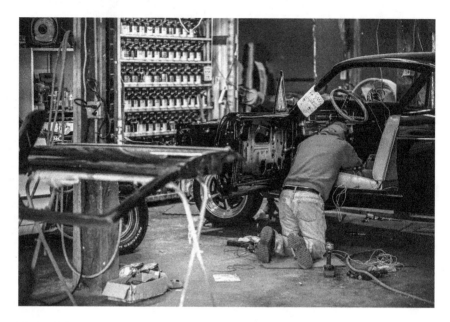

Figure 5.1 Automotive industry. *Source:* Fancycrave.com

its plant and "other assets of the company, such as vehicles." Although the MNE had been the market leader in Venezuela for 35 years, it found itself increasingly ensnared in the nation's political and economic turmoil. Competitors suffered a similar fate. Ford wrote off its Venezuelan investments in early 2015, having stopped production. Toyota Motor Corp reported its plant was operating normally, but it was "only producing based on orders that come in."

Industry statistics painted a grim picture. In 2016, Venezuela's total auto production had fallen to an all-time low of less than 3,000 vehicles. The car industry lacked raw materials, and it was not alone. Food-makers and pharmaceutical firms experienced similar hardship under the nation's command economy, centrally planned by a government instating complex controls over currency and production.

Based on

https://www.rt.com/business/385387-venezuela-general-motors-plant/

1. *How could an attractive investment transition to an economic nightmare? What are the signs of political risk, as well as the potential remedies?*

5.0   Introduction

A nation's political and legal systems not only set regulatory standards, award subsidies and grants, or impose taxes, quotas, and tariffs, they also create free trade agreements, common markets, and other political and economic unions. These activities impact capital flow and, consequently, the business world.

The relationship between foreign governments and international businesses is often fragile. Although hosting an MNE may result in higher economic growth and improved economic well-being, some large international companies dictate the terms of their operations by getting involved in local politics. Corrupt foreign officials similarly prey upon MNEs. For example, they may accept corporate bribes and award contracts unfairly.

In our culturally and legally diverse world, international business law seeks to standardize and regulate global business practices. Institutions, such as the World Trade Organization, act as mediators. Navigating the international political landscape is challenging nonetheless, armed with proper understanding, firms can succeed abroad and offer foreign nationals much needed products, services, and opportunities, including those their host government cannot provide. Figure 5.2 displays each country's level of political freedom, according to Freedom House's 2019 ratings (Freedom House, 2019).

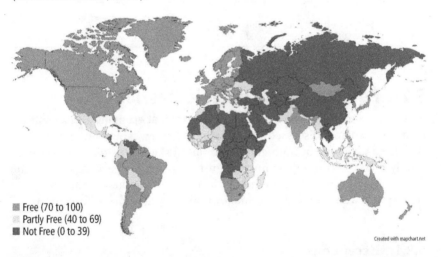

■ Free (70 to 100)
Partly Free (40 to 69)
■ Not Free (0 to 39)

Created with mapchart.net

Figure 5.2 Map of Political Freedom (Freedom House, 2019). (Aggregate score: 0 = least free, 100 = most free)

5.1 Overview of Political Systems

Fundamentally, there are two main political systems: **democratic** and **nondemocratic** (see Table 5.1).

TABLE 5.1 Democratic and Non-Democratic Systems	
Democratic System	**Non-democratic System**
✔ Leaders elected by majority vote, consensus, or direct referendum.	✘ Leadership does not change by election or popular vote. It is gained by inheritance or force (e.g., totalitarian system or dictatorship.)
✔ Periodical elections ensure leaders are accountable to their constituencies.	
✔ Economic and policy issues are debated, not only for the leadership's decision-making process, but also for the voting population.	✘ Regime changes are abrupt and possibly violent when a group seeks to overthrow the leadership in a coup d'état.
	✘ Policy issues are not openly debated, therefore their costs and benefits are not apparent to the population.
✔ "Equality" and "freedom" have been identified as important characteristics, although there is no specific, universally-accepted definition of democracy.	✘ The interests of the dictator or ruling group may not reflect majority interests. These self-serving objectives are often accomplished at the expense of citizens.
✔ There is usually freedom of expression, freedom of press and freedom to organize political parties	✘ It is against the law to criticize the leader and the party in power.
✘ May be slow in terms of decision making, since all decisions need to be debated and agreed upon.	✔ Decision-making is faster, since the decision flow is top-to-bottom.
Examples: United States, Germany, France, India, South Africa	*Examples:* China, Iran, Cuba, Saudi Arabia, Egypt

5.2 Political and Economic Overlap

Economic systems also have two variants: a **market economy** and a **centrally planned economy**, discussed in an earlier chapter. Nowadays, most countries have elements of both economic variants, and it is difficult to find a purely market economy or purely centrally planned market (such as the former Soviet Union.) Nonetheless, a nation's economic stance tends to correspond with one of the two major political systems (see Table 5.2).

5.2.1 Exceptions

Although market economies typically accompany democratic political systems and vice versa, there are cases where non-democratic societies such

TABLE 5.2 Market and Centrally Planned Economies		
Economic System	Market	Centrally Planned
Decision Makers	"The Market"	Planning Authorities
(Typical) Political System	Democracy	Totalitarian

SPOTLIGHT

Market Authoritarianism and Democratic Socialism

Many of the Persian Gulf countries such as the United Arab Emirates (UAE), Qatar, and Bahrain have a market economy, but the political system is totalitarian.

In Europe, social democratic parties play an important role and have been in power for decades.

---

as China have market-driven economies. Similarly, many democracies such as Denmark, Finland and Sweden have strong tendencies for socialist economic systems.

A **socialist economic system** is a structure that is somewhere in between a full market economy and a full centrally planned economy. Typical characteristics are the following.

- Several major social functions, such as **healthcare** and **education**, are the responsibility of the government
- The government also develops the country's **infrastructure**, including roads, airports, electric power systems, water resources, telecommunication, etc.
- Private firms have the possibility of participating in many different manufacturing and service industries.
- Financial resources for government investments must come from taxes. (Therefore, the marginal tax rate is quite high.)
- Some of the government owned firms get subsidies from the public sector; as a result, there is less emphasis on profitability and efficient resource use.

5.2.2 The Soviet Union

The quintessential example of intertwined political and economic transition is the former Soviet Union (Union of Soviet Socialist Republics), a communist regime with a centrally planned economy. Although the Soviet Union was technically a union of 15 republics, its economy was **centralized** and the **Communist Party** dominated the union's **single-party political system** until 1990. **Satellite countries**, such as Poland, the Czech Republic, Slovakia, Hungary, Romania and Bulgaria, were formally independent from the Soviet Union, but their political and economic states were heavily influenced and controlled by the Soviet Union. Their democratization and economic liberalization occurred in two stages:

1. *1980s.* Economic pressure built on the Soviet Union. It became difficult to support the various republics and satellite countries of Central Asia and Eastern Europe, and the Soviet Union's control of these satellite countries weakened.
2. *1990s.* These countries began restructuring their economic and political system toward a market economy and a democratic political system.

The transition of East European economies to market economies became a reinforcing cycle that started with East Germany's unification with West Germany and continued with the dissolution of the former Soviet satellite countries that joined in the reform process. In addition, many of the Central Asian Soviet republics became independent states from Russia and began the process of transition to market-based economies. Russia also began restructuring its economy.

5.3 Supranational Organizations

A **supranational organization** is an international group or union that has an influence over its member states. While some supranational organizations do not have an enforcement authority, many play an important role in the political and economic environments of member states by setting the stage for collective decision-making.

5.3.1 Political Union

A **Political Union** is a supranational organization that represents the maximum level of integration among countries and occurs when a group of states adopts not only common economic and monetary practices, but also a common political policy. Some examples of political unions are the United Arab Emirates (UAE) and the European Union (EU).

The **European Union** (EU) began as the **European Economic Community** (EEC), established by six countries in 1958. It was then an economic union that sought to prevent future conflict among European nations by fostering commercial interdependence among member states. It has since expanded to include 28 member states, which share a **single market**, a **common currency** (the Euro), and **policy agreements** in certain areas, including climate, health, and security.[1] The EEC changed its name to the EU in 1993, reflecting the consortium's development from a purely economic union to a partially political one.

5.3.2 United Nations (UN)

The **League of Nations**, predecessor to the United Nations, was founded in the wake of the first world war. Its mission, as stated in the **Treaty of Versailles**, was "to promote international cooperation and to achieve peace and security." However, the League proved to be ineffective. After failing to prevent a second world war, it ceased its activities.

In 1945, following the second world war, delegates from 50 countries founded the **United Nations** (UN) after signing the **UN Charter** at a conference in San Francisco. The organization officially came into being that October.

Nowadays, the UN has 193 **Member States**. It seeks to address international issues such as peace and security, climate change, sustainable development, human rights, disarmament, terrorism, humanitarian and health emergencies, gender equality, governance, and food production. It also acts as a forum in which its members can express their views, and these dialogues take place in subdivisions of the UN, such as the General Assembly, Security Council, and Economic and Social Council. These subdivisions, in addition to the Trusteeship Council, the International Court of Justice, and the UN Secretariat, form the UN.

Representatives from all UN member states meet in the General Assembly Hall in New York each September. Decisions of the **General Assembly** (GA) on peace and security, admission of new members, and budgetary matters require a two-thirds majority, whereas other decisions require only

SPOTLIGHT

Democratic Variety

The United States is a democracy with a president, two chambers of Congress (bicameralism), and state laws (federalism). Other political systems differ.

The Japanese government is an example of a **unitary system**—although the nation has state-like **prefectures**, they cannot make their own laws. The governments of Sweden, South Korea, Singapore, and New Zealand practice **unicameralism**. In other words, they have one-chamber legislatures.

Lastly, England, Japan, and many other countries have **parliamentary systems**. Their legislative seats are proportionately allocated to each political party based on the number of votes received. Their **prime ministers** are not directly elected by the people; they are the head of the **ruling party** or **coalition**. By contrast, Russia and France have **semi-presidential systems**. These countries have both a president and a prime minister.

a simple majority. The GA is headed by a president, elected annually. In conjunction with the Security Council, the GA also appoints the UN leadership, or the **Secretary-General**, for a five-year, renewable term.

To maintain international peace and security, the **Security Council** (UNSC) can impose sanctions and authorize the use of force. The UNSC has 15 members, and each has one vote. Five of its members—France, Great Britain, Russia, China, and the United States—are **permanent** and have veto power. The remaining ten members are non-permanent. The UNSC is headed by a rotational presidency that changes monthly.

The **International Court of Justice** uses international law to settle legal disputes submitted to it by member states. It also offers advice on legal questions referred to it by specialized agencies and subdivisions of the UN. A new Internal Justice System was introduced in 2009. It seeks to act as a faster, more transparent, and more decentralized system favoring informal resolutions rather than litigation.

Debate—
Supranational Organizations

As exemplified by the EU's evolution, countries, especially those plagued by war or other hardship, do not often join politically without first forming an economic union, in which member states remain competitive and autonomous. Although some states are eager to reap the benefits of joining long-established institutions, other leaders question their value.

Pros

- *New Opportunities.* Nations may more easily form new economic and cultural partnerships with other members of an international organization.
- *Conflict Resolution.* International organizations often include dispute resolution mechanisms; their legal infrastructure helps reduce the possibility of violent conflict among member states.
- *Cultural Preservation.* Some international organizations do not have an official language. This symbolic choice denotes member states' equality in terms of soft power and quells fears of cultural imposition.

Cons

- *Communication Barriers.* Due to the language and cultural diversity of member states, miscommunication is a common risk.

- *Inequality.* Smaller nations contend that large and powerful countries dominate international organizations and make decisions without thoroughly consulting their smaller counterparts.
- *Shared Wealth.* Larger, wealthier nations may contribute more to an international organization's funding yet receive fewer benefits than developing nations. Some world leaders regard this disproportionate tradeoff as 'unfair.'
- *Joining and Leaving.* When new nations want to join an international organization, they may need to meet certain qualifications. For example, a country must be in "Europe" to join the EU, or to join the UN, an applicant nation must garner approval from both the Security Council and the General Council. In either case, the subjective process may bar applicants' entry. Conversely, long-time members may become entrenched in the organization's legal, economic, and organizational infrastructure. Leaving the organization becomes a complex and difficult task, as Britain has discovered in its bid to leave the EU.
- *Sovereignty and Collective Interests.* All member states in an international organization must set aside their own interests in pursuit of a collective good. Some nations view the prioritization of other nations' desires over their own as a challenge to their ability to autonomously govern themselves. For example, in the case of the IMF and the World Bank, critics claim borrower countries cannot receive much-needed capital without having 'pre-packaged' policies, or 'conditionalities,' imposed on them. Whereas the institutions in question aim to foster long-term economic health by deregulating, liberalizing, and privatizing, loan recipients perceive the efforts as a challenge to their sovereignty.

5.4 Major Legal Systems

Adhering to the legal system of each country is one of the first steps to entering into that country's market. Of course, there are many gray areas between what is legal and ethical in each culture. If a manager is not careful in dealing with these issues appropriately, it can become costly for the organization and the individual. Overall, organizations must assess these differences, and managers must become protectors of an ethical identity throughout the organization. These topics are discussed in a later chapter.

5.4.1 Common & Civil Law Systems

The two most prominent legal systems are **common law** and **civil law**. The World Bank Group outlines their central differences as follows (see Table 5.3).

TABLE 5.3 Common and Civil Law Characteristics

Feature	Common Law	Civil Law
Written Constitution	Not always	Always
Judicial Decisions	Binding	Not binding on third parties; however, administrative and constitutional court decisions on laws and regulations binding on all
Legal Scholars' Writings	Little influence	Significant influence in some civil law jurisdictions
Freedom of Contract	Extensive—only a few provisions implied by law into contractual relationship	More limited—a number of provisions implied by law into contractual relationship
Court System Applicable to Public Private Partnership (PPP) Projects	In most cases a contractual relationship is subject to private law and courts that deal with these issues	Most PPP arrangements (e.g., concessions) are seen as relating to a public service and subject to public administrative law administered by administrative courts

Civil Law. Civil law systems were inherited from Roman law. As described in the table above, civil law systems give precedence to written law, and a systematic codification of general laws. This is the most widespread system of law in the world. Countries such as Russia and Spain have civil law systems.

Common Law. Common law is founded not on laws made by legislatures but on judge-made laws, which are generally based on previous judicial

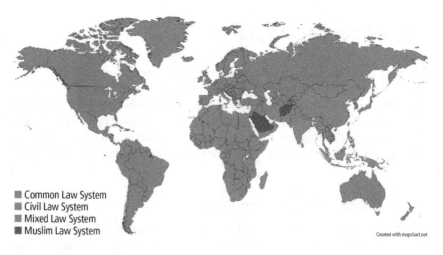

■ Common Law System
■ Civil Law System
■ Mixed Law System
■ Muslim Law System

Created with mapchart.net

Figure 5.3 Map of legal systems of the world.

decisions. Great Britain and the United States are examples of nations with common law systems.

Muslim Law. These systems are generally autonomous but of a religious nature and predominantly based on the Koran.

Mixed-Law Systems. In many countries, two or more systems apply cumulatively or interactively. For example, the Japanese legal system mixes elements of common and civil law. In other nations, civil and Muslim law may be mixed.

5.4.2 International Law

International law supersedes domestic law and addresses a range of humanitarian issues, including human rights, disarmament, international crime, migration, the treatment of prisoners, the use of force, and war.

International law directly affects the MNEs in its regulation of global commons, such as the environment and sustainable development, international waters, global communications, and world trade. For example, the **United Nations Commission on International Trade Law** (UNCITRAL) seeks to modernize and harmonize the rules on international business, while the **United Nations Convention on the Law of the Sea** (UNCLOS) governs the world's waters.

5.4.3 Treaties

Multilateral treaties such as the North American Free Trade Agreement (**NAFTA**), now known as the United States-Mexico-Canada Agreement (USMCA), further exemplify the convergence between politics, law, and international trade. A **bilateral trade agreement** (BTA) governs certain aspects of trade between two countries, such as the United States and Mexico. Similarly, a **regional trade agreement** (RTA) regulates trade between two or more governments. In addition to NAFTA, the Central American-Dominican Republic Free Trade Agreement (CAFTA-DR), the **European Union** (EU) and the **Asia-Pacific Economic Cooperation** (APEC) are all examples of RTAs. Whereas there were only 50 trade agreements in 1990, there were more than 280 in recent years. These agreements are increasing not only in number but also in complexity, and MNEs must ensure their organizations are compliant.

5.5 Global Intellectual Property Issues

Intellectual Property (IP) includes patents, trademarks, and copyrights. These assets enable organizations to distinguish themselves from competitors, add value, cultivate brand loyalty, attract partners and investors, access new markets, and generate revenue through new venues such as licensing. Thus, businesses have a strong incentive to protect their IP. Similarly, governments grant creators these rights as an incentive to produce and spread ideas that will benefit society.

Yet IP rights are only valid in the country or region in which they have been granted; therefore, MNEs must apply for IP rights in each country where they operate or want to do business. There are some exceptions to this general rule. For example, the **Berne Convention** (1888) provides automatic protection for copyright and famous trademarks, and it further states that trade secrets are confidential by nature.

Another important agreement is **TRIPS**, or the Trade-Related Aspects of Intellectual Property Rights. It was developed in 1994 during the Uruguay Round of the WTO negotiations and establishes the minimum standards of IP protection and enforcement each government must grant to fellow WTO members. Note that less-developed nations receive more leniency than developed nations in terms of IP violations.

5.6   The WTO and Mediation

One of the World Trade Organization's major activities is dispute settlement and **mediation**. More than 500 disputes have been brought to the WTO since 1995.

Rulings are made by a panel and endorsed or rejected by the **Dispute Settlement Body** (DSB), a special convening of the WTO's General Council. A seven-member **appellate body** handles appeals.

However, the WTO prefers to settle disputes through **consultations** rather than pass judgement. As of 2008, less than half of its cases reached the full panel process; the majority were settled "out of court" or remained in a prolonged consultation phase. Disputes may also be settled by **arbitration**.

5.7   Trends

5.7.1   *Nationalism, Separatism, and Isolationism*

Chapter 1 discussed globalization, the increasing exchange across national borders and cultures. Whereas this phenomenon defines international business and relations as a long-term trend, short-term exceptions exist. **Nationalism**, **separatism**, and **isolationism** surface as social movements, with well-known contemporary examples including Britain's bid to leave the EU (**Brexit**), Catalonia's bid for independence from Spain, and rising popular support for nationalist parties worldwide. When embraced by political parties and elected officials, these sentiments may be embedded in law, affecting global business in turn.

These movements are, in part, a product of economic and social imbalance. When a nation experiences low economic growth for prolonged periods, foreign nationals and MNEs may become the politicized targets of protectionist policies and cultural backlash.

5.7.2 Sources of Political Instability & Risk

As famously argued by Samuel Huntington in 1991, democracy is thought to occur in **waves** and **reversals**. These terms categorize cyclic shifts over time. During democratic waves, such as that spanning from the 1970s to the 1990s, most nations exhibited democratic values; by contrast, non-democratic values and practices are prominent during reversals, such as the era Huntington identifies as the "first reversal," between 1920 and 1945. The Soviet Union's disbanding occurred during a democratic wave, and Hitler, Mussolini, and Stalin rose to power during a reversal .

The occurrences that trigger politically and socially destabilizing events are case-specific and generally unpredictable. However, economic decline, growing inequality, corruption, political repression, failing infrastructure and social services typically preclude revolutions, such as the **Arab Spring** that swept the Middle East and North Africa (MENA) in 2010 and 2011.

Yet, as the World Bank stated in a 2015 article, "Judging by economic data alone, the revolutions of the 2011 Arab Spring should have never happened."[2] In other words, those involved in international business must not only consult quantitative measures of stability, but also qualitative factors like inequality, corruption, and political efficacy.

5.8 Conclusion

As demonstrated in this chapter, economic, political, and legal systems are deeply interconnected, whether the scale is domestic, international, or global.

MNEs must know how their actions will affect the host countries' political spheres. For example, international businesses may bolster political stability by generating economic growth, reducing resource scarcity, and promoting humane employment practices. A socially responsible business operating in less developed nations will empower its citizens and strive to improve their standards of living.

MNEs must also remain up-to-date with international law, as well as the legal landscapes of their home and host nations. Beyond this minimum requirement, MNEs should develop an internal code of ethics honoring the "people" and "planet" facets of TBL. By training employees to act in accordance with this code, organizations can ensure they act in the best interest of all shareholders and bolster sustainability.

TBL Connection
U.S. Tech Companies Reconsider Saudi Ties, 2018

The controversy over the death of a Saudi Arabian journalist, Jamal Khashoggi, prompted Silicon Valley to reconsider its ties to the world's largest oil exporter. On October 2nd, 2018, Khashoggi, who often was critical of his home country's government, entered the Saudi Arabian consulate in Istanbul and never left the building. Subsequently many tech leaders including Steve Case, the co-founder of AOL, and Dara Khosrowshahi, the CEO of Uber, announced that they were not going to attend Saudi Arabia's annual investment forum in Riyadh.

The controversy highlighted the extent to which tech startups rely on Saudi Arabian investors. The kingdom's Public Investment Fund, for example, invested $3.5 billion in Uber and has a seat on its board. While companies like Uber cannot simply ignore political issues and have to respond to demands of their employees and customers with regard to their ethical stances, they also cannot easily give up hundreds of millions of dollars in fees and consultancy work.

Based on

https://www.voanews.com/a/us-tech-companies-reconsider-saudi-investment/
    4626218.html

https://www.cnn.com/2018/10/22/middleeast/jamal-khashoggi-murder-cynics
    -analysis-intl/index.html

1. *Silicon Valley's TBL responsibilities for "people" and "profit" are in conflict. Why do international corporations need to address ethical questions that relate to politics? How should Uber respond to similar issues moving forward?*

Chapter Review

Key Terms

- Democratic
- Non-democratic
- Totalitarian
- Coup d'état
- Market Economy
- Centrally Planned Economy
- Socialist

- Transition Economy
- Liberalization
- Privatization
- Communist Party
- Political Union
- Single Market
- Common Currency
- Policy Agreement
- United Nations
- Security Council
- International Court of Justice
- Common Law
- Civil Law
- NAFTA (USMCA)
- EU
- APEC
- Berne Convention
- TRIPS
- Mediation
- Consultation
- Arbitration

Questions & Assignments

Questions

1. In the 1930s, American legislators passed a "neutrality act" to avoid entanglement in European wars. How might isolationist political and legal decisions such as this affect businesses, particularly international trade and MNEs? What are the costs and benefits of a neutrality policy, with respect to domestic markets, foreign markets, and international trade? Lastly, what are the implications for the modern world?

Assignments

1. Select a foreign nation that interests you, then use the CIA Factbook (online) to learn about its political and legal systems. Who's the head of government? What are the major political parties and their beliefs? Is it politically stable? When is the next major election? How might these factors shape foreign investment, trade, and venture capitalism?
2. Although this chapter focuses on the international political system, you likely have the most influence over your domestic political af-

fairs: find out about a new foreign policy of your choice, whether domestic law or a treaty in the making. What are the domestic and international implications? What recommendations and criticisms can you provide? (If it's a domestic law that will be voted on by your elected representative, you may even want to seek out opportunities to get involved locally.)

Notes

1. As a result of Brexit, with the UK leaving the EU, the number of EU members will change.
2. For details of the article, please see *Middle-class Frustration Fueled the Arab Spring, October 21, 2015*, published by the World Bank: http://www.worldbank.org/en/news/feature/2015/10/21/middle-class-frustration-that-fueled-the-arab-spring

Suggested Reading

Transparency International's Corruption Perceptions Index (2017).
https://www.transparency.org/news/feature/corruption_perceptions_index_2017

Freedom House Annual Report, "Democracy in Crisis" (2018).
https://freedomhouse.org/report/freedom-world/freedom-world-2018

"League of Nationalists," *The Economist* (November 19, 2016).
https://www.economist.com/international/2016/11/19/league-of-nationalists

Michael Gordon, "Forecasting Instability: The Case of the Arab Spring and the Limitations of Socioeconomic Data," Wilson Center (2018).
https://www.wilsoncenter.org/article/forecasting-instability-the-case-the-arab-spring-and-the-limitations-socioeconomic-data

Yves Doz and C.K. Prahalad. "How MNCs Cope with Host Government Intervention," *Harvard Business Review* (1980).
https://hbr.org/1980/03/how-mncs-cope-with-host-government-intervention

References

Barker, T. S., & Cobb., S. L. (1999). A survey of ethics and cultural dimensions of MNCS. *Competitiveness Review, 9*(2), 11–18.

Buller, P. F., & McEvoy, G. M., (1999). Creating and sustaining ethical capability in the multi-national corporations. *Journal of World Business, 34*(4), 326–343.

De George, R., (1993). *Competing with integrity in internal business.* New York, NY: Oxford University Press.

Freedom House (2019). *Democracy in retreat.* Retrieved from https://freedomhouse .org/report/freedom-world/freedom-world-2019

General Motors accuses Venezuela of illegally seizing its car plant. (2017). Retrieved from https://www.rt.com/business/385387-venezuela-general-motors-plant/

H&M accused of failing to ensure living wage for supply chain workers. (2018). Retrieved from https://www.edie.net/news/7/H-M-accused-of-failing-to-en-sure-living-wage-for-supply-chain-workers/

Huntington, S. P. (1991). *The third wave: Democratization in the late twentieth century.* Norman: University of Oklahoma Press.

Lister, A. B. (2018, October 23). Khashoggi's murder shows that the cynics have won. Retrieved from https://www.cnn.com/2018/10/22/middleeast/jamal -khashoggi-murder-cynics-analysis-intl/index.html

Quinn, M. (2018, October 23). US Tech Companies Reconsider Saudi Investment. Retrieved from https://www.voanews.com/a/us-tech-companies-reconsider -saudi-investment/4626218.html

CHAPTER 6

Cultural and Social Environments

LEARNING OBJECTIVES

- Define **culture** and its components.
- Understand foreign cultures through various **analytical lenses**.
- Understand the cultural importance of **language** and **religion** and their implications on global business activities.
- Learn the role of **social structures** of countries in business operations.

Opening Case

Walmart Underestimates Cultural Differences

In 2006, Walmart Inc., a successful multinational retailer, pulled out of the German market after nearly a decade. The company had several major weaknesses since the American executives had a limited understanding of what German customers were looking for. First, the company selected unpopular

Global Business, pages 119–139
Copyright © 2019 by Information Age Publishing
All rights of reproduction in any form reserved.

Figure 6.1 Walmart logo.

locations for its stores. The troubles followed when it failed to recognize that German and American cultures differed significantly. Various Walmart practices common in the U.S. stores, such as staff members morning chants, and the requirement to smile at customers were viewed as strange by Germans. The company also failed to establish good relationships with labor unions which are important in the German retail business sector. Finally, German stores like Aldi offered high-quality groceries for lower prices than Walmart. Thus, the company ended up losing millions of dollars and became a popular international business example of how not to enter or do business in foreign markets.

When Walmart faced similar challenges in Japan and South Korea, management had to reconsider their expansion strategies. The company is now less aggressive in imposing American corporate culture on non-American employees. Many stores around the globe even have a different name. Seventy percent of the company's international sales come from stores with names like Asda in Britain and Seiyu in Japan.

Based on

https://www.nytimes.com/2006/08/02/business/worldbusiness/02walmart .html?ei=5088&en=e01e99c3081724c5&ex=1312171200&partner=rssnyt& pagewanted=print

https://www.cbc.ca/radio/undertheinfluence/passport-revoked-when-brands -fail-internationally-1.3942237

1. *How could have the knowledge of German culture helped Walmart succeed?*
2. *What business practices are influenced by culture (marketing, staffing, etc.)?*

6.0   Introduction

The key characteristic of global business is the need to interact with people across national boundaries. A business person must understand foreign cultures for the following reasons:

- Adjusting to the local environment
- Learning new ways of accomplishing goals
- Relating to peers, clients, businesses, and local people

- Avoiding embarrassing mistakes
- Improving the likelihood of success

6.1   Culture—A Nation's Social Characteristics

What is "culture"? There is no single, universal definition of culture. Throughout the last century, several definitions have evolved to identify what culture entails or encompasses. Some prominent definitions are the following.

- Sir Edward B. Taylor defined culture as " the complex whole which includes knowledge, beliefs, arts, morals, law, customs, and any other capabilities and habits acquired by [a human] as a member of society." He also warned about the complexity of defining culture due to the comprehensive characteristics that need to be included if the term is used to generalize groups of people.[1]
- Anthropologist Alfred Kroeber defines culture "as a set of shared attitudes, values, goals, and practices that characterizes an institution, organization or group" (Kluckhohn & Strodtbeck, 1961).
- In 2002, the **United Nations Educational, Scientific and Cultural Organization** (UNESCO) defined culture as follows: "... culture should be regarded as the set of distinctive spiritual, material, intellectual and emotional features of society or a social group, and that it encompasses, in addition to art and literature, lifestyles, ways of living together, value systems, traditions and beliefs" (UNESCO, 2002).
- Other authors have recognized culture as a synonym of civilization, defining the overall characteristics that identify a group of people or community as local culture.
- For Ruth Benedict, a sociologist, "culture, like an individual, is a more or less a consistent pattern of thought and action" (Benedict, 1989).

SPOTLIGHT
Cultural Differences in Business

European and Chinese businesspeople value relationships differently. Similarly, although some assume Europeans from different countries assign the same level of importance to relationships, differences exist from one western culture to another.

Watch the following video to learn more.
https://www.youtube.com/watch?v=VMwjscSCcf0

- Anthropologist Clifford Geertz sees culture as "the means by which people communicate, perpetuate and develop their knowledge about attitudes towards life" (Clifford, 1973). If behaviors can be understood and predicted, managers are able to direct multicultural organizations better to their goal.
- Kluckhohn and Strodtbeck define culture as a shared, commonly held body of beliefs and values that define the "shoulds" and "oughts" of life ((Kluckhohn & Strodtbeck, 1961).
- Hofstede defines culture as "the collective programming of the mind which distinguishes one group or category from another" (Hofstede, 1984).

6.2   The Importance of Cultural Understanding

As demonstrated by Walmart in the opening case, the differences in how people interact with each other can cause several challenges in cross-cultural business relations. It may be uncomfortable to interact with a businessperson of a different culture for the very first time. One might not know how to begin a conversation, how to greet the other person, how to negotiate with the other culture, or how to interact socially with them. When interacting with people from other cultures, it is imperative to know about the "Dos and Don'ts" in that culture in order to avoid mistakes, embarrassment and potentially loss of business opportunities.

Individuals can be categorized according to their cultural perspectives as follows:

- *Ethnocentric.* Individuals judge others by their own cultures. They believe that their culture is superior to other traditions and think others should learn from them.
- *Polycentric.* Individuals easily adopt and immerse themselves into a foreign culture.
- *Geocentric.* Individuals keep their own cultural attributes, but adjust to the culture of the country they live in.

How these cultural approaches can be used by managers as alternative styles are discussed in a later chapter. However, it is common that most people have tendencies to consider their own way of doing things as the right approach and often disapprove of alternative belief systems or behaviors. In other words, people look through their own lenses and see everything with a filter. Someone else who wears a different color lenses could see the same thing differently. As a result, there is a potential for misunderstanding, misjudgment or conflict.

When doing business in any other culture, there are many cross-cultural challenges that need to be addressed. For example, due to the extreme population boom, industry growth, and technological advantages, China has become a market in which many foreign companies are investing. Many Westerners experience tremendous difficulties when trying to conduct business in China because the two cultures are quite different. The cultural barriers such as communication, different objectives and means of cooperation, and operating methods of each side have led to failed business collaborations. The differences between China and the United States are not only due to cultural aspects, but also due to differences in economic and political systems. It is, however, important for business people to learn how to deal with cultural misunderstandings and cross-cultural differences around the world.

6.3   Characteristics of Culture

Assessing cultural impact is the first step for organizations to examine when managing in a cross-cultural environment. The second step is to understand the different characteristics that conform a culture.

Culture is shared, learned, organized, and dynamic.

- *Shared.* Culture must be acknowledged as common by more than one person.
- *Learned.* Culture is transmitted through the process of learning and interacting with the surrounding environment or from one generation to the next.
- *Organized* (or systematic). Culture is not a random assortment of elements, but a well-organized system of values, attitudes, beliefs, and behavioral meanings related to each other.
- *Dynamic.* Culture changes over time, sometimes very slowly and sometimes faster, but it rarely stays the same.

It is important not to confuse culture with other aspects of individual behavior. In his 1980 Dimensions of Culture assessment (see Figure 6.2), Geert Hofstede presented three different levels of mental programming that explained how individuals behave in regular circumstances (Thomas & Peterson, 2014).

The first level, named **universal** or biological, comprises all human nature expected behavior such as eating when hungry or sleeping when tired.

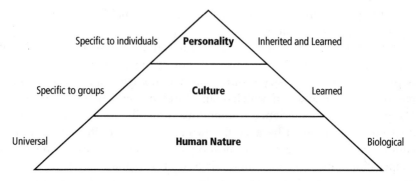

Figure 6.2 Dimensions of culture.

Hofstede suggested that all individuals share this level of attributes across cultures since birth.

The second level, **culture**, refers to those behaviors that are learned and specific to a particular group of individuals.

The third level, **personality**, reflects the characteristics that are specific to the individual, and are not shared among a group of people. This level is a product of inherited and learned behavior.

The importance of identifying the different levels of individual behavior is that confusing one group with another can lead to misinterpretation of a culture and will impact organizational performance. Businesspeople must be able to differentiate the types of behavior and their roots, before generalizing anything as cultural behavior.

6.4 Dimensions of Culture

Another study by Hofstede allows to further understand differences in national and organizational cultures. His research identified six dimensions that shape the national culture which we explore below.

6.4.1 Individualism vs. Collectivism

In the 1970s, Henri Tajfel proposed that humans understand the social world by categorizing themselves into groups.[2] He claimed that an individual's identity is shaped by group membership. There are **in-groups** to which a person belongs, as well as **out-groups** to which the person does not belong, whether by choice or exclusion. In-group members share some commonality and are reciprocally loyal to one another. By providing emotional and material support to other members, an individual can reasonably expect to receive the same support.

The difference between **individualist** and **collectivist** mindsets can be understood as a difference in how narrowly or expansively a person defines in-group membership. In other words, how large is the group to which an individual offers loyalty and support? In-groups of individualists are relatively small, perhaps limited to themselves and close family members, whereas in-groups of collectivists are larger (Hofstede & Bond, 1984). This dynamic has important psychological and cultural implications. For example, individualists tend to craft personal identity independent of group membership, but collectivists define themselves based on their connection and contribution to the group.

Similarly, group orientation affects cultural values and social perception. When Kagitcibasia and Berry (1989) asked Chinese and Australian subjects to analyze social episodes for an experiment, Chinese subjects (collectivists) emphasized common feelings, social usefulness and acceptance of authority. Australians (individualists) emphasized competitiveness, self confidence and freedom.

Neither individualism nor collectivism is inherently preferable. Nor are all collectivist and individualist cultures equal and unchanging. For example, although both the Chinese and Japanese cultures have been defined as collectivists, Chew and Puttic found they value individualism differently in the workplace (1995). Yeh similarly asserted that the Taiwanese practice collectivism differently in the home and workplace (1988a and 1988b), and Tayeb discovered that, among the collectivist nations of Japan, India, and Iran, only the Japanese practiced collectivism in the workplace (1994).

In business, collectivists and individualists may act differently. Individualist employees might prefer to work independently, while collectivist employees emphasize teamwork and group harmony. Those engaged in international business must be sensitive to cultural differences in group-orientation when managing and negotiating.

6.4.2 Power Distance

This dimension alludes to the hierarchical relationships between subordinates and leaders. The **Power Distance index** can be viewed as an organizational leadership style that varies from autocratic to participative. Effectively, **Low Power Distance** organizations are characterized by leadership styles that empower subordinates and treat them in a very proximate way. **High Power Distance** organizations have cultures where the leadership styles are more authoritarian, with less regard for any initiatives from subordinates.

6.4.3 Uncertainty Avoidance

To what degree are members of a society anxious about the unknown? How do they attempt to cope with anxiety by minimizing uncertainty? In cultures with **high uncertainty avoidance**, people prefer explicit rules (e.g., about religion and food) and formally structured activities. Employees tend to remain longer with their employers. In cultures with **low uncertainty avoidance**, people prefer implicit or flexible rules or guidelines and informal activities. Employees tend to change employers more frequently.

6.4.4 Masculinity and Femininity

The value is placed on traditional male or female roles, as understood in most Western cultures. In so-called "**masculine**" cultures, people (whether male or female) value competitiveness, assertiveness, ambition, and the accumulation of wealth and material possessions. In so-called "**feminine**" cultures, people value relationships and quality of life.

6.4.5 Long Versus Short-term Orientation

Each society has a **time horizon**—the importance attached to the future, past, and present. In **long-term oriented societies**, people value actions and attitudes that affect the future: persistence/perseverance, thrift, and shame. In **short-term oriented societies**, people value actions and attitudes that are affected by the past or the present, such as protecting one's own face, respect for tradition, and reciprocation of greetings, favors, and gifts.

6.4.6 Indulgence vs. Restraint

An **indulgent society** allows relatively free gratification of basic and natural human desires related to enjoying life and having fun, whereas a **restrained society** suppresses the gratification of those needs and regulates it using social norms.

The Figure 6.3 compares Hofstede's dimensions for South Korea and the United Kingdom.

6.5 Major Components of Culture

Several different factors affect a country's culture. These components include:

- *Aesthetics.* The sense of beauty and good taste, art, clothing, buildings, music, etc.

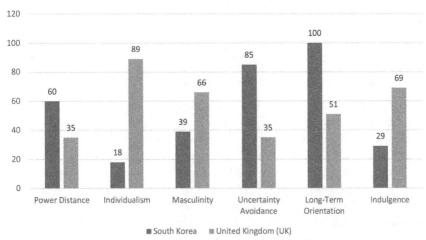

Figure 6.3 Dimensions of culture. *Data from:* https://www.hofstede-insights.com/product/compare-countries/

- *Attitudes and beliefs.* Including those regarding time, change, risk-taking, proper distance between people, money or material wealth, work, political philosophy, achievements, etc.
- *Education.* Vocational/technical versus liberal arts, importance of human capital, focus on higher education vs. family business, etc.
- *Language.* Spoken and non-spoken, also called 'silent' language.
- *Religion.* Beliefs concerning the afterlife, supreme being(s), worship, rituals, etc.
- *Social Structure.* Family Size, respect for the elderly, national identity, legal structure, political and economic systems, role of government in everyday life, etc.

Furthermore, components of culture can be classified as **material components** such as art, clothing, and eating utensils, or as **nonmaterial components** such as language, values, and traditions. Some cultural components such as music and food can be easily identified; they are visible like a tip of an iceberg. Others, like assumptions, norms, and expectations may remain out of an individual's awareness. Those aspects of culture can be compared to the part of an iceberg that is under water. While those aspects are less visible, they often constitute the majority of the cultural components. It is important for multinational businesses to recognize that not all aspects of culture may be easily recognized. Developing business relationships and understanding the culture of someone from a foreign country is likely to take time, effort, and open-mindedness.

6.5.1 The Role of Language
(Spoken and unspoken language)

Language, spoken or written, constitutes an essential means of communication. The role of the English language around the world has become quite significant. Many countries such as China require that high school graduates have English language knowledge. However, only six percent of the world's population speak it. In terms of the number of people speaking a language, Chinese is far ahead of English. Hindi and Spanish closely follow it as shown in Figure 6.4. It is, therefore, important not to underestimate the ability of speaking a foreign language. The knowledge of a local language might allow a foreign businessperson to grasp cultural nuances, demonstrate respect for the local culture, and develop more meaningful connections. It is also important for businesspeople to understand the body

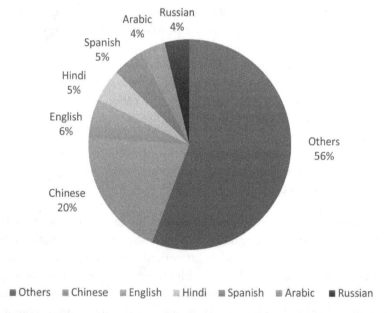

▪ Others ▪ Chinese ▪ English ▪ Hindi ▪ Spanish ▪ Arabic ▪ Russian

Figure 6.4 World population by language. *Source:* Mike W. Peng estimate based on data in (a) *The Economist Atlas, 2005,* London, England: The Economist Books; (b) Graddol, D. (2004), The future of language, *Science, 303,* 1329–1331; (c) Huntington, S. (1996). *The clash of civilizations and the remaking of world order.* New York, NY: Simon & Shuster.

SPOTLIGHT
Mis-Translation in MNE Marketing

Many successful multinationals have experienced translation failures which led to poor business outcomes. HSBC's "Assume Nothing" slogan translated in many countries as "Do Nothing." In 2009, the bank was forced to spend $10 million to change its slogan to "The world's private bank" which had a better translation. When KFC first opened in China in the 1980s, its "finger-lickin' good" slogan was accidentally translated to "eat your fingers off." Despite the unappetizing translation, KFC still managed to become the No.1 quick-service restaurant in China today. Braniff Airlines faced issues advertising its brand-new leather seats in Latin America. Their "Fly in Leather" slogan ended up being translated to "Fly Naked," sending the wrong message to customers. These examples suggest that something as simple as translation might go wrong and result in quite significant costs to the company.

Based on

https://www.businessnewsdaily.com/5241-international-marketing-fails.html

language (sometimes referred to as the 'silent' language). A friendly gesture in one country might mean something else, or even be offensive, in another country. For instance, while Americans and Italians use their arms while talking, Japanese might find the excessive use of hand gestures impolite. A "thumbs up" gesture in one language might be a sign of approval, whereas it could indicate the number "one" in countries such as Germany and Russia, or it could be a rude gesture in the Middle East where it is equivalent to the "middle-finger" gesture.

Debate—MNEs and International Businesspeople Must Adopt English as a Primary Business Language

Is there a common ground?

Pros

- *Prevalence.* English already plays a major role in global business operations.

- *Simplicity.* A single language would simplify global business communications.

Cons

- *Identity.* Business people and MNEs should be able to use language of their culture.
- *Interference.* A requirement or expectation to speak English represents an attempt by English-speaking nations to assert dominance over other cultures.

6.5.2 Role of Religions on Culture

Another important aspect of culture is **religion**. Merriam Webster's Dictionary defines religion as "the service or worship of God or the supernatural, or commitment or devotion to religious faith or observance."[3]

Many religions have a rich history. Some have maintained deeply-held beliefs for more than a thousand years. Because they generally prescribe a moral or ethical code of conduct, promote certain social values, and define shared customs or observances, a society's predominant religion often reflects or shapes the larger culture. On the other hand, members of a minority religion may belong to a smaller "subculture" with beliefs divergent from the majority. And, because religion is highly personal, individual beliefs may also differ. Along these lines, global businessmen and women should take caution never to assume a "one-size-fits-all" mindset.

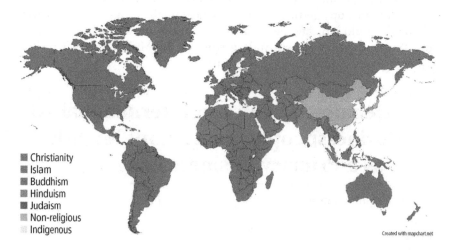

Figure 6.5 Prevailing Beliefs: Map displays the largest religious group in each country.

Eight out of ten people around the world identify with a religion. In 2010, about 32% of people identified as Christians, 23% identified as Muslims, 16% were unaffiliated, 15% identified as Hindus, and 7% identified as Buddhists. The smaller religious groups included various **folk religions** (African traditional religions, Native American religions, etc.), Judaism, Sikhism, Jainism, and other religions (Pew Research Center, 2012). Since religion constitutes a significant aspect of personal life and identity for many people, it has an impact on work lives as well. The business implications of Christianity, Islam, and Hinduism are considered below.

Christianity is a major monotheistic religion. Its adherents, Christians, believe in in the teachings of Jesus Christ who is the Messiah sent by God. It is estimated that about 50% of Christians are Catholic, 37% are Protestant, 12% are Orthodox, and 1% belong to other denominations such as Jehovah's Witnesses (Pew Research Center, 2012). Some sociologists suggest that the Protestant tradition has had the most significant business implications. **Max Weber**, a German sociologist, associated Protestantism with capitalism. Protestant values emphasize hard work and frugality and both of those qualities lead to the "expansion of capitalist enterprises" (Hill & Hult, 2015).

Islam is another monotheistic religion. It is the second largest, as well as the fastest growing religion in the world. Its followers, Muslims, believe that there is only one God (Allah) and that Muhammad is his prophet. Islam also acknowledges other prophets such as Jesus Christ and Moses. The two major branches of Islam are Sunni (87%–90%) and Shia (10%–13%) (Pew Research Center, 2012). Islam has five religious acts, or pillars, that include Shahada, Salat, Zakat, Sawm, and Hajj. Shahada is the faith—it is the testament that "there is no God but Allah and Muhammad is his Prophet." Salat constitutes prayer five times a day, facing the holy city of Mecca in Saudi Arabia. Zakat can be explained as charity or sharing of wealth with those who are less fortunate. Sawm is fasting during the holy month of Ramadan; while sick, pregnant, and elderly do not have to fast, others are expected to not eat or drink during the day. The last pillar, Hajj, is the pilgrimage to Mecca.

Islam is not against trade; it supports free enterprise, honest profit-making, and protection of private property. It also emphasizes following contractual obligations. Islam's holy book, the **Koran**, however, prohibits the payment or receipt of interest (Hill & Hult, 2015). One way in which Islamic banks earn money without interest is by employing profit-sharing systems. For example, if a company takes out a loan, it is repaid without paying the interest. However, a share of the company profits are paid to the bank.

Hinduism is the oldest religion in the world. Major traditions within Hinduism are Vaishnavism, the worship of God Vishnu, and Shaivism, the worship of the God Shiva (Pew Research Center, 2012). Hindus believe in reincarnation, or rebirth after death, as well as karma. **Karma** suggests that actions of an individual affect this individual's future and following lives. Hindus also consider cows sacred; many of them, therefore, are vegetarian. They value spiritual achievements over material achievements. Max Weber, therefore, argued that Hindus might be less likely to engage in entrepreneurial activity (Hill & Hult, 2015). It is also important to note that Hinduism supported the **caste system** which still has some impact on today's Indian society. Some individuals might have a hard time getting promoted if they come from a lower caste. India, however, has been developing economically and many aspects of its society continue undergoing social and cultural changes; today, businesses do not necessarily follow various Hindu traditions (Hill & Hult, 2015).

A closer look at the world's major religions reveals that an individual's religious beliefs may affect the way in which that individual views wealth and entrepreneurship. Religion might also impact the banking system of a country and the way in which companies promote individuals. It is, therefore, important for MNEs to study the religion of the host country.

At its core, understanding foreign cultures relates to caring about people, the first aspect of the Triple Bottom Line. Some companies failed in foreign markets despite having all the business tools necessary to succeed. For instance, by underestimating the importance of culture and the global trend to protect it, Nike, Inc. ended up being criticized for its apparel. Consider the Spotlight about Nike.

SPOTLIGHT
Nike Accused of Cultural Exploitation

In 2012, Nike, Inc., a famous athletic footwear and apparel brand, was accused of cultural insensitivity and exploitation. The cause was a pair of patterned women's leggings. Customers from Australia and New Zealand pointed out that the tattoo-like pattern on the leggings resembled the traditional male tattoo of Samoa, called pe'a. The tattoo has a significant cultural meaning in Samoan society and represents manhood. A member of New Zealand's parliament expressed that there should have been a consultation with those who have the ownership of the pattern. A Change.org petition with 750 signatures eventually forced Nike, Inc. to stop selling the item.

Based on
https://www.huffingtonpost.com/2013/08/15/nike-tattoo-leggings_n_3763591.html

1. *What could have Nike done differently to avoid the negative situation?*

6.6 The Role of Social Structure on Culture

In addition to different political, legal and economic systems, the social structure of a nation affects its culture and the type of interactions people have with each other. We cannot assume that business negotiation styles in China are the same as in Canada. These societies are vastly different, not only in their political and economic systems but also their history, societal priorities, and the social fabric of their culture. Even neighboring countries have different cultures. For instance, despite many similarities, there are key cultural differences between South Korea and its neighbor North Korea. These differences are mainly due to varying political, legal and economic philosophies that manifest themselves in social structures. Therefore, we expect to observe different types of cultural characteristics in these two countries.

A country's **social structure** depends on two broad categories:

1. *Individualism versus Collectivism.* As discussed earlier in this chapter, in some societies such as the U.S., individual freedom is more valued than the group harmony, whereas in other cultures such as Japan, the desire of the group or a team plays a more important role than a person's individual preferences. One of the implications of this difference is the growth of entrepreneurs in the U.S. where risk-taking by an individual in anticipation of high profit is encouraged, whereas in a more "group-oriented" culture, there is less incentive to take risks.

2. *Social Stratification (Grouping of people in some type of hierarchy).* In some societies, there used to be clear and distinct "classes" based on wealth, political influence, and family heritage.

   For instance, in British society, people were classified based on their income and education into upper, middle or lower class. Currently, the UK parliament has an upper house, known as House of the Lords that primarily represented the hereditary upper class; the lower house, known as the House of Commons represented everyone else in society. The other well-known example of societal class is the "caste" system in India where people were stratified in a group (or caste) based on the family in which they were born into. In such a strict classification, social mobility from one group to another was restricted and people's occupations and marital choices were strongly influenced by their caste associations. Such clear societal classifications have been diminishing in recent decades. In fact, the caste system in India has been illegal for decades, but there are still signs of such groupings in rural areas in India.

Other characteristics of a society, such as individual freedom, the size of a family, the treatment of minorities, and the history of a nation, have an influence on culture and business practices.

6.7   High and Low Context Cultures

Anthropologist Edward T. Hall distinguished between **high-** and **low-context cultures** (see Figure 6.6; Hall, 1959).

- *High-context.* These cultures rely heavily on nonverbal communication and cues. In such cultures the tone of voice, facial expressions, and eye movements are important. Relationships are built slowly, and productivity often depends on those relationships. African, Asian, Arab, Central European, and Latin American cultures are typically considered to be high-context.
- *Low-context.* These cultures rely primarily on explicit communication; nonverbal elements of communication play a less significant role. In such cultures, communication is more direct, and disagreements are typically not personalized (Neese, 2016). Cultures with Western European roots are typically low-context.

The differences between high-context and low-context cultures have business implications. For instance, businesspeople from high-context cultures may prefer personal agreements instead of legal documents. People from those cultures also tend to prefer in-person communication, as opposed to electronic correspondence. While the distinctions between high- and low-context cultures do not apply to everyone, they are useful to consider. For instance, a businessperson from Western Europe may want to be more mindful of the body language and tone of voice when working in the Middle East.

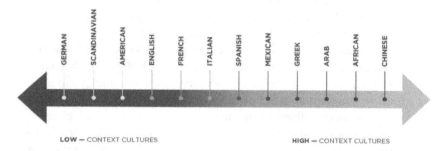

Figure 6.6   High- and low-context cultures.

6.8 The Role of Stereotyping, Prejudice, and Discrimination

In a business setting, just like in personal life, it is not uncommon to classify people by various attributes such as the department they work for or their country of origin. Such classifications provide a point of reference. It is, however, important to be aware of stereotyping and prejudice. **Stereotypes** are over-generalized ideas and beliefs about a particular group of people, while **prejudices** are negative feelings about an individual based on that individual's group membership. If someone, for instance, holds the stereotype that Italians are expressive, and Chinese are diligent, they may view individuals from those cultures through limiting lenses, instead of taking the time to learn who they truly are (MacLachlan, 2011). The example above is a rather simple case, but many people around the world experience challenges in the workplace due to stereotypes based on ethnicity, race, gender, sexual orientation, and other identity characteristics. The most harmful expressions of stereotypes and prejudice may lead to **discrimination**, unjustified negative behaviors towards members of outgroups (Stangor, 2014).

Stereotypes, prejudice, and discrimination create an unwelcoming environment in business settings which can range from awkward social interactions to avoidance. This type of environment may affect employee morale and productivity by alienating them from the organization. In an international business setting specifically, such behaviors may prevent managers from establishing professional connections abroad and thus successfully overseeing operations of foreign subsidiaries. Furthermore, the lack of cultural awareness and sensitivity may damage a company's reputation and affect the profitability in a long run. A diligent study of foreign cultures and business practices, as well as open-mindedness may allow businesspeople to avoid those challenges.

6.9 Conclusion

Culture represents an important but complex aspect of international business. Cultural insensitivity and ignorance has led many MNEs to financial losses and damaged reputation. Those issues could have been prevented by carefully studying the culture of the host country and understanding the cultural components such as language, religion, traditions, and expectations. Finally, culture is a dynamic aspect of every society that transforms and changes along with economic and political shifts. In other words, culture is not static. Understanding a certain culture, therefore, should not be viewed as a one-time research assignment, but rather as a diligent and continuous study.

TBL Connection
Paying Tribute to China

In November of 2018, the well-known luxury brand, Dolce & Gabbana released three short videos on Chinese social media to promote the upcoming fashion show in Shanghai. The videos featured an Asian model in a D&G dress attempting to eat pizza, spaghetti, and cannoli with chopsticks and embarrassingly failing. The male narrator of the video mispronounced words in a way that mocks Chinese accent. The controversial ad brought to light a history of offensive remarks made by Stefano Gabbana. The company later announced that the show which was supposed to have more than 1,000 guests was cancelled, and the designers released an apology video.

While mainstream media has hinted that the Chinese market is generally becoming increasingly challenging to succeed in, the issue seems to stem from the limited efforts some Western brands put into understanding the Chinese market. A 2018 Tencent study concluded that over half of Chinese Gen Z do not view a brand's foreign origin as a "plus point." The results of the study suggest that international brands have to develop a more sophisticated understanding of modern China. Amid the D&G failure, another high-fashion brand, Louis Vuitton, published a Weibo post about the beauty of Chinese calligraphy and highlighted their luggage collaboration with artist Xu Bing. MiuMiu similarly made a Weibo post about their collaboration with art director Tu Nan. Both brands earned positive feedback from online users.

Multinationals that succeed in China not only avoid cultural insensitivity at all costs, but also try not to fixate on the past and focus on collaboration. They avoid cliché motifs, representing a nostalgic view of the country and try to understand modern Chinese audiences instead. For example, Coca-Cola launched a campaign illustrating how the country has changed over the years to celebrate the 40th anniversary there.

From a TBL perspective, multinationals cannot afford to be culturally insensitive. Such a mistake would affect the Profit aspect of the TBL, by both offending customers in the foreign country and damaging the firm's reputation worldwide. The examples above illustrate that succeeding internationally is possible by carefully studying the local market and its intricacies. Massive mistakes, as was the case with D&G, however, are not easily forgotten.

Based on
https://www.npr.org/sections/goatsandsoda/2018/12/01/671891818/dolce-gabbana-ad-with-chopsticks-provokes-public-outrage-in-china
https://jingdaily.com/tribute-china/

1. *How can D&G regain the trust of its Chinese customers? What was unique about MiuMiu and Louis Vuitton's approaches to Chinese market?*

Chapter Review

Key Terms

- Globalization
- Culture
- Ethnocentrism
- Geocentrism
- Polycentrism
- Individualism vs. Collectivism
- Power Distance
- Uncertainty Avoidance
- Masculinity and Femininity
- Long vs. Short-term Orientation
- Indulgence vs. Restraint
- Material cultural components
- Nonmaterial cultural components
- Religion
- High-context vs. Low-Context
- Stereotype
- Prejudice
- Discrimination

Questions & Assignments

Questions

1. Select a foreign culture you are not very familiar with and identify Hofstede's cultural dimensions that best characterize it. Do you foresee changes in any of the dimensions? If so, what kind?
2. Conduct research on the business implications of Confucianism, Judaism, and Buddhism (which were not thoroughly discussed in the text).

Assignment

1. Get together with someone from a different culture and lean about the culture of that individual. Present your findings to the class from three perspectives: ethnocentric, geocentric, and polycentric. If you were an international business manager, which perspective would you try to employ? Why?

Notes

1. For the full article, please see: https://ocw.mit.edu/courses/anthropology/ 21a-01-how-culture-works-fall-2012/readings/MIT21A_01F12_Sir_Edwrd _cul.pdf
2. Tajfel, H. (1970). Experiments in intergroup discrimination. *Scientific American, 223*, 96–102.
3. For other definitions of religion, please see: http://wordcentral.com/cgi-bin/ student?religion

Suggested Reading

Bersin, Josh (2012). *How does leadership vary across the globe?* Retrieved from https://www.forbes.com/sites/joshbersin/2012/10/31/are-expat-programs -dead/#3ce52bd82304

Eglash, Ruth. (2013). *New Coca-Cola ad campaign mired in sensitive Israeli identity politics.* Retrieved from https://www.washingtonpost.com/news/worldviews/wp/ 2013/05/23/new-coca-cola-ad-campaign-mired-in-sensitive-israeli-identity -politics/?utm_term=.2ef1df50d529

Molinsky, Andy. (2016). *Cultural differences are more complicated than what country you're from.* Retrieved from https://hbr.org/2016/01/cultural-differences-are -more-complicated-than-what-country-youre-from

References

Benedict, R. (1989). *Patterns of culture.* Boston, MA: Mariner Books.

Brooks, C. (2013, October 07). *Lost in translation: 8 international marketing fails.* Retrieved from https://www.businessnewsdaily.com/5241-international-marketing -fails.html

Chew, I. K. H., & Putti, J. (1995). Relationship on work-related values of Singaporean and Japanese managers in Singapore. *Human Relations, 48*(10), 1149–1170.

Clifford, G. (1973). *The interpretation of cultures.* New York, NY: Basic.

Hall, E. (1959). *The silent language.* Garden City, NY: Doubleday.

Hill, C. W. L., & Hult, G. T. M. (2015). *Global business today* (9th ed.). New York, NY: McGraw-Hill Education.

Hofstede, G. (1984). *Culture's consequences: International differences in work-related values* (Vol. 5). SAGE.

Huffpost. (2017). *Nike pulls tattoo leggings after offending pacific community.* Retrieved from https://www.huffingtonpost.com/2013/08/15/nike-tattoo-leggings_n _3763591.html

Intercultural Communication: High and Low Context Cultures. (2016, May 16). Retrieved from https://online.seu.edu/high-and-low-context-cultures/

Kluckhohn, F., & Strodtbeck, F. L. (1961). *Variations in value orientation.* New York, NY: Row Perterson Company.

Kagitcibasia C., & Berry, J. W. (1989). Cross-cultural psychlogy: Current research and trends. *Annual Review of Psychlogy*. Retrieved from https://www.annual reviews.org/doi/abs/10.1146/annurev.ps.40.020189.002425

Landler, M., & Barbaro, M. (2006). *Wal-Mart finds that its formula doesn't fit every culture*. Retrieved from https://www.nytimes.com/2006/08/02/business/ worldbusiness/02walmart.html?ei=5088&en=e01e99c3081724c5&ex=131217 1200&partner=rssnyt&pagewanted=print

Luo, J. (2018). *Paying tribute to China: How western brands can avoid cultural insensitivity*. Retrieved from https://jingdaily.com/tribute-china/

MacLachlan, M. (2011). *Impact of stereotypes on international business: Cross cultural awareness is key*. Retrieved from https://www.communicaid.com/cross-cultural -training/blog/impact-of-stereotypes-on-international-business-cross-cultural -awareness-is-key/

Neese, B. (2016). *Intercultural communication: High- and low-context cultures*. Retrieved from https://online.seu.edu/high-and-low-context-cultures/

Passport revoked: When brands fail internationally. (2017). Retrieved from https:// www.cbc.ca/radio/undertheinfluence/passport-revoked-when-brands-fail -internationally-1.3942237

Peng, M. (2009). *Global business*. Cengage South-Western.

Stangor, C. (2014, September 26). Principles of Social Psychology—1st International Edition. Retrieved from https://opentextbc.ca/socialpsychology/part/ chapter-12-stereotypes-prejudice-and-discrimination/

The Pew Forum. (2012). *The global religious landscape*. Retrieved from http://assets .pewresearch.org/wp-content/uploads/sites/11/2014/01/global-religion -full.pdf

Xu, Y. (2018, December 1). *Dolce & Gabbana ad (with chopsticks) provokes public outrage in China*. Retrieved from https://www.npr.org/sections/goatsandsoda/ 2018/12/01/671891818/dolce-gabbana-ad-with-chopsticks-provokes-public -outrage-in-china

Ye, Michelle (1988, June). Taoism and modern Chinese poetry. *Journal of Chinese Philosophy*. Retrieved from https://onlinelibrary.wiley.com/doi/abs/10.1111/ j.1540-6253.1988.tb00596.x

CHAPTER 7

Business Ethics and Corporate Social Responsibility

LEARNING OBJECTIVES

- Define **international business ethics** and **corporate social responsibility**
- Understand what **ethical dilemmas** are and how they affect multinational operations
- Identify the **consequences** and **issues** related to **corruption**
- Identify the basic principles and consequences of the **U.S. Foreign Corrupt Practices Act**

Global Business, pages 141–155
Copyright © 2019 by Information Age Publishing
All rights of reproduction in any form reserved.

Opening Case

Bolivia Legalizes Child Labor, Attempting to Make It Safer

In 2014, Bolivia lowered the age children could legally work for themselves or their families to 10. Children can work for others when they are 12. Previously, Bolivia's minimum working age was 14. The United Nations and the International Labor Organization have set the minimum age to legally work at 14. These organizations and activists have urged Bolivia to change back the law.

However, supporters of the new legislation say that the law guarantees legal protections and fair wages for children, who have been working regardless of laws against it. In addition, in a country with a 39 percent poverty rate, the children's wages are often income families need to survive. Bolivian president Evo Morales has resisted calls for repeal. He's reiterated his support for

Figure 7.1   Bolivian child shoe-polisher. *Source:* Alberto https://upload.wikimedia .org/wikipedia/commons/4/4b/Child_labor_in_Bolivia_Shoe-Shine_Boy.jpg

children and adolescents and unveiled new decrees and mandates to protect them. For example, a new decree provides free legal aid to victims of violence, and mandated paid leave for the parents critically ill children. The law already includes provisions for children to be paid minimum wage, just like an adult, and to have the same rights as workers.

The Bolivian Union of Child and Adolescent Workers (UNATSBO) claims that children and adolescents have to work because their families don't have enough money. They also claim that the law gives them the opportunity to be recognized and to be more protected as young workers. However, they also recognized that this is not the ideal situation. Parents need to have better jobs so they can actually support their families.

Voices that condemn the law argue that a child who is working doesn't have the proper time to dedicate to school, that it's going to trap people in a cycle of poverty because they're never going to be able to get an education that could move them out of it. The minimum wage should be increased for adults so that they're able to support their families.

Based on

https://www.npr.org/2014/07/30/336361778/bolivia-makes-child-labor-legal-in-an-attempt-to-make-it-safer

https://www.nbcnews.com/news/latino/bolivia-wrestles-protecting-child-workers-young-10-n840616

https://www.dol.gov/agencies/ilab/resources/reports/child-labor/bolivia

Additional Resource

The International Labor Organization: http://www.ilo.org/global/lang—en/index.htm

1. *How should a foreign business from a country where child labor under 14 is illegal conduct their operations if they must be operate in Bolivia? Explain and provide at least three different actions for the company to undertake.*

2. *Does the above scenario present an ethical dilemma? Explain.*

7.0   Introduction

Demands for businesses to conduct their business ethically and to be socially responsible have increased due to evolving communications, technological advancement as well as the expectations of market participants. Beyond bringing economic value to shareholders, modern companies are expected to support and advance the interests of their stakeholders. This trend has resulted in the development of concepts such as business ethics, and corporate social responsibility (CSR). International businesses face more challenges than domestic businesses because they operate in countries and locations that have different economic levels of development, different socio-cultural structures, and even different laws. Thus, multinational business face ethical dilemmas more often than purely domestic business.

An **ethical dilemma** is also known as a moral dilemma. It refers to a problem in the decision-making process between two possible options, neither of which is absolutely acceptable from an ethical perspective.[1] Global ethical dilemmas are extremely complicated challenges that do not have simple solutions and cannot be easily solved. The opening case describes the situation in Bolivia regarding child labor laws. The scenario highlights a potential ethical dilemma for a foreign company operating in Bolivia.

In this chapter, the definitions of business ethics, the present history and applications of CSR are also presented. Corporations deal with a wide variety of social issues in their operations, directly or indirectly. Advancing communications and technology in the era of globalization is demanding businesses to operate ethically and contribute to the wellbeing of stakeholders.

7.1 Business Ethics and Globalization

Corporations increasingly operate in a global environment. Critics suggest that globalization leads to the exploitation of developing nations and workers, destruction of the environment, and increased human rights abuses. They also argue that globalization primarily benefits the wealthy and widens the gap between the rich and the poor.

Proponents of globalization argue that open markets lead to higher standards of living for everyone, higher wages for workers worldwide, and economic development in impoverished nations. Most of the large corporations are multinational in scope and may face legal, social, and ethical issues globally. Another issue is the marketing of goods and services in the international marketplace. For example, some companies continue to market products in other countries such as cigarettes to youth, while such practices have been banned in the home country.

Businesses have taken various steps to address some of the challenges described above through Corporate Social Responsibility (CSR).

7.1.1 Business Ethics

Business ethics focuses on the moral judgments and behavior of individuals and groups within organizations. It is a form of applied ethics or professional ethics. It examines ethical principles, morals, and problems that take place in all types of business environments. Thus, the study of business ethics may be regarded as a component of the larger study of corporate social responsibility (Buchholtz & Carroll, 2012). Kirk Hanson, the Executive

SPOTLIGHT
Cigarette Advertising in Developing Countries

The Guardian reported that research by campaigners and experts in more than 22 countries found cigarettes are being sold and promoted near schools.

Stalls and shops full of vibrantly colorful branding sell single cigarettes at pocket money prices alongside sweets and candies. Marlboro cigarettes made by Philip Morris and British American Tobacco brands such as Pall Mall, Kent, Dunhill and Lucky Strike were being sold and promoted within 300 meters (1,000 ft) or closer to schools in nearly all the countries researchers examined in a series of studies. Brands made by Japan Tobacco and Imperial were seen near schools in a smaller number.

In countries like Peru, Indonesia and India, the Guardian correspondents saw banner ads above stalls near a primary school and were told that tobacco company reps visit with free cigarettes and new promotional material every few months.

Both Philip Morris International (PMI) and British American Tobacco (BAT) deny the allegations and said they have strict rules against targeting children.

Based on

https://www.theguardian.com/world/2018/mar/09/how-children-around
-the-world-are-exposed-to-cigarette-advertising

Director of the Markkula Center for Applied Ethics states that "business ethics is the study of the standards of business behavior which promote human welfare and the good."[2]

7.2   Ethical Issues in Global Business

Ethics are a set of guiding principles to distinguish between right and wrong behaviors. In recent decades, companies, whether domestic or multinational have been paying more attention to their employees' ethical conducts by developing **ethical strategies**. Such strategies identify morally-acceptable actions for their organizations and clearly design a formal framework for a **code of conduct** for their employees.

MNEs face different ethical issues particularly when they operate in countries with different cultural, political, social and legal systems. How these factors affect the strategies of MNEs will be discussed in a later chapter.

7.2.1 Sources of Unethical Business Behaviors

Most countries and cultures differ in terms of legal and ethical standards. Common points of divergence include **wage laws**, **employment practices**, and **bribery**. The **1977 Foreign Corrupt Practices Act** (FCPA)[3] holds American companies legally accountable for bribing foreign officials in order to win contracts or permissions from their governments. Yet **grease payments**, which expedite delivery, remain a common ethical gray area.

Whereas a developed nation may ban certain practices, a less developed nation may not. The low cost of manufacturing goods in countries with few regulations concerning wages, working hours, or environmental pollution attracts investors seeking to profit from the legality of unethical practices.

Some people in businesses are often involved in unethical behaviors. Some of the key reasons for such conducts are:

1. Lack of personal ethics where there could be a "bad apple" in the organization
2. Lack of an internal code of conduct in the organization that could lead to unethical behavior by leaders, managers and co-workers
3. Pressure to achieve unreasonable goals by unintentionally encouraging employees to engage in questionable practices
4. Widespread corruption in a society where people feel that "everybody cheats and I don't want to fall behind"

SPOTLIGHT
H&M Accused of Failing to Employ
Fair Living Wage Approach

The Clean Clothes Campaign (CCC), an alliance championing ethical garment production, accused H&M of paying its workers in Bulgaria, Turkey, Cambodia, and India wages below the poverty line. The alliance specifically stated that H&M did not follow through on their commitment to offer a fair living wage to all of the strategic suppliers by 2018. The retail giant refuted the CCC's claims and suggested that all of their suppliers are required to pay the workers at least a minimum wage, following the national laws.

Based on

https://www.edie.net/news/7/H-M-accused-of-failing-to-ensure-living-wage-for-supply-chain-workers/

1. *What are some issues with H&M's argument, assuming it follows the labor laws of the host countries?*

7.2.2 The Corruption Perceptions Index

Transparency International is an international non-governmental organization based in Berlin, Germany. In 1995 the organization started to publish the **Corruption Perceptions Index** (CPI). The index is based on business people opinion surveys and or performance assessments from a group of analysts. Therefore, some scholars question the validity of the index. Nevertheless, other scholars argue that despite the inherent bias of surveying small groups of people, the index is a useful measure to provide a sense of the level of corruption in a particular country (Charron, 2016; Clark, 2009). Transparency International generally defines **corruption** as "the misuse of public power for private benefit."[4]

The CPI ranks countries on a scale from 100 (very clean) to 0 (highly corrupt). For example, according to the 2018 CPI, Denmark, Singapore and New Zealand were perceived as the least corrupt countries in the world, whereas, Somalia ranked at 10 out of 100 in 2018. See Figure 7.2.

7.3 Corporate Social Responsibility

Corporate Social Responsibility or **CSR** is broadly defined as the "economic, legal, ethical, and discretionary expectations that society has of organizations at a given point in time" (Buchholtz & Carroll, 2012). The United Nations has stated that the concept of CSR is directly interchangeable with an organization's corporate responsibility for citizenship, social enterprise, sustainability, and corporate ethics (Post, 2013). Through the concept of CSR, businesses and organizations are given moral, ethical, and philanthropic

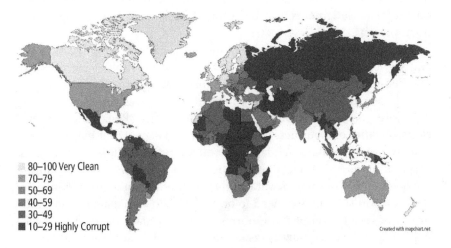

80–100 Very Clean
70–79
50–69
40–59
30–49
10–29 Highly Corrupt

Created with mapchart.net

Figure 7.2 2018 Corruption Perceptions Index.

responsibilities in addition to the traditional responsibilities of earning a fair return for investors and complying with the required laws. In other words, the traditional view that suggests that the primary and sole responsibility of a corporation is to its owners has been broadened.

Corporate social responsibility demands organizations to be responsible for other constituencies such as employees, suppliers, customers, the local community, state, and federal governments, environmental groups, and other special interest groups, in addition to their shareholders. The various groups affected by the actions of an organization are usually called **stakeholders**. Freeman (2010) stated that stakeholders are "any group or individual who can affect or is affected by the achievement of the firm's objectives" (Freeman, 2010).

The stakeholder theory is directly related to Freeman's statement as it describes the need for MNEs to focus on incorporating internal and external stakeholders into their business decisions. The **stakeholder theory** discusses that a MNE's internal stakeholders (owners, customers, and suppliers) and external stakeholders (the government, environment, and local communities) are vital to the success of any organization (Lopez-De-Pedro & Rimbau-Gilabert, 2012). When a multinational company views all stakeholders as integrated members, the incorporation of a code of ethics facilitates the development and adaption of sustainability and CSR initiatives across all business functions and departments (Adams, Tashchian, & Shore, 2001; Asgary & Mitschow, 2002; Sethi, 2005).

Although CSR is directly related to business ethics, the concept is somewhat different. While CSR encompasses the economic, legal, ethical, and discretionary responsibilities of organizations, business ethics focuses on the *moral* judgments and behavior of individuals and groups *within* organizations.

The **economic responsibility** of business corporations is to produce goods and services efficiently, profitably, and to keep shareholder interests. On the other hand, society's expectation is that business corporations will produce goods and services that are needed and desired by customers and sell those goods and services at a reasonable price. Regarding the **legal responsibilities** of a business corporation, it is expected that businesses will comply with the established laws. The **ethical responsibilities** of a business corporation include societal expectations that go beyond the law. Thus, it is expected that businesses will conduct their affairs in a fair and just way. In other words, businesses need to be proactive to anticipate and meet the norms of society even if those norms are not formally enacted in law. Finally, one of the **discretionary responsibilities** of a business corporation is to behave as a good citizen.

7.3.1   The History of Corporate Social Responsibility

The nature and scope of corporate social responsibility has changed over the years. The concept of CSR has been in wide use since the 1960s. However, while the economic, legal, ethical, and discretionary expectations placed on business corporations may differ, it is probably accurate to say that all societies at all points in time have had some degree of expectation that business corporations would act responsibly.

At the beginning of the twentieth century, a backlash against large corporations began to gain momentum. Big business was criticized as being too powerful and for practicing antisocial and anticompetitive practices. Laws and regulations, such as the **Sherman Antitrust Act**,[5] were enacted to rein in the large corporations and to protect employees, consumers, and society. The labor movement also called for greater social responsiveness on the part of business. Between 1900 and 1960, businesses gradually began to accept additional responsibilities other than (a) making a profit and (b) obeying the law.

In the 1960s and 1970s, the civil rights movement, consumerism, and environmentalism affected society's expectations of business. Based on the general idea that those with great power have great responsibility, many called for the business to be more proactive in ceasing societal problems and starting to participate in solving them. Some legal mandates were placed on businesses that related to equal employment opportunity, product safety, worker safety, and the environment.

Furthermore, most stakeholders expect corporations should go beyond their economic and legal responsibilities and take proactive actions related to the advancement of society. This view of corporate social responsibility is becoming more prevailing perspective in the global community.

7.3.2   Arguments For and Against Corporate Social Responsibility

The **economic argument** against CSR is closely associated with the American economist Milton Friedman, who argued that the primary responsibility of business is to make a profit for its owners, while complying with the law. According to this view, the self-interested actions of millions of participants in free markets will lead to positive outcomes for society. If the operation of the free market cannot solve a social problem, it becomes the responsibility of the government, not the business, to address the issue.

The **competitive argument** recognizes the fact that addressing social issues creates additional cost to a business that in turn will hurt the competitive position of the business relative to other businesses. This argument is particularly relevant in a globally competitive environment if businesses in

SPOTLIGHT
"What Really Motivates People to be Honest in Business?"

Each year, one in seven large corporations commits fraud. Why? To find out, Alexander Wagner takes us inside the economics, ethics and psychology of doing the right thing. Join him for an introspective journey down the slippery slopes of deception as he helps us understand why people behave the way they do.

Learn More

https://www.ted.com/talks/alexander_wagner_what_really_motivates_people_to_be_honest_in_business/details

Time: 13:29

Source: Lisa Termini [CC BY-SA 4.0 (https://creativecommons.org/licenses/by-sa/4.0)], from Wikimedia Commons

one country expend assets to address social issues, but those in another country do not. The effects of increased sustainability through integrated stakeholder partnerships can lead to increases in financial performance as well as greater brand image recognition and competitive advantages (Asgary & Li, 2014; Porter & Kramer, 2006).

Finally, some argue that businesses are ill equipped to address social problems. This **capability argument** suggests that business executives and managers are typically well trained in the ways of finance, marketing, and operations management, but not well versed in dealing with complex societal problems. Thus, they do not have the knowledge or skills needed to deal with social issues. This view suggests that corporate involvement in social issues may actually make the situation worse. Part of the capability argument also suggests that corporations can best serve societal interests by sticking to what they do best, which is providing quality goods and services and selling them at an affordable price to people who desire them.

There are several arguments in favor of corporate social responsibility. One view, held by critics of the corporate world, is that since large corporations create many social problems, they should attempt to address and solve them. Those holding this view criticize the production, marketing, accounting, and environmental practices of corporations. They suggest that corporations can do a better job of producing quality, safe products by conducting their operations in an open and honest manner.

A very different argument in favor of corporate social responsibility is the **self-interest argument**. This is a long-term perspective that suggests corporations should conduct themselves in the present in a manner that ensures a promising operating environment in the future. Therefore, companies must look beyond the short-term benefits and recognize that investments in society today will be beneficial in the future. Furthermore, it may be in the corporate world's best interests to engage in socially responsive activities because, by doing so, the corporate world may forestall governmental intervention in the form of new legislation and regulation.

Finally, some suggest that businesses should assume social responsibilities because they are among the few private entities that have the resources to do so. The corporate world has some of the brightest minds in the world, and it possesses tremendous financial resources. Wal-Mart, for example, has annual revenues that exceed the annual GNP of some countries. Thus, businesses should utilize some of their human and financial capital in order to "make the world a better place."

Corporate social responsibility is a complex topic. There is no question that the legal, ethical, and discretionary expectations placed on businesses are greater than ever before. Few companies totally disregard social issues and problems. Most purport to pursue not only the goal of increased revenues and profits, but also the goal of community and societal betterment. Research suggests that those corporations that develop a reputation for being socially responsive and ethical enjoy higher levels of performance. However, the ultimate motivation for corporations to practice social responsibility should not be a financial motivation, but a moral and ethical one.

Debate—CSR

Should businesses go above and beyond legal requirements when they operate abroad?

	Pros	Cons
Utilitarian Argument	✔ Corporation created and continued to create many social problems. Therefore, the corporate world should assume responsibility for addressing these problems.	✘ Taking on social and moral issues is not economically feasible. Corporations should focus on earning a profit for their shareholders and leave social issues to others.
Competitive Argument	✔ In the long run, it is in the corporations' best interest to assume social responsibilities to ensure future success and potentially avoid governmental regulation.	✘ Social responsibility creates additional costs placing corporations at a competitive disadvantage relative to corporations that are not socially responsible.
Capability Argument	✔ Large corporations have huge reserves of human and financial capital. They should devote at least some of their resources to addressing social issues.	✘ Those who are most capable should address social issues. Those in the corporate world are not equipped to deal with social problems.

7.4 Conclusions

The role of businesses in the global environment continues to grow and evolve. Increased information technology and communications demand transparency. In order to succeed, businesses and multinational corporations need to adhere to strong ethical standards, and embrace corporate social responsibility. While this trend places a great responsibility on businesses, it also represents a great opportunity to turn this need into a competitive advantage, to make a difference, and be a good citizen. Conducting businesses ethically is rewarded by the end-users, which in turn impact the bottom line. Global businesses can utilize their capabilities to have a positive impact on society by managing their operations ethically and contribute to the society's wellbeing.

TBL Connection
Socially Responsible Disney

The Walt Disney Company, founded in 1923, has been recognized internationally for their films and entertainment parks, and also for their Corporate Social Responsibility (CSR) initiatives and programs. In 2017,

Fortune named the company as one of the "World's Most Admired Companies." The 2017 Disney's CSR report revealed the main issues the company is focusing on: environmental stewardship, international labor standards, healthy living, workplace practices, and strategic philanthropic and community engagement.

With regard to environmental stewardship, the company is working to reduce waste and emissions. For example, one such initiative includes purchasing half of the electricity for Disneyland Paris from renewable sources. To better support workers internationally, the corporation continues to monitor working conditions. One of the workplace initiatives of Disney includes recruiting and hiring more women and veterans and promoting employee volunteering. The company also promotes healthy living by incorporating healthy messages in their media content, and revamping menus. Finally, through strategic philanthropic engagement, Disney supports various special projects around the globe. In 2017, the Disney Conservation Fund awarded more than $8 million in grants to organizations that protect wildlife across the globe.

Based on

https://www.thewaltdisneycompany.com/wp-content/uploads/2017 disneycsrupdate.pdf

https://www.smartrecruiters.com/blog/top-20-corporate-social-responsibility -initiatives-for-2017/

1. *Why do you think companies such as Disney spend so much money on being more socialy responsible?*
2. *Do you think consumers care more for socially responsible companies?*

Chapter Review

Key Terms

- Business ethics
- Corporate Social Responsibility (CSR)
- Ethical dilemma
- Moral dilemma
- International Labor Organization
- Foreign Corrupt Practices Act (FCPA)
- Corruption
- Bribery

- Corruption Perception Index
- Grease payment
- Sherman Antitrust Act

Questions & Assignments

Questions

1. Do you consider the use of plastic straws and bottled water a CSR related issue? If yes, how is it related to CSR? What would be possible solutions to reduce their use?
2. Identify the best and worst cities in the United States in terms of CSR performance. Discuss the reasons for the differences and illustrate with examples.
3. Discuss corporate social responsibility and examine two companies from them same industry in which one proactively adheres to CSR and the other does it reactively.
4. Select a multinational company you are familiar with and evaluate its CSR initiatives. How does its CSR compare to that of other companies in the industry?

Assignments

1. Discuss the feasibility of implementing CSR programs or initiatives in China, USA, and a small developing country. Describe in which country stakeholders can influence company's action more. Illustrate with examples.
2. Research the current CSR debates in EU countries of your choice. Compare and contrast your findings to CSR practices in the USA.

Notes

1. https://corporatefinanceinstitute.com/resources/knowledge/other/ethical-dilemma/
2. https://www.scu.edu/ethics/about-the-center/people/kirk-o-hanson/
3. https://www.justice.gov/criminal-fraud/foreign-corrupt-practices-act
4. https://www.transparency.org/about
5. https://www.ftc.gov/tips-advice/competition-guidance/guide-antitrust-laws/antitrust-laws

Suggested Reading

The World's most Ethical Companies
    https://www.worldsmostethicalcompanies.com/

Xerox Corporate Responsibility Report
    https://www.xerox.com/corporate-social-responsibility/2018/
Patagonia's Environmental and Social Responsibility Report
    https://www.patagonia.com/environmentalism.html
Transparency International
    https://www.transparency.org/
    https://www.bentley.edu/centers/center-for-business-ethics

References

Adams, J. S., Tashchian, A., & Shore, T. H. (2001). Codes of ethics as signals for ethical behavior. *Journal of Business Ethics, 29*(3), 199–211.

Asgary, N., & Li, G. (2014). Corporate social responsibility: Its economic impact and link to the bullwhip effect. *Journal of Business Ethics, 135*(4), 665–681.

Asgary, N., & Mitschow, M. C. (2002). Toward a model for international business ethics. *Journal of Business Ethics, 36*(3), 239–246.

Buchholtz, A. K., & Carroll, A. B. (2012). *Business & Society: Ethics & Stakeholder Management*: South-Western Cengage Learning.

Charron, N. (2016). Do corruption measures have a perception problem? Assessing the relationship between experiences and perceptions of corruption among citizens and experts. *European Political Science Review, 8*(1), 147–171.

Clark, D. (2009). Adjustment Problems in Developing Countries and the U.S.–Central America–Dominican Republic Free Trade Agreement. *The International Trade Journal, 23*(1), 31–53.

Freeman, R. E. (2010). *Strategic management: A stakeholder approach*: Cambridge University Press.

Lopez-De-Pedro, J. M., & Rimbau-Gilabert, E. (2012). Stakeholder Approach: What Effects Should We Take into Account in Contemporary Societies? *Journal of Business Ethics, 107*(2), 147–158.

Porter, M. E., & Kramer, M. R. (2006). The link between competitive advantage and corporate social responsibility. *Harvard Business Review, 11.*

Post, J. E. (2013). The United Nations global compact: A CSR milestone. *Business & Society, 52*(1), 53–63.

Sethi, S. P. (2005). Voluntary codes of conduct for multinational corporations. *Journal of Business Ethics, 59*(1), 1–2.

GLOBAL AND ECONOMIC
ENVIRONMENTS
1. Globalization
2. Global Economic Environment
3. Trade Theories and the Role of
   Governments in Trade
4. Global Financial System and Risk

CURRENT ISSUES IN GLOBAL BUSINESS
12. Environmental Changes and Global Business
13. Disruptive Innovation and Global Business
14. Sustainability, Social Enterprise, and Impact
    Investment

FIRM-LEVEL MANAGEMENT
  8. International Business Strategy
  9. Entry Modes Into Foreign Markets
 **10. The Internationalization Process
       of the Firm**
 11. Cross-Cultural Management

2

POLITICAL, CULTURAL, AND ETHICAL
ENVIRONMENTS
5. Political and Legal Environments
6. Cultural and Social Environments
7. Business Ethics and Corporate
   Social Responsibility

CHAPTER 8

International Business Strategy

LEARNING OBJECTIVES

- Describe the key elements of **strategy formulation** by considering **internal** and **external factors**.
- Describe **alternative strategies** available to multinational enterprises
- Describe and apply **SWOT** and **PESTEL** analyses to structure international strategy for a firm while considering location specific factors.
- Identify the **dynamic factors** and their interaction for **market entry planning** and **operational approach** in international strategy.
- Describe the **Tripod** and **5W** strategic models

Global Business, pages 159–179
Copyright © 2019 by Information Age Publishing
All rights of reproduction in any form reserved.

Opening Case

Timberland

Timberland is a multinational company headquartered in Stratham, New Hampshire, that produces and sells high-end sporting clothing. Nathan Swartz established the company by buying a major share of the Abington Shoe Company of Boston in 1952. In 1995, he purchased the remaining share, and moved the manufacturing to New Hampshire. In 1973, the company's name changed to Timberland. In the 1980s, the company began expanding internationally. Timberland merged with the VF Corporation in 2011.

Timberland introduced waterproof boots to the market in 1973. Timberland became known for its high-quality outdoor boots, but it began to introduce other products such as apparel, backpacks, sunglasses, and other related products for outdoors in the 1980s. Timberland products are made both in the United States and in the Dominican Republic. One major issue that Timberland faces is how to fight against "fake" Timberland products. Counterfeit products are produced and marketed under the Timberland brand in other countries.

Regarding the corporate structure, Timberland maintains its brand within the VF Corporation. Currently it operates stores in many different countries around the world. The company has stores in the UK, Argentina, Chile, Brazil, Spain, and South Africa just to name a few. Timberland boots, footwear, and other clothing items are made for outdoor and cold weather. They are

Figure 8.1 Timberland boots. *Source:* Dough4872, https://commons.wikimedia.org/wiki/File:Timberland_6_inch_boots.jpg

also relatively expensive sporty and outdoor products. Timberland's premium waterproof boots, for example, cost around $190 per pair.

Based on

https://www.vfc.com/brands/outdoor/timberland

1. *Why should a firm develop objectives before focusing on location selection?*

2. *Should Timberland adjust their products for each market to address the weather and living condition of each country? What are the arguments for and against changing product and design for each market?*

3. *Considering Timberland's situation, what should their pricing strategy be for various global markets? Should prices be adjusted to match the purchasing power of specific markets or should the prices be kept constant globally? You can use resources available in Globaledge https://globaledge.msu.edu/ for an analysis of the business environment of the country of choice in your answer. Focus on risk and attractiveness of the country.*

8.0   Introduction

This chapter explains the process of strategic planning. Various dynamic aspects of international strategy are integrated to describe the development of international business strategy within the context of the overall business strategy of a firm. Finally, applications of the tripod model are discussed.

8.1   Strategy

Strategy is a roadmap for the future of an organization. It provides guidance for various stakeholders including investors, management, and other people working in the organization. Strategy sets the vision for the future of the enterprise and the objectives of the organization along with guidance as to how they will be achieved. The main goal of a firm is value creation for the owners, both in the short-term and in the long-term, while considering the interests of other stakeholders and society. For State Owned Enterprises

SPOTLIGHT
Apple & Foxconn

Many MNEs work with partners overseas in low-income countries such as India, Indonesia, and China to reduce cost of their supplies. However, these partners may not give adequate wages and more importantly, not have a proper working environment. One example is Apple's subcontractor Foxconn in China. Foxconn's salaries and work conditions are far from desirable. Watch the video below to learn more.

https://www.youtube.com/watch?v=TmLsV9cSk0o

Figure 8.2 Strategic planning elements.

(SOEs), the main objective is the creation of both social benefits and private benefits, such as job creation and financial returns. SOEs are common in many centrally planned economies and even in a few mixed economies.

Strategy formulation is a complex process that requires building a vision for the future of the organization, evaluating the firm's core competence, determining the strength and weaknesses, as well as identifying the external environment in terms of opportunities and threats. Then, it requires developing an action plan, and continuous evaluation of progress toward achieving the plan's objectives (see Figure 8.2). Appropriate implementation not only necessitates analysis and development of an action plan, but it also requires effective execution. An effective execution alone may need a number of factors and processes that take into account changes in the culture of the organization, leadership, reorganization, and reallocation of resources.

A **strategy** must have at least three clear objectives: financial, competitive and CSR (see Figure 8.3). The **financial objectives** analyze the financial situation of the firm and ways to improve it. Normally financial performance such as the return on investment (ROI) and the return on assets (ROA) are benchmarked against industry averages to show how well the firm is performing financially. Improvement in financial performance and profitability is achieved by increasing sales, cutting costs, or a combination of both. An increase in sales can come from an aggressive domestic market expansion via the introduction of new products, marketing efforts, upgrades in the technology used, and new design. Cost rationalization focuses on a more efficient use of resources. An example of market expansion is to expand into new international markets. The **cost cutting approach** of international expansion focuses on analyzing the value chain to determine which part or parts of the firm's value chain can operate more efficiently through the use of technology, relocation to lower cost countries, outsourcing, and off-shoring.

One way that firms can reduce cost is to move their production site to the places with lower cost of resources, particularly labor, such as China and

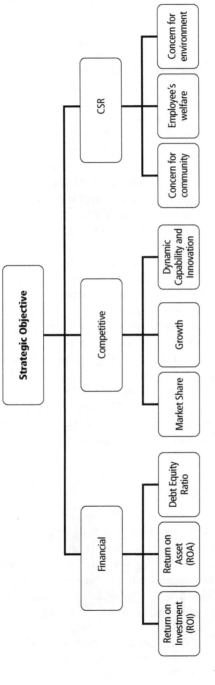

Figure 8.3 Strategic objective.

India. In the manufacturing sector, off-shoring has become a way to reduce the cost of production. To increase revenue, firms need to tap into new markets in order to expand the market size. Both methods increase a firm's profit, which pushes the target profit even higher. International market expansion leads to higher revenue, which could increase the profit of the company.

The main strategic objective focuses on determining success and positioning the firm relative to its competitors. At times, the financial and competitive objectives maybe at odds with each other. For example, competing for market share may require incremental costs in the short term, such as investment in research and development (R&D), which takes years before it yields new products or technology. However, without investment in R&D, the firm would be leveraging its future for saving costs in the short term. Nevertheless, such strategy would not be sustainable and would be detrimental to the firm's long-term success and well-being.

Finally, the strategy of a firm should consider employees, the community where it operates, and the environment. Creating a good working environment leads to a dedicated workforce. It is commonly believed that employees are one of the most important intangible assets of an organization. In addition, being a good neighbor and helping to improve the community where the firm operates is important in building goodwill. Many firms encourage (and some firms require) their employees to do volunteer work within their communities. Lastly, commitment to the environment should be an integral part of the strategy of firms. It is a legal requirement to avoid air and water pollution. Therefore, going beyond the legal requirements and attempting to reduce the company's carbon footprint is a socially responsible activity. In many emerging economies, environmental laws are quite lax. Nevertheless, MNEs should not take advantage of lax regulations and move polluting factories to those countries. It is important to recognize that the world is a close system and pollution in one location impacts other countries and locations.

8.1.1 SWOT Analysis

An action plan requires the analysis of internal and external factors. A firm must analyze their own strengths and weaknesses. They also need to search for external opportunities, and potential threats they may have to mitigate or prevent. The Strength–Weakness–Opportunity–Threat analysis is called a **SWOT analysis**, and it is a common analytical tool used for crafting a strategy (see Figure 8.4). The example below shows the various items that can be considered in each category.

Example: Technology has created both threats and opportunities. In the retail industry, firms that did not develop a competitive e-commerce platform have lost their competitive advantage, i.e., Toys 'R' Us. On the other hand, firms that quickly embraced this new technology, such as Amazon and Netflix, have succeeded both financially and in terms of growth.

The aim of a SWOT analysis is to provide a path for the positioning of a firm in the future. Once the firm determines its strengths, then it can build on those strengths to improve its competitive position. The identification

SPOTLIGHT
Zara

Zara is a Spanish clothing and accessory company with annual revenues of around 25 billion Euro (as of 3/15/ 2019, one Euro is equal to $1.13). Zara is a division of Inditex, the largest apparel company in the world. Inditex has other apparel divisions. Zara has around 7,000 stores in 50 countries. The company's success is based on the strategy of providing products consumers want when they want them. The core competency and strategy is the cutting of the lead-time between design, manufacturing and distribution. This concept is called "instant fashion." Since fashion changes quickly getting product to market is a key success factor for the industry. In the clothing industry, the time between design and production is normally around one year but for Zara it is weeks. Zara is also known for "trendy products" that require short time from design to availability in stores. In contrast to many clothing firms, Zara works with small number of company owned factories to be able to implement this type of strategy and shorten the supply chain.

Based on

https://www.inditex.com/about-us/our-brands/zara

Zara store-front in Barcelona. *Source:* M. Samii [Owned by author]

Strength (example)	Opportunity (example)
• Market share	• Global market
• Financial condition	• Cost cutting through use of technology
• Dedicated employees	• Merger and acquisition
• Name recognition	
• Technology	
Weakness (example)	**Threat (example)**
• Lack of new products	• New competitors
• High debt	• Government regulation
• Legacy product and technology	• Change in consumer attitude

Figure 8.4 Sample SWOT analysis.

of weaknesses requires the firm to find ways to eliminate those weaknesses so competitors are not able to exploit them. The identification of external opportunities requires a strategy to take advantage of those opportunities. Finally, the identification of threats requires rethinking of the strategy to build defensive mechanisms to prevent those threats from impacting the firm in the future.

8.1.2 PESTEL Model

To analyze external factors, a firm must consider several facts and trends about Political, Economic, Social, Technological, Environmental and Legal factors (or **PESTEL**). It is important to perform a detailed analysis of these factors for planning purposes. This type of analysis is especially important when developing international strategy for activities in foreign countries. The differences between the domestic and international environment are quite significant. The limited knowledge of decision-makers on various factors of a foreign country makes it imperative to obtain detailed knowledge of PESTEL factors prior to mapping a specific country strategy.

Example: Regardless of whether a firm is considering entering into a country to sell their product or establish operations, an assessment of the political and economic risk of expanding there is necessary. Political change can be risky, but it can also be an opportunity. Since the 1980s, China has evolved toward an open-door policy for MNEs. MNE operations in China brought considerable opportunities in terms of the advantage of cheap labor and a very large and growing consumer market. However, as of 2018, the possibility of a tariff war started to affect the economic relation between the United States and China, which changed from a cooperative relationship to a confrontational one.

8.1.2   Tripod Model

Another strategic planning model is the **tripod model** of strategy formulation (see Figure 8.5). The tripod model proposed that strategy must be approached from three dimensions:

1. Resource Based View
2. Industry Based View
3. Institution Based View (Peng, 2001, 2013)

Resource Based View (RBV). This view focuses on the internal resources that the firm has that differentiate it from its competitors. Some of the resources are tangible assets, such as financial resources, plants and equipment, and technology while some other assets are intangible such as management capabilities and brand recognition. One can argue that intangible assets are as important as tangible assets in building firm level competitive advantage. Both tangible and intangible assets are accumulated over time. While tangible assets are easy to see and their accumulation over time is recognizable, the intangible assets are more difficult to recognize. Over time, their accumulation would provide a competitive advantage for the firm and would differentiate it from its competitors (Peng, 2001, 2002; Peng, Wang, & Jiang, 2008).

Industry Based View. By contrast, this view focuses on the external factors that impact the operation of the firm within a particular industry. This includes the stage of the industry life cycle, the dynamic changes of industry (DCI), and the competitive nature of the industry. The industry analysis also requires evaluation of the competitive structure of the industry including the number of competitors. The degree of industry concentration is an important dimension of the competitive structure of an industry. When there are large numbers of firms within an industry and products are not

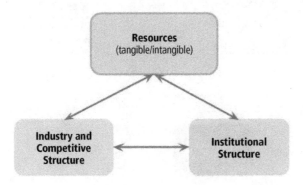

Figure 8.5   Strategy formulation approach.

differentiated, there is much less competition within the industry in terms of marketing. Going international when an industry has reached its maturity stage with lower growth rate may provide an opportunity for increasing sales.

Institution Based View. This final view focuses on the institutional aspects in the process of strategy formulation. The institutional aspects include government regulation and legal aspects. The institutional view also looks at the informal aspect of institutions, which include culture, social norms, and the social value system. A new government regulation at home may make the firm's operation more difficult and could pressure the profit margin of the firm. Similarly, pressure could arise from social norms and changes in the value system pushing the firm to look internationally. An example is the institutional pressure exerted on the U.S. tobacco industry in the early 1980s. The U.S. government began regulating this industry due to health concerns as well as the increase in health care costs related to cigarette smoking. The public also began campaigning against smoking in the United States, leading to a change in the attitude toward smoking in the country. In order to maintain their profit margin, several tobacco companies shifted their focus to international markets, particularly to developing countries where the anti-smoking culture had not yet developed and where government regulations and the legal system were less negative towards tobacco companies.

The tripod model can be further expanded to add two more dimensions (see Figure 8.6). These are the **dynamic capability** and the **system-based view**. The concept of dynamic capability implies the ability of an enterprise

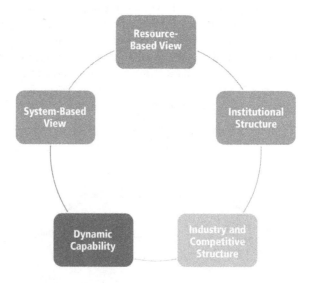

Figure 8.6 Tripod Model extended.

to build assets, both tangible and intangible, for future growth as well as the ability to be nimble to make necessary adjustments to external changes. International strategy is particularly important in this regard because of the dynamic and continuously changing global business environment.

A more dynamic and comprehensive view requires an understanding of the strategy implications on other parts of the enterprise and the external system. It also implies the ability to internalize changes in the external system to the firm level system. For example, a firm's strategy of international expansion impacts its risk. Diversification of operations and sales avoids risk of dependency on only one location and one market. However, it also creates incremental risk due to the country specific risk of a new location. In particular, if the strategy requires financial investment in terms of foreign direct investment, requiring additional capital could increase cost of capital.

8.2   International Strategy

International strategy focuses on how a firm benefits from internationalization in achieving its objectives. A firm can have multiple objectives, which include increasing sales, lowering cost, increasing its competitive position, or acquiring knowledge through internationalization. The international strategy of a firm must focus on achieving those objectives by exploring the potential in other countries.

Market expansion is an important motivation for the internationalization of a firm. The international market and, in particular, emerging economies with their increasing per capita income and a large population provide an incredible market potential. China and India together have a population of about 2.4 billion people. While their per capita income is relatively low, in the last decade their rate of growth has been three times that of most developed Western countries. This growth rate has provided a great opportunity for companies that are interested to increase their sales and their revenue.

Firms also go international in order not to lose sales if their customers move overseas

> *Example:* In the 1980s when several Japanese car manufacturers (Toyota and Honda) moved their production facilities to the United States, the tire producer Bridgestone, realized that in order to remain close to Toyota and Honda they had to set up operations in the United States. Thus, Bridgestone acquired Firestone.

Reducing cost is another potential reason for MNEs to look into operating internationally. Many companies have set up offshore activities to take advantage of cheaper labor costs overseas. The cost differential along with lower overhead requirements for operating in a number of developing countries, particularly in China, has been the driving force for many companies currently operating there. Another approach for international cost reduction is the business process of **outsourcing**. Particularly outsourcing services and the operational side of certain activities in order to reduce costs has become the norm.

> *Example:* India is one of the many attractive locations for outsourcing activities. The country is well positioned for those activities due to the large English speaking and well-educated population. Many companies have outsourced back-office activities such as accounting, payroll, document maintenance, and customer service to India. This has reduced cost significantly because of the labor cost differential between the U.S. and India.

8.2.1   5W Model

The international business strategy of a firm must address five main questions called the 5 Ws of international business strategy (see Figure 8.7):

1. **Why** *is a firm going international?* This is the key question to be asked by the firm. Much of the subsequent decisions are based on the answer to this question. The main reasons for international expansion, as was explained previously, are: 1) increase in revenue, 2) reduction in cost, 3) risk diversification, and 4) a combination of these factors.

2. **Which** *activities will go abroad?* The firm needs to do a value chain analysis to ensure that the international strategy fits well with the overall competitive strategy. Value chain analysis requires the disaggregation of activities to basic components. Once this is done, the firm must decide which activities should move overseas and which ones should be kept domestic.

3. **What** *is the best ownership structure?* Or what should be the appropriate scale of going abroad? The decision to whether a firm would use its financial resources or would rather limit its international financial exposure is a key decision. In other words, should the firm start conservatively by limiting capital investment abroad or should it go full scale and try to dominate the foreign market quickly? The answer to these questions determines the mode of entry and operation. Various options would include export, strategic alliance, licensing, joint venture, and wholly owned subsidiary. Exporting and strategic alliances including franchising and licensing are a low cost way of going international with limited risk. While a joint venture and wholly owned subsidiary have higher financial risk for the firm and require the firms to be highly familiar with the business

Figure 8.7   5Ws of international strategy.

environment of the country. These latter modes of entry have the advantage that the firm has control of the operation and decision-making process in the location, which can ensure a strategic and operational fit with the operations in other locations.

4. **Where** *should the various activities be located?* Location selection is an important strategic decision. The objective of the firm is to determine the best foreign location. Each foreign location offers certain advantages. If the objective is sales increase, then countries with high per capita income and fast economic growth become the target. However, if the firm is considering cost, then locations that provide cost advantage with cheap labor or cheap natural resources become the target of the firm. At the same time, several issues, such as cultural differences, location specific risk factors, availability of infrastructure, and government regulations must be considered when selecting a location.

Multinational firms normally operate in multiple countries. Each part of the supply chain of a MNE, such as research and development, production, sales, and after sale service, are located in a different country based on the comparative advantage of the country. This will optimize the supply chain and take advantage of what each location has to offer by minimizing cost and maximizing sales revenue.

5. **When** *is the best time to enter the foreign market?* When entering a new location, a firm must ask the following question: should we enter now or wait to enter later? Waiting would provide additional information and time for evaluating the risk. This suggestion is particularly valuable for high-risk locations. The *wait and see* strategy is also important for countries that are in temporary economic or political turmoil. However, waiting involves additional cost. The cost of delay could potentially be a lost opportunity. In many cases it is important for a firm to seize a strategic opportunity since a delay would have an opportunity cost. Therefore, firms must compare the benefits of delay and the associated cost. A cost benefit analysis of a strategy is the answer to *when*.

These decisions are important and should consider the resources available to the firm. Nevertheless, the competitive structure of the industry and institutional aspects of countries should also be considered.

8.3　Topology of Operational Strategies

While in a broad sense firms develop an international strategy, the form of the strategy is different depending on the industry structure, the need for local responsiveness, and the requirements for international integration. In general, a firm can adopt three potential approaches for operation strategy. They are a global strategy, a multi-domestic strategy, and an international strategy. Each of these strategies is briefly discussed below.

Global Strategy. This strategy views the world as one market. A global strategy works best when (a) there is very little need to adjust for local needs and (b) a firm meets the same competitors in various countries. The advantage of a global strategy is that the firm is able to reduce its cost structure by standardization in various markets and to compete effectively on a cost and price basis through the achievement of economies of scale.

Multi-Domestic Strategy. The opposite of global strategy. When the need to adjust to local requirements including cultural aspects and competitive structure is high, there is not much benefit in standardization to achieve economies of scale. In this situation, competition is highly localized and therefore the competitive strategy must be built around the local attributes. In such cases, firms provide a great deal of flexibility to local management to make the necessary changes in product, services and the strategy in general to improve the competitive position in that country or location.

International Strategy. This strategy is used when a firm needs to make adjustments to its core competency to improve its local competitiveness. It is a strategy that represents a middle ground between a global strategy and

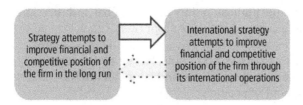

Figure 8.8 Fit between General Strategy and International Strategy.

a multi-domestic strategy. With an international strategy, a firm determines the country specific strategy based on the core competencies. Core competencies such as technology, brand recognition and management capability are the basis of the strategy. However, the difference between international strategy and global strategy is that the local managers have some flexibility to adjust and improve the operations in each location. In addition, usually there is feedback from the headquarters.

Firms may change their approach based on the circumstances and their accumulation of experience. A firm may initially begin with a global strategy and change it later to a multi-domestic strategy when management realizes that in a particular market it is difficult to compete unless they make certain adjustments based on local needs. Many fast food companies that entered China started with a fixed menu, but adjusted over time to the local tastes.

Sometimes a firm enters a new market using the home-country functional strategy such as marketing or a financial strategy, but later adjusts it as needed to increase competitiveness. Learning experience and knowledge accumulation is an intangible asset that helps the internationalization of the firm by improving its competitive position in the global marketplace.

Figure 8.9 Elements of strategy.

Based on the understanding of the global industry and competitive structure, a firm would need to adopt one of the above approaches. However, there are cases in which a firm may use a mixed strategy for the various products or divisions. A firm could have a global strategy for some products, a multi-national for others, and adopt an international strategy for yet another segment of products.

SPOTLIGHT
McDonald's

McDonald's, a global company with revenues of around $22 billion, and 3600 stores operating in over 100 countries, follows an international strategy by using the brand and signature Golden Arches while adjusting to the needs and cultural requirements of the countries in which it operates. In India, where a large percentage of the population is vegetarian, and beef consumption is not customary, McDonald's local Indian partners introduced a veggie burger and the signature "Chicken Maharajah". The international strategy has enabled the company to growth and become the largest chain of fast food in the world.

The competitive structure of the European restaurants and the coffee shop industry is quite different than in the U.S. The European taste in food is more about quality and ambiance than speed and low prices. The demand for restaurants and coffee shops is mostly in the city centers where the real estate cost is high requiring higher margins per visit. Also, the competition in Europe is with local family owned restaurants and coffee shops instead of other food or coffee chains.

In Europe, McDonald's has focused on expanding the McCafe line, which is an upscale coffee shop located at the entrance of existing McDonald's restaurants. It offers espresso coffee and regular coffee. Since McCafes are at the entrance of existing MacDonald's stores they give it an image of an upscale restaurant. McCafe originally started in Australia where it became success. After, it expanded to the rest of the world particularly to Europe. There are currently over 850 McCafes in Germany and 317 in Italy alone. McCafe's prices for espresso and other drinks are considerably higher than regular coffee prices generating the required margin for operation in the costly city centers.

Based on

https://www.statista.com/statistics/515700/number-of-mccafe-stores-in-europe

1. *Should McCafe adjust the products for each market to adapt to local eating habits?*

2. *What are the arguments for and against changing product design and characteristics for each market for McDonald's in particular?*

8.4   Internalization Theory

Buckley and Casson used a broad-based intellectual framework based on the original work of Ronald Coase to analyze multinational operation aspects such as technology transfer and international trade, as well as the location of multinational enterprises in their internationalization strategies. The combined effects of location and internalization strategies explained the division in certain markets between domestic producers, local subsidiaries of MNEs, exports from foreign-owned plants, and exports from MNEs. Internalization is a general principle that explains the boundaries of organizations. It applies not only to the geographical boundaries of the firm, but also to other boundaries such as the firm's product range or diversification.

By using this approach, the multinational firm was viewed as a complex system of interdependent activities linked by flows of knowledge and intermediate products (Buckley & Casson, 1998, 2009; Coase, 1988).

This view of the multinational firm was a radical departure from the **neoclassical economic view** of the firm as a unitary black box devoted entirely to production, whose inputs and outputs were related by a simple production function. The new vision of the firm emphasized the internal division of labor, involving specialized functions comprising not only production but also marketing and R&D. The power of the **internalization concept** was such that it was believed that using a global system view would make it possible to analyze a very wide range of practical issues in international business. Two distinct forms of internalization were identified:

1. *Operational Internalization.* This process involves intermediate products flowing through successive stages of production and the distribution channel.
2. *Knowledge Internalization.* It is the internalization of the flow of knowledge emanating from R&D. The gains from R&D internalization can be substantial and they stem from asymmetric information.

Debate—Global Versus Multidomestic Strategy

GLOBAL	
Pros	**Cons**
✔ Lower Cost	✘ Might backfire in certain markets for cultural and operational reasons
✔ Standardization	
✔ Holistic Brand Image	✘ Might be challenging to implement in regions with limited resources

MULTIDOMESTIC	
Pros	**Cons**
✔ Individualized approach might result in greater financial returns ✔ Implementation might provide useful insights relevant to the overall operations of the company	✘ Higher Cost ✘ Delayed Entry into Foreign Market(s)

8.5   Conclusion

To be successful, firms must have a strategy that provides a roadmap for the future. An international business strategy provides direction so firms can take advantage of opportunities outside their home country to improve financial performance, increase market share, and maintain a competitive position. This is achieved by sales expansion, cost reduction, and/or risk reduction.

International markets provide both advantages and challenges. It is important for firms that are planning to go international or are operating internationally to have a clear vision about the reason for going international and in which location to establish various activities of their supply chain. A successful international strategy requires analysis of company resources both tangible and intangible, the competitive nature of the industry, and the social and economic conditions of the target country.

Finally, in any strategy it is an imperative to decide the degree of control from the headquarters to the subsidiaries. That is, whether the managers of each location make decisions independently (multi-domestic strategy) or the headquarters tightly coordinate the activities of each location (global strategy). In most cases, a combination of coordination and control from the headquarters with some degree of autonomy for each subsidiary (international strategy) is adopted.

TBL Connection
Tesla

Tesla Motors is an electric car manufacturer based in Palo Alto, California founded in 2003. Elon Musk, one of Tesla's co-founders, currently serves as the CEO. The company's sales have grown significantly over the years. In the third quarter of 2018, the total vehicle deliveries have increased by 221% year over year. Today, Tesla is a multinational enterprise with sales offices in Canada, UK, Netherlands, Japan, China, and Australia.

Tesla's strategy has differed from other car manufacturers since its inception. Instead of trying to reach the mass market by producing affordable cars, the company focused on developing an environmentally-friendly product, disrupting the status quo. Tesla's business model includes three major components: direct sales, service, and supercharge network. It relies on proprietary showrooms and attempts to speed up the adoption rate of electric cars by building stations that allow to fully charge a Tesla vehicle in 30 minutes. From a TBL perspective, Tesla is unique. Instead of simply adopting a strong CSR policy, like many modern companies, Tesla put a concern for the planet at the core of its operations. Beyond bringing a unique product to the market, Tesla placed a significant pressure on other car manufacturers, many of which are now working on developing vehicles that do not harm the environment. It is important to note, however, that despite significant success and potential, the performance of Tesla and other electric car manufacturers is dependent on the price of gasoline and availability of rebates by state and federal governments. Those challenges will be of great consideration in the years to come.

Based on

https://www.investopedia.com/articles/active-trading/072115/what-makes-teslas-business-model-different.asp

https://www.fool.com/investing/2018/11/15/teslas-staggering-growth-in-3-charts.aspx

1. *How do challenges Tesla faces differ from those of traditional car manufacturers like Ford, General Motors, and others?*

Chapter Review

Key Terms

- SWOT analysis
- PESTEL analysis
- Tripod Model
- 5W Model
- Resource Based View (RBV)
- Institution Based View
- Global Strategy
- Multi-domestic Strategy
- International Strategy

Questions & Assignments

Questions

1. Why should firms develop objectives before focusing on location selection?
2. Why should a firm have financial and strategic targets while taking into account environmental and social factors?
3. What are tangible and intangible resources of a firm?
4. How does the degree of industry concentration of a country influence the development of a strategy for the country for a firm operating there?
5. Why should a firm analyze the institutional factors of a foreign country before entering to that country?

Assignments

1. Select a country (China for example) analyze the attractiveness and risk for a particular business by looking at:
   - Cultural differences with United States
   - Political system and risk
   - Economic conditions and forecast
   - Tariff structure
   - Exchange rate stability

   Recommend whether McDonald should expand its operation, hold and not put additional resources there or exit the area. You can use material and concepts from pervious chapters. You should use Globaledge https://globaledge.msu.edu/ for your analysis.
2. Tesla, as discussed in the TBL Connection, is a newcomer to the car industry. Evaluate the financial, competitive, environment and social performance in the last few years. What recommendation do you have for Tesla? What is the mission of Tesla? Has the company succeeded in achieving the mission?

Suggested Reading

What is Global Strategy?
> http://www.global-strategy.net/what-is-global-strategy/

Forbes: International Business Strategy
> https://www.forbes.com/sites/85broads/2011/07/01/international
> -business-strategy-a-journey-of-its-own/

Corporate Social Responsibility in International Marketing
> https://smallbusiness.chron.com/corporate-social-responsibility
> -international-marketing-55963.html

References

Buckley, P. J., & Casson, M. C. (1998). Analyzing foreign market entry strategies: Extending the internalization approach. *Journal of International Business Studies*, 539–561.

Buckley, P. J., & Casson, M. C. (2009). The internalisation theory of the multinational enterprise: A review of the progress of a research agenda after 30 years. *Journal of International Business Studies, 40*(9), 1563–1580.

Coase, R. H. (1988). The nature of the firm: influence. *Journal of Law, Economics, & Organization*, 33–47.

Kristina Zucchi, C. (2018, October 27). *What makes Tesla's business model different?* Retrieved from https://www.investopedia.com/articles/active-trading/072115/what-makes-teslas-business-model-different.asp

Peng, M. W. (2001). The resource-based view and international business. *Journal of management, 27*(6), 803–829.

Peng, M. W. (2002). Towards an institution-based view of business strategy. *Asia Pacific Journal of Management, 19*(2/3), 251.

Peng, M. W. (2013). *Global strategy* (3rd ed.). Mason, OH: South-Western, Cengage Learning.

Peng, M. W., Wang, D. Y. L., & Jiang, Y. (2008). An institution-based view of international business strategy: A focus on emerging economies. *Journal of International Business Studies, 39*(5), 920–936.

Sparks, D. (2018, November 16). *Tesla's staggering growth in 3 charts*. Retrieved from https://www.fool.com/investing/2018/11/15/teslas-staggering-growth-in-3-charts.aspx

CHAPTER 9

Entry Into a
Foreign Market

Opening Case

International Entry by Huawei, a Chinese Technology Enterprise

Huawei Technologies, the leading telecommunication equipment manufacturer in China was founded in 1988. Nearly 58% (4.8 billion USD) of their

Global Business, pages 181–204
Copyright © 2019 by Information Age Publishing
All rights of reproduction in any form reserved.

Figure 9.1   Huawei. *Source:* Open Grid Scheduler, https://www.flickr.com/photos/opengridscheduler

total revenue comes from foreign markets. The internationalization of Huawei illustrates how a hi-tech enterprise uses different modes of entry in different host markets.

After 8 years of operation Huawei's first internationalization step was to provide customized design for Hong Kong's Hutchison Telecoms in 1996. Subsequently, Huawei entered the Russian market by setting up a joint venture "Beto-Huawei" in 1997. At that time, Huawei was the first Chinese company with the biggest investment in Russia. After 2000, Huawei rapidly expanded to Thailand, Singapore, Malaysia, the Middle East, South America, and Africa. Since 2001, Huawei's products are sold in West Europe market through local agents.

Huawei has used different market entry modes and strategies in different countries. Initially, Huawei's market selection strategy was to target markets with weak telecommunication infrastructure but with great developing potential. In terms of entry modes, products were exported to South America, Asia and Africa. The main factors influencing the decision to export were geographical distance and local market conditions. However, in West Europe and North America Huawei used a variety of contractual entry modes such as franchising, co-research, co-production and co-sales (reciprocal agreements to sell products in each other's markets). In North America, Huawei set up joint venture with 3Com to take advantage of R&D capabilities. The fact that Huawei is a Chinese company, an emerging market illustrates that the internationalization process is not limited to U.S. and European companies (Wu & Zhao, 2007).

1. *Describe how Huawei's internationalization process and selection of foreign market entry modes was adapted to different locations.*

2. *Why would Huawei use an export mode entry in some markets and not in others? Elaborate.*

3. *In your opinion what were the determining factors to decide which mode of entry to use in different markets? Are such factors unique to hi-tech companies?*

9.0   Introduction

This chapter explains important factors in selecting entry modes and key aspects in their management. It details the circumstances in which each entry mode into a foreign market is most appropriate and the advantages and disadvantages that each provides. The choice of which entry mode to use in entering international markets should match the company's international strategy. Some companies want entry modes that give them tight control over activities abroad because it fits their strategy, while others might not require an entry mode with central control. Generally, the selection of an entry mode is aligned with an organization's structure and available resources.

9.1   Strategic Factors in Selecting an Entry Mode

Because entering a new market requires an investment of time and money, and because of the strategic implications of the entry mode, selection must be done carefully. The following aspects should be considered when selecting the right entry mode into a foreign market.

9.1.1   Political and Legal Environment

Political instability in a target market increases the risk exposure of assets. Significant political differences and instability cause companies to avoid large investments in favor of entry modes that shelter assets. The legal system of the selected country influences the choice of entry mode. For example, certain import regulations such as high tariffs or low quota limits can discourage exports but encourage foreign direct investment. Finally, companies must continuously monitor government policies, which may affect the mode of entry of choice.

9.1.2   Market Size

The size of a potential market influences choice of entry mode. Rising incomes in emerging and developing markets encourage investment entry modes because a firm can prepare for growing demand and better understand the market in those locations. For example, growing demand in China is attracting investment in joint ventures, strategic alliances, and wholly owned subsidiaries. If the company believes that a market will remain small they may prefer to export or another mode of entry such as licensing or franchising.

9.1.3 Cultural Environment

Culture can differ greatly, and managers can feel less confident in their ability to manage operations in the host country. If the cultural differences are large, companies may avoid investment entry modes in favor of exporting or a contractual mode. On the other hand, cultural similarity may encourage confidence and thus the likelihood of investment. Therefore, it is important that managers are knowledgeable about the culture of the target market.

9.2 Entry Modes

An **entry mode** is the institutional arrangement by which businesses get products, technologies, human skills, or other resources into a market. Companies seek entry to new marketplaces for manufacturing, selling products or services. Entry mode selection depends on market experience, level of control desired, and market size. As companies gain international experience, they select entry modes that require deeper involvement. Through this process, they must accept greater risk in return for potentially higher profits and greater control over operations and strategy. They initially explore the advantages of licensing, franchising, management contracts, and turnkey projects. Once they become comfortable in a market, joint ventures, strategic alliances, and wholly owned subsidiaries become viable options. Advances in technology and transportation allow small companies to undertake entry modes requiring more commitment to the local market (Daniels, Radebaugh, & Sullivan, 2014; Hill & Hult, 2015; Wild & Wild, 2015).

9.2.1 Export–Import

The most common method of buying and selling goods internationally is **exporting** and **importing**. These means are the easiest way to expand internationally and globalize. Many companies start their international exposure through exporting their products or services to a neighboring country and then use other entry modes as their knowledge and comfort level increases.

Exporting requires a low level of investment, it is a relatively low risk entry mode, but also has a lower return when compared to other entry modes.

The company retains operational control, but relinquishes marketing and sales control to hosts. Companies often underestimate the level of dedication that is needed to successfully export products. Resources are needed to address the increased activities necessary to support exporting. Management and staff may need to dedicate time to deal with a different language, different culture, and a different time zone. Financial personnel will need to process the different exchange rate transactions and implement various accounting changes.

Many times, a company will choose a foreign agent or distributor that may not meet their expectations. Other common pitfalls include failure to modify the product to meet the requirements of the foreign market, or not modifying the warranties or the instructions into the language of their new customers.

A logical approach to exporting is to research and analyze international opportunities and develop a coherent export strategy. A firm with such a strategy pursues export markets rather than waiting for orders to arrive. In identifying a potential market, it is essential to determine through market research whether demand exists in the target market or foreign country. Companies also must have thorough knowledge of the regulations in the target market as well as the exporting regulations of the home country. Meetings with potential distributors, buyers, and other stakeholders are also important. Initial contact should focus on building trust and cooperation. Some companies use intermediaries to get their products in a market abroad. Other companies perform all their export activities themselves, with an infrastructure that bridges the gap between the two markets. Different export models are described below:

Direct exporting. In this modality, a company sells directly to buyers in a target market. The company usually has the personnel and organizational structure to handle the exporting function in-house. They often promote their products by attending trade fairs and making personal visits to foreign retailers and wholesalers

Indirect exporting. In this modality, a company sells to intermediaries who resell to buyers in a foreign market. The choice of intermediary may depend on the ratio of international sales to total sales, available resources, and the growth rate of the foreign market. In general, the distributors take ownership of merchandise when it enters their country and accept the risks associated with local sales, and sell to retailers, wholesalers, or end users through their own channels of distribution. This reduces an exporter's risk but also its control of their products.

Agents. These are individuals or organizations that represent one or more indirect exporters in a foreign market. Usually agents receive

commissions on sales. They may represent several indirect exporters and might focus their promotional efforts on the products of
the company paying the highest commission.

Export Management Companies (EMCs). EMCs export on behalf of indirect exporters, operating contractually, either as an agent or as a
distributor. EMCs provide services on a retainer basis. Usually they
provide more sophisticated services such as market information
gathering, promotional strategies formulation, handle promotions,
arrange shipping, and coordinate export documents.

Advantages

- *Feasibility.* Exporting is relatively simple if there is foreign demand
  for the product.
- *Experience.* Company begins to build international knowledge and
  experience.
- *Low Risk.* The risk associated with this entry mode is lower for the
  company.

Disadvantages

- *Low Return on Investment (ROI).* ROI from exporting is not as high as
  in other modes.
- *Loss of Control.* MNE has less control over the product's marketing or
  handling abroad.
- *Limited Foreign Interaction.* If a company exclusively relies on agents
  and EMCs, they will not develop international skills and experience.

SPOTLIGHT

**How can I learn about complying with U.S.
export licensing and other regulations?**

Visit the Export.gov website. The following link provides more information. https://www.export.gov/Export-FAQs

Summarize your findings.

9.2.2 Licensing

Some products simply cannot be traded in open markets because they
are intangible.

Licensing is an agreement between two companies, where the licensee
or the company that pays another company, or the licensor, for the right to

use their intangible asset, such as a patent, trade secrets copyrights (brand name or company name), technical knowledge, product formulation, or specialized processes, for a specified period of time. Licensors receive royalties, license fees, or some other form of compensation payments based on a percentage of revenue generated by the property. Licensing is a global entry and expansion strategy, with considerable appeal. It can offer an attractive ROI, if the necessary performance clauses are included in the contract. The only cost is signing the agreement and policing the implementation.

Example. General Electric licensed Asian suppliers to manufacture certain grades of copper clad laminates when the product became a commodity. It did not make sense for this product to be manufactured in the United States. Cheaper labor and good access to natural resources enabled this product to be manufactured in Asia, then imported and sold in the United States in a market where they would not be able to compete had this agreement not been in place. Licensing is widely used in the fashion industry.

Advantages
- *Low Cost.*
- *Avoids Barriers.* Licensors circumvent tariffs, quotas, or similar export barriers.
- *Low Risk.* Licensing limits political risk and risk of expropriation.
- *Licensee Upgrades.* Licensees can upgrade existing production technologies.
- *Black Market Prevention.* Can reduce likelihood of product appearing on the black market.

Disadvantages
- *Limited Market Control.*
- *Limited Financial Gains.* Financial gains are limited by the royalty rate.
- *Increased Competition.* Licensees can become competitors.
- *Restricted Activities.* It may restrict a licensor's future activities.

SPOTLIGHT
The Licensing Industry Merchandisers' Association

The Licensing Industry Merchandisers' Association (LIMA), founded in 1985, is the industry trade group of the $80 billion licensing industry. Check their website to learn more about the licensing process:

http://www.licensing.org/education/intro-to-licensing/types-of-licensing/

9.2.3 Management Contracts

Companies can provide technical specifications or managerial expertise to a **subcontractor** or local manufacturer for a specific period of time. The subcontractor then oversees production. The supplier of expertise is compensated with either a lump-sum payment or a fee based on sales.

Advantages
- *Specialization.* The licensing firm can specialize in product design and marketing, while transferring responsibility for ownership of manufacturing facilities to others.
- *Limited Resource Use.* The licensing firm has limited commitment of financial and managerial resources.
- *Speed.* The licensing firm has quick entry into target countries, especially when the target market is too small to justify significant investment.
- *Host Country Development.* Help nations develop skills of local workers and managers.

Disadvantages
- *Increased Competition.* Suppliers with expertise may encourage a strong new competitor in the local market.
- *Public Criticism.* Companies may open themselves to public criticism if workers in contract factories are poorly paid or labor in inhumane circumstances.

9.2.4 Turnkey Projects

A **turnkey project** entails designing, constructing, and testing a production facility for a client. Turkey projects are often large-scale and often involve government agencies. They are used to transfer special process technologies or production-facility designs to a client (e.g., power plants, telecommunications, and petrochemical facilities).

Advantages
- Specialization. Firm specializes in core competency to exploit opportunities.
- Product Quality. Governments can obtain designs for infrastructure from the world's leading companies.

Disadvantages
- *Political Motives.* Company may be awarded a project for political reasons rather than for technological expertise.
- *Increased Competition.* May create future competitors.

SPOTLIGHT
Outsourcing

Outsourcing is the practice of contracting for the manufacture of goods or services outside of the home country. This arrangement works best when transportation costs and inventory management are not major factors. The goods may need to travel in bulk back to the home country, then repackaged into smaller orders before shipment to customers. With production in a foreign facility, product in transit, and stock in the home country, inventory management can be complicated and cost prohibitive to accurately track in detail.

Drawbacks of this method include the loss of operational control, cultural barriers, costs, and dependence on another company.

9.2.5 Franchising

Franchising is a form of licensing in which one company (parent company or franchiser) allows another company (franchisee) to use their trademark and also assists them in the operation of the business for an extended period. Franchisers typically receive compensation as flat fees, royalty payments, or both. This entry mode is common in the fast food industry. McDonald's reliance on franchising to expand globally is a case in point. Franchising has great appeal to local entrepreneurs anxious to learn and apply Western-style marketing techniques. Franchising takes advantage of well-known company logos allowing products to be introduced into areas where the product would not have been popular if the name did not have a high level of recognition. It also keeps the product consistent.

Example: Since their inception in 1974, Subway restaurants have focused on franchising and have experienced phenomenal growth. There are more than 37,000 SUBWAY® locations throughout the world. In recent years, about 70% of the new franchises are purchases by existing owners. The investment capital required to open a franchise is anywhere between $84,300 and $258,300 (Subway.com, 2014). The specialty retailing industry e.g., The Body Shop also favors franchising as a market entry mode.

Franchising differs from licensing in three ways.

1. Provides greater control over the sale of a product in a target market.
2. Licensing is common in manufacturing industries; franchising is primarily used in the service sector.

3. Although licensing normally involves a one-time transfer of property, franchising requires ongoing assistance from the franchiser.

With the single currency and a unified set of franchise laws, franchising is growing in the EU. In Eastern Europe, expansion through franchising suffers from a lack of capital, high interest rates and taxes, bureaucracy, restrictive laws, and corruption.

Advantages
- *Low Cost.*
- *Low Risk.*
- *Speed.* Allows for rapid geographic expansion.
- *Local Expertise.* Uses cultural knowledge and know-how of local managers.

Disadvantages
- *Difficult to Manage.* Cumbersome to manage many franchisees in several nations.
- *Inflexible.* Franchisees can experience a loss of organizational flexibility in franchising agreements.

EXERCISE

What are the main aspects related to the foreign location a company should consider when expanding overseas using a franchising mode of entry? Elaborate.

Hint: The following questions should be asked of would-be franchisers before expanding overseas:

- Will local consumers buy your product?
- How tough is the local competition?
- Does the government respect trademark and franchiser rights?
- Can your profits be easily repatriated?
- Can you buy all the supplies you need locally?
- Is commercial space available and are rents affordable?
- Are your local partners financially sound and do they understand the basics of franchising?

9.2.6 International Joint Ventures

An **international joint venture** (**IJV**) is a business arrangement in which two or more companies from different countries share ownership of another company. Joint ventures are an entry strategy for a single target country in which the partners share ownership of a newly created business entity. If they invest together in downstream business activities, then it is a forward integration joint venture. If the parties invest together in upstream business activities, then it is called a backward integration joint venture.

The more companies are involved in the IJV, the less control each has over the newly formed company. About 50% of international joint ventures fail for various reasons. Partners may have different objectives for the joint venture, a different sense of priority of the joint venture, or disagreements over control may occur. Other sources of friction include cultural clashes or resentment arising when one company thinks it is unfairly doing the majority of the work while the other partners are not as dedicated. An international joint venture with a local partner represents a more extensive form of participation in the foreign markets than either exporting or licensing.

Advantages
- *Shared Knowledge.* Allows for risk sharing and possibly combining complementary strengths, especially local market knowledge of the foreign country partner.
- *Shared Strengths.* Joint ventures also allow partners to achieve synergies by combining different value chain strengths. For example, through a joint venture a company may access the local distribution network.
- *Learning Opportunity.* A company can use the joint venture experience to learn about a new foreign market environment.
- *Overcome Barriers to Entry.* A joint venture may be the only way to enter a country or region if laws prohibit foreign control but permit joint ventures (as it used to be in China and India), or if import tariffs are high.

Disadvantages
- *Shared Risk.* Joint venture partners must share rewards as well as risks.
- *Partner Conflict.* There is the potential for conflict between partners. Corporate cultures and other interests of a foreign partner may clash.
- *Increased Competition.* A dynamic joint venture partner can evolve into a stronger competitor.
- *Loss of Control.* Sharing means less control than in 100 percent ownership. Loss of control over a joint venture's operations can also result when the local government is a partner in the joint venture.

9.2.7　International Strategic Alliances

An **international strategic alliance** is an agreement between two or more companies from different countries to cooperate in business, enabling the business to take place but they do not form a separate company. Without this cooperation, the business would not be possible. The terms strategic alliances, strategic international alliances, and global strategic partnerships (GSPs) are often used interchangeably.

This arrangement helps companies to spread or reduce costs, gain access to needed resources, sidestep government regulations, and minimize political and economic risk. It allows a company to concentrate on their core competencies while addressing competitive concerns. Like joint ventures, strategic alliances can be formed for short or long periods, depending on the goals of the participants. Strategic alliances can be established between a company and the suppliers, buyers, and even competitors; sometimes the partner purchase each other's stock.

Global strategic alliances are attractive for several reasons:

- High product development costs in the face of resource constraints may force a company to seek one or more partners.
- The technology requirements of many contemporary products mean that an individual company may lack the skills, capital, or know-how.
- Partnerships may be the best means of securing access to national and regional markets.
- Partnerships provide important learning opportunities.

SPOTLIGHT
Cooperative Strategies in East Asia

Japanese Keiretsu

Japan's Keiretsu represent a special category of cooperative strategy. A Keiretsu is an inter-business alliance or enterprise group that resembles a clan or fraternity of business families that work together to gain market share.

Keiretsu exist in a broad spectrum of markets, including the capital, primary goods, and component parts markets. Keiretsu relationships are often cemented by bank ownership of large blocks of stock and by cross-ownership of stock between a company and its buyers and nonfinancial suppliers. Furthermore, Keiretsu executives can legally sit on each other's boards, share information, and coordinate prices in closed-door meetings of "presidents' councils." Thus, Keiretsu are essentially cartels that have the government's blessing. While not a market entry strategy per se, Keiretsu played an integral role in the international success of Japanese companies as they sought new markets.

Korean Chaebol

South Korea has its own type of corporate alliance groups, known as Chaebol.

Like the Japanese Keiretsu, Chaebol are composed of dozens of companies, centered around a central bank or holding company, and dominated by a founding family. However, Chaebol are a more recent phenomenon, dating from the early 1960s. The Chaebol were a driving force behind South Korea's economic miracle; GNP increased from $1.9 billion in 1960 to $238 billion in 1990.

Advantages
- *Shared Cost.* Share the cost of an international investment project.
- *Shared Strengths.* Tap into competitors' specific strengths.

Disadvantages
- *Increased Competition.* Can create a future local or even global competitors.
- *Partner Conflict.* Conflict can arise and eventually undermine cooperation.

Debate—The Merits of the Keiretsu

Divide the class into two teams. Each team has 10 minutes to prepare, 5 minutes to present their arguments, and 5 minutes to refute the opposing team. Use these additional readings:

An Economic Introduction to the Japanese Keiretsu System
   https://www.thoughtco.com/intro-to-the-japanese-keiretsu
   -economics-system-1148018
How Eight Conglomerates dominate Japanese Industry
   https://www.smithsonianmag.com/innovation/how-eight
   -conglomerates-dominate-japanese-industry-180960356/

Team A

The *Keiretsu* violates anti-trust laws because it is anti-competitive.

Team B

American companies should increase alliances patterned after the Japanese Keiretsu because of Japanese success in the auto and electronics industries.

9.2.8 Wholly Owned Subsidiaries

A **wholly owned subsidiary** can be established by purchasing or acquiring (**brownfield investment**) an existing company or by establishing a new company from the ground up (**greenfield investment**). In other words, a wholly owned subsidiary is a foreign company that is separate from the parent company but fully owned by it. This structure allows the company to retain the most control, but it is also the riskiest entry mode. Large companies with vast experience and with available resources to start-up and operate the subsidiary usually select this entry mode. It is much more labor intensive than the other internationalization methods mentioned so far.

Whether an international subsidiary is purchased or newly created depends on its operations. For example, for high-tech products, a company may build new facilities because state-of-the-art operations are hard to locate.

Advantages
- *Complete Control.* Managers have complete control over day-to-day operations access to valuable technologies, processes, and other intangible properties within the subsidiary in the foreign market.
- *Coordinated Subsidiaries.* Companies can coordinate activities of their subsidiaries (if more than one).
- *Speed.* Acquisition allows for instant market access.
- *Technology Transfer.* Provides opportunities for technology transfer back to the parent company.

Disadvantages
- *Expense.* Costly, therefore not always viable for small- and medium-size firms.
- *High Risk.* Requires substantial resources; thus, risk exposure and political risk are higher than other entry modes.
- *Time Cost.* A major drawback of a greenfield investment is the time it takes to construct new facilities, hire and train employees, and launch production.
- *Integration Difficulties.* Problems may arise from efforts to integrate acquisitions into parent company.
- *Host Country Criticism.* Investment and ownership in some foreign countries may create suspicion about the foreign company exploitation. American companies in particular may be targets of accusations about "**cultural imperialism.**"

9.3   Foreign Direct Investment (FDI)

Foreign direct investment (FDI) is defined as an investment made by a firm or individual in one country into business interests located in another country. Generally, FDI takes place when a company establishes a foreign business operation or acquires foreign business assets, including establishing ownership or controlling interest in a foreign company. The purchase-or-build decision of companies is of utmost strategic importance.

Adequate facilities are sometimes unavailable, and a company must go ahead with a **greenfield investment**. Greenfield investments have their own drawbacks such as obtaining the necessary permits and financing and hiring local personnel can be difficult in some markets. When companies gain experience outside the home country via exporting, licensing, franchising, or other entry modes, often they realize that a more extensive form of participation in the foreign country is necessary. For example, setting up and owning production in a market is desirable when the total cost of production is lower than at home. Companies producing products with high shipping costs prefer to invest and produce in locations where shipping costs can be eliminated or at least reduced significantly. A business may also make a greenfield investment if there are no suitable target in the foreign country to acquire. This is favorable in situations where businesses can gain local government-related benefits by starting up from scratch in a new country, as some countries provide subsidies, tax breaks or other benefits in order to promote the country as a good location for FDI. The top 5 recipients of inward greenfield FDI in the European Union are real estate, software & IT services, communications, consumer products, automotive components, and original equipment manufacturers (European-Commission, 2017)

Businesses may be more inclined to acquire an existing foreign business in situations where it is difficult to enter a foreign market. Buying an overseas business simplifies the processes involved in building from scratch. For example, the acquired business usually already has its own personnel, allowing the acquiring company to avoid having to hire and train new employees. Moreover, the acquired company may already have a good brand name and other intangible assets, which can help the business to gain a good customer base. Acquiring a foreign company can also provide the **parent company** with easier access to host country financing. However, when acquiring a foreign business there might be unexpected surprises in terms of the challenges of integrating the acquisition to the parent company.

Foreign direct investment (FDI) figures reflect investment flows out of the home country as companies invest in or acquire plants, equipment, or other assets. This allows companies to produce, sell, and compete locally in key markets. Most governments set the threshold for an investment to be called FDI at anywhere from 10 to 25 percent of stock ownership in a company abroad. The U.S. Commerce Department sets it at 10 percent.

9.3.1   The Impact of FDI

The investments and operations of MNEs may affect a country's **balance of payments**, economic growth, and employment objectives in ways that are positive or negative for both home and host countries. MNEs may use technology that cannot be easily transferred from one industry to another. In addition, they may use resources that were either underemployed or unemployed in the host country. In such scenario, both home and host countries can gain from FDI.

As manufacturers seek lower-cost foreign production sites, home countries claim that FDI outflows create jobs abroad at the expense of jobs in the home country. However, MNEs gain valuable knowledge in their foreign operations that can be shared across their entire organizations, and if successful abroad they can re-invest profits at home.

Host countries gain through the transfer of capital and technology; through the import of technology and managerial ability. The presence of MNEs may increase the number of local companies operating in host-country markets by serving as role models for local talent to emulate, which helps create new jobs. However, critics argue that FDI inflows often displace domestic investment and drive up local labor costs. They claim that MNEs have access to lower-cost funds than local competitors do and that MNEs can spend more on promotion activities. In addition, while it is true that MNEs often source inputs locally, critics claim that they also destroy local entrepreneurship.

9.3.2   FDI Inflows and Outflows

Foreign Direct Investment (FDI) flows record the value of cross-border transactions related to direct investment during a given time period. **FDI net inflows** are the value of inward direct investment made by non-resident investors in the reporting economy. **FDI net outflows** are the value of outward direct investment made by the residents of the reporting economy to external economies. By studying FDI inflows and outflows, we can determine the patterns of international investment. There are several reasons for the increase in worldwide FDI.

Political and economic system changes in many countries opened new markets. These changes encouraged FDI in those markets through mergers and acquisitions (brownfield investments) and building new production sites (greenfield investments).

FDI inflows changed significantly since the 1980s when developing countries began to receive significant FDI inflows. Developing countries are attracting a lot of FDI inflows but have not surpassed developed countries. FDI inflows to developing countries account for about 41% of total world

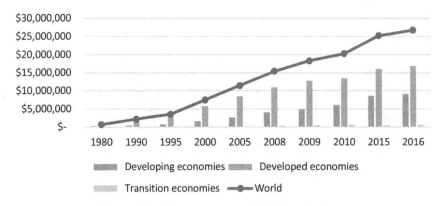

Figure 9.2 FDI inflows in million USD. *Source:* UNCTAD database, 2018

FDI inflows. By comparison, developed countries account for 55%. The remaining roughly four percent of global FDI goes into countries across Southeast Europe in various stages of transition from communism to capitalism (see Figure 9.2).

Europe receives slightly more FDI net inflows than America and Asia, whereas in comparison Africa has received significantly less FDI inflows (see Figure 9.3).

Outward FDI presents a differing pattern from inward FDI. FDI net outflows from developed economies are the highest. As Figure 9.4 shows, even though FDI outflows from developing countries have increased, the rate is much lower compared to outflows from developed countries. A dip in FDI outflows happened around 2005 and since then it has slowly been recovering.

In terms of geographical region as Figure 9.5 indicates, FDI net outflows from Asian nations have been increasing, which coincides with the rise of countries such as China, India, South Korea, and others.

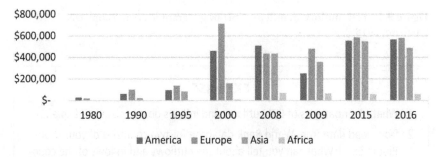

Figure 9.3 FDI inflows in million USD by geographic area. *Source:* UNCTAD database, 2018

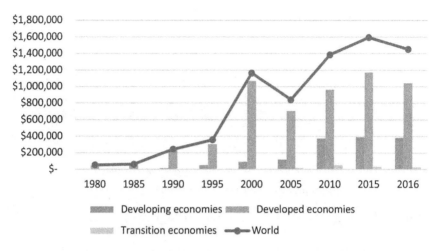

Figure 9.4 FDI outflows in million USD. *Source:* UNCTAD database, 2018.

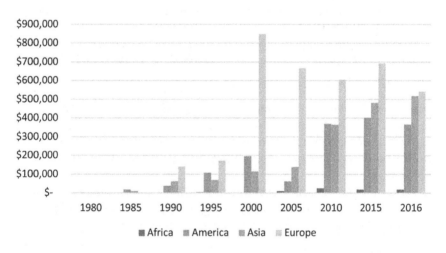

Figure 9.5 FDI outflows in million USD by geographic area. *Source:* UNCTAD database, 2018.

EXERCISE

1. What other patterns of FDI outflows and inflows do you observe? Explain.

2. Download data from World Bank database for two countries of your choice. Plot in Excel. What can you tell about the outflows and inflows of the countries of your choice?

9.3.3 Government Intervention in Foreign Direct Investment

Many companies invest abroad because they wish to control activities in the local market. Yet complete ownership does not *guarantee* complete control. Companies are still at the mercy of the local country rules, regulations and the political environment. Countries may have strict policies regarding how much ownership they allow foreign companies. A country may demand shared ownership in return for market access, as is the case of China. Governments may use such requirements to shield workers and industries from exploitation or domination by large multinationals. In other words, countries enact laws, create regulations, or construct administrative hurdles for foreign companies. A bias toward protectionism or openness is rooted in a nation's culture, history, and politics. FDI tends to raise output and enhance standards of living. Besides philosophical ideals, countries intervene in FDI for practical reasons.

9.3.4 Host Country Reasons for Controlling FDI Inflows

Control Balance of Payments

The effect on the host country of a single foreign direct investment may be positive or negative. Thus, governments must learn to maximize the benefits while minimizing the long-term adverse effects of FDI flows. Many governments see intervention as the only way to keep their balance of payments under control. Host countries get a balance of payments boost from initial FDI flows if these encourage exports. However, when companies repatriate profits, they deplete the foreign exchange reserves of their host countries; these capital outflows decrease the balance of payments. Consequently, a host nation may prohibit or restrict nondomestic firms from removing profits. On the other hand, host countries conserve their foreign exchange reserves when international companies reinvest their earnings in local manufacturing facilities. This also improves the competitiveness of local producers and boosts a host country's export, thus improving its balance of payments position.

Obtaining Resources and Benefits

Countries encourage FDI in technology because it increases productivity and competitiveness. Management skills and employment FDI allows talented foreign managers to train local managers in how to operate the local facilities.

9.3.5   Home Country Reasons for Controlling FDI Outflows

There are fewer concerns regarding the outflow of FDI among home nations because they tend to be prosperous, industrialized nations. However, investing in other nations sends resources out of the home country and can lessen investment at home. Outward FDI may damage a country's balance of payments by reducing exports otherwise sent to international markets. Jobs resulting from FDI outflows may replace jobs at home. On the other hand, outward FDI can increase long-run competitiveness of the home country companies.

9.3.6   Policy Instruments to Control Foreign Direct Investment

Host countries commonly offer tax incentives or low-interest loans to attract investment. This in turn may spur **bidding wars** between locations vying for investment. Another way to attract investment is the development or improvement of the local infrastructure.

Host countries can also restrict FDI by imposing ownership restrictions that prohibit nondomestic companies from investing in certain industries or owning certain types of business.

Another restriction is a requirement that nondomestic investors hold less than a 50% stake in local firms. However, more countries are eliminating such restrictions because companies can choose another location. Host countries can also restrict FDI through certain performance demands that dictate the portion of a product's content that originates locally in order to be exported.

The home countries also promote or restrict FDI. In terms of promotion, home countries offer **insurance** to cover the risks of investments abroad. Many countries have special agencies that grant **loans** to firms wishing to increase their investments abroad. They may offer **tax breaks** on profits earned abroad or negotiate special tax treaties.

Home countries restrict FDI by imposing **differential tax rates** that charge income from earnings abroad at a higher rate than domestic earnings. Sanctions are another way of restricting domestic firms from making investments in certain nations.

9.4   Conclusion

Companies that wish to expand internationally can use a variety of entry modes. Each mode of entry has distinct advantages and disadvantages associated with it. Entry modes can be ranked on a continuum representing increasing levels of investment, commitment, and risk. Exporting is the easiest mode to expand internationally. Licensing can generate revenue flow with little new investment; it can be a good choice for a company that possesses advanced technology, a strong brand image, or valuable intellectual property. Contract manufacturing and franchising are two specialized forms of licensing that are widely used in global marketing. International joint ventures and strategic alliances represent an important market entry strategy that may involve business partners in several different country markets.

A higher level of involvement outside the home country involves foreign direct investment, which can be used to establish company operations outside the home country through greenfield investment, acquisition of a minority or majority equity stake in a foreign business, or taking full ownership of an existing business entity through merger or outright acquisition.

Finally, the chapter discusses foreign direct investment (FDI) in detail. Many factors influence a company's decision to invest in markets abroad. Depending on the philosophy of the home or the host nations and the impact of FDI on their economic health, a firm can be encouraged or dissuaded to invest in a nation.

TBL Connection
Green FDI: Korea's Way to Achieve Green Growth

Following the proclamation of Lee Myung-bak, President of the Republic of Korea, in 2008 Korea embarked on a far-reaching green growth strategy. This marked a significant change in the country's official political agenda, which until then was not necessarily focused on environmental protection. The first Five-Year Plan for Green Growth (2009-2013) and the National Strategy (2009–2050) set the respective short and long-term policy framework specifying that in particular a shift in both public and private investments is required. In this context, FDI is seen as one of the engines to stimulate economic growth and the adoption of environmentally friendly technologies. FDI in green growth industries has been prioritized since the foreign investment promotion plan from February 2011. The green growth strategy is successful as long as these two criteria are fulfilled:

- FDI needs to facilitate (long run) economic growth.
- FDI needs to support the clean-up of existing industrial sectors by either helping to change the current domestic industrial composition or by introducing technologies that reduce industrial emission intensities (Hille, Shahbaz, & Moosa, 2018).

1. *Investigate the Korean economy. What are the main industrial sectors in the country? How would you describe Korea's investment potential?*
2. *What type of FDI should Korea encourage in order to fulfill their green-growth strategy? Be specific and explain your reasoning.*
3. *What other initiatives or policies that complement the green FDI strategy would you suggest? Elaborate.*

Chapter Review

Key Terms

- Modes of Entry
- Exporting
- Licensing
- Contract manufacturing
- Outsourcing
- Turnkey investment
- International joint venture
- International strategic alliance
- Wholly owned subsidiary
- Foreign Direct Investment (FDI)
- FDI inflows/outflows
- Home and Host country
- Greenfield investment
- Brownfield investment

Questions & Assignments

Questions

1. Select two countries. What are the main industrial sectors in the selected countries? How would you describe investment potential of the selected countries?
2. What type of FDI should developing countries encourage? Select a developing country and describe some of the policies the country could consider to encourage FDI.
3. Select a multinational company and investigate how the company has expanded abroad. What types on entry modes were used? Why were those modes of entry selected?

Assignments

1. Research and examine a firm that expanded internationally and succeeded, and another firm that also expanded internationally, but faced many challenges.
2. Describe the advantages and disadvantages of three entry modes used to expand to a developed country and to a developing country.
3. Identify a case where government intervened causing FDI to increase. Also, identify a case where government policies prevented FDI.

Suggested Reading

The 2018 World Investment Report published by UNCTAD
https://unctad.org/en/PublicationsLibrary/wir2018_en.pdf

A Basic Guide to Exporting
https://www.export.gov/article?id=Why-Companies-should-export

The Top 125 Global Licensors
https://www.licenseglobal.com/top-125-global-licensors-0

The American Association of Franchisees and Dealers (AAFD) Story
https://www.aafd.org/the-aafd-story/

A Record $2.5 Trillion in Mergers Were Announced in the First Half of 2018
https://www.nytimes.com/2018/07/03/business/dealbook/mergers
-record-levels.html

Strategic Alliances: a real alternative to M&As?
https://assets.kpmg/content/dam/kpmg/ie/pdf/2018/01/ie-strategic
-alliances-a-real-alternative-to-ma.pdf

References

Daniels, J. D., Radebaugh, L. H., & Sullivan, D. P. (2014). *International business: Environments and operations* (15th ed.). Upper Saddle River, NJ: Pearson.

European-Commission. (2017). In focus: China's expansion in the EU. *Geenfield Investment Monitor,* (1). Retrieved from https://ec.europa.eu/epsc/sites/epsc/files/greenfield-investment-monitor-1.pdf

Hill, C. W. L., & Hult, G. T. M. (2015). *Global business today* (9th ed.). New York, NY: McGraw-Hill Education.

Hille, E., Shahbaz, M., & Moosa, I. (2018). The Impact of FDI on Regional Air Pollution in the Republic of Korea: A Way Ahead to Achieve the Green Growth Strategy?

Subway.com. (2014). The History of Subway. Retrieved from http://franchise.subway.com/subwayroot/about_us/history.aspx

Wild, J. J., & Wild, K. L. (2015). *International Business:the Challenges of Globalization* (8th ed.). Upper Saddle River, NJ: Pearson.

Wu, D., & Zhao, F. (2007). *Entry modes for international markets: Case study of Huawei, a Chinese technology enterprise* (Vol. 3).

The Internationalization Process of a Firm

Global Business, pages 205–224
Copyright © 2019 by Information Age Publishing
All rights of reproduction in any form reserved.

Opening Case

Starbucks: The Internationalization of Coffee House Chains

In 1987, Howard Schultz bought Starbucks with the help of a few investors. The company then consisted of six stores and one roasting plant in Seattle, WA. Today, Starbucks is not only a global brand but also an internationalization success story.

Four years after going public, the company began their expansion to Asia. Once Starbucks started internationalizing, it expanded rapidly to many different regions. Starbucks currently operates about 21,000 stores in over 60 countries. The company divides its operations into three regional clusters the Americas; China and Asia-Pacific (CAP); and EMEA (Europe, Middle East, and Africa.)

Starbucks entered the neighboring country Canada (Vancouver) as a first step. The motivation to expand to Canada can be explained based on cultural (psychic distance), as well as geographical closeness, using the Uppsala Model and Hofstede's cultural dimensions. Canada is also one of few coun-

Figure 10.1 Starbucks. Source: By Kure-UserKurefile, https://commons.wikimedia .org/w/index.php?curid=1657996

tries Starbucks entered by wholly-owned stores instead of licensed or franchised stores. Wholly-owned subsidiaries (or stores) have given Starbucks the opportunity to retain full control and full revenues of its business in Canada. After the success in Canada, Starbucks focused expansion in the CAP region, followed by the EMEA region. Starbucks only continued the expansion in the Americas in 2003.

In the CAP region, Starbucks started operations in Japan, Singapore, the Philippines, Malaysia, New Zealand, Taiwan and Thailand. A common question raised when looking at Starbucks' internationalization process is why the company expanded to Asian countries first instead of staying within the Americas or expanding to other Western countries.

At that time, Japan had already been a major importer of coffee. In addition, Japan, was the second largest economy in the world, which benefitted the company's entry. Finally, the Starbucks brand had a status symbol for Japanese youth interested in the American lifestyle. However, since Starbucks had no prior experience in Asian markets, the company entered the majority of the countries in the region via licensing agreements with joint venture (JV) partners. The Asian expansions between 1996 and 1998 can be explained by the Eclectic paradigm or OLI model. Moreover, by utilizing joint venture partners Starbucks built a reliable network of business relationships.

While Starbucks successfully extended operations in the CAP region, it also started to expand to the EMEA region. In Europe, the company acquired 65 stores in the UK. Soon after, Starbucks began to internationalize in the Middle East, a culturally and geographically distant region from the United States. There, Starbucks partnered with Alshaya Retail, a family-owned business from Kuwait. 15 years after the Canadian expansion, Starbucks entered more countries in the Americas region, namely Mexico and Puerto Rico in 2002. (Source: https://www.starbucks.com/about-us/company-information)

1. *How can the OLI paradigm explain the expansion process of Starbucks to the EMEA region? Elaborate. Why did Starbucks wait so long to expand in the Americas? Explain your reasoning.*

10.0 Introduction

This chapter describes the internationalization process as well as how value creation has been enhanced by internationalization. In the context of internationalization, the foreign country where a company invests is called the host country, whereas the home country is where a company's headquarters are and where the company came from.

The increase in international business in the last few decades can be attributed to many factors. Some of the factors that have contributed to the changes in globalizing the business landscape are the following:

- The emergence of new technologies, as well as advances in the information and communications industries, have flattened the playing field especially for small and medium size companies by providing them easier access to the global market.
- The continuous development of emerging markets such as Brazil, Russia, India, China (also known as BRIC countries), and other economies in Asia, Africa and South America has created great opportunities for international business activities.
- In addition to the growth of the middle class in emerging economies, the disintegration of the Soviet Union and the subsequent opening of new markets in Eastern and Central Europe added hundreds of millions of new customers throughout the world for new products and services.
- Multinational corporations from emerging economies have become global players and are competing with multinationals from developed countries.

Companies internationalize their operations for different reasons. Such efforts provide a great potential for creating more value for the company. Although there is no agreement on the definition of internationalization, there are several theories that try to explain why there are global business activities and how these activates create value for the organizations.

10.1 Value Creation through International Business

Profit maximization is one of the most important goals for every business. The bottom line can improve either by increasing revenues or by reducing costs. In general, firms invest in foreign markets to increase revenues or to access lower cost inputs such as labor or raw materials. Such investments by firms in foreign markets contribute the profitability of the multinational companies, and also may improve the economy of the host countries in the long-term. The next section explains how internationalization can enhance a company's profit by increasing revenues and reducing costs.

10.1.1 Enhancing Revenue Through a Market Seeking Strategy

Firms can increase profits through increasing sales. International expansion in search of new markets to increase profits is particularly important when demand in the company's home country (**domestic market**) is saturated or decreasing, but demand exists abroad. Especially in small markets, the domestic market may be maturing, so foreign markets would provide revenue-enhancing opportunities.

By determining the **target sales**, a company can estimate the level of demand that would be required to reach the domestic and foreign sales targets. In general, firms understand the domestic demand because they know the environment in which they operate. On the other hand, if international sales are successful, a firm may choose to focus on foreign sales to increase the foreign sale target in the future. Because of different cultures, tastes, government policies, economic systems, the nature of competitions and other factors, it is more difficult for companies to estimate the demand for their products in foreign markets especially if they do not know the market. Thus, a firm may choose to focus more on clearly identified foreign sales. For instance, many American companies prefer to start selling their products in Canada instead of other countries. This is not only because of Canada's proximity, but also because of the perceived similarities between Canada and the United States. One common way to internationalize is exporting to or investing in a new market. An increase in international activities will eventually increase foreign sales.

SPOTLIGHT
Market Comparison

The Czech Republic (Czechia), a member of the European Union, is a land-locked central European nation that shares its western border with economic powerhouse Germany. The Czech Republic shipped $180.2 billion worth of goods around the globe in 2017. Based on estimates from the Central Intelligence Agency's World Factbook, Czechia's exported goods and services represent 79.1% of the total country' economic output or Gross Domestic Product. Given Czechia's strategic location in central Europe, it should come as no surprise that 88.6% of Czech exports by value were delivered to fellow European countries. Smaller percentages were sold to customers in Asia (6.6%), North America (2.7%) and Africa (0.9%).

By contrast, the United States offers the largest consumer market on earth with a GDP of $20 trillion and 325 million people. Household spending is the highest in the world, accounting for nearly a third of global household consumption. The country is consistently ranked among the best internationally for its overall competitiveness and ease of doing business.

Based on
http://www.worldstopexports.com/czech-republic-top-10-exports/
https://www.selectusa.gov/why-invest

10.1.2 Minimizing Cost through a Resource-Seeking Strategy

Companies may also go abroad in order to gain access to resources that may not be readily available in the domestic market or may be costly in their home country. As domestic resources may be depleted and become more expensive, a firm might begin to look for foreign resources that are less costly.

The resources could be **natural resources** such as oil, copper, coco beans or water; **man-made resources** such as electricity, electronics; **human resources** such as a talented, highly educated human capital, or cheap labor. China and India have attracted many foreign businesses due to their low wage labor. Some of the oil producing countries such as United Arab Emirates or Saudi Arabia attract foreign companies to their oil reserves. Many companies go to Japan, Germany or the U.S. because of access to their superior technological markets. China's abundant, low skilled, inexpensive labor force encourages producers to relocate there. India's highly educated, low wage labor force draws companies who outsource customer service, software development, and other technical positions.

With the **resource-seeking strategy**, firms get additional resources from other countries that are cheaper than the home one. With the additional resources, the costs of the firm are reduced. However, many firms need to withdraw the investment from one country and invest in another country because the resources in the host country become expensive. For example, the cost of Chinese labor force was low two decades ago. However, the labor cost in China has increased in recent years and many firms are moving their plants to other countries with lower labor cost. In the long run, the firm gets access to the resources from other countries, and the amount of the resources left in that country is reduced. When the resource is used, the resource availability will be lower, and it will become scarcer. Therefore, the cost of the resource will increase again and push the firm to go for another round of resource-seeking strategy.

This process demonstrates that the conditions of the foreign countries where companies operate is dynamic and therefore the company's strategy also needs to be dynamic in order to adjust to the new conditions.

10.1.3 Strategic Asset-Seeking Strategy

A company might seek access to local knowledge, capabilities, technological resources and innovations. The **strategic asset-seeking** motive is based on the idea that international presence gives companies a major information advantage over other companies. It is often argued that access to specific knowledge and capabilities in the host country are an important reason for direct investment. If strategic asset-seeking is a major motive for internationalization, the country characteristics used as selection criteria may include innovation level, sophistication of demand, availability of related and supporting industries and the presence of innovation clusters in the relevant industry. For example, many companies in emerging economies try to take advantage of technological advancements in Japan, Germany or the United States.

While a company must consider the innovation capacity of a potential host country in a specific industry, some general evaluations can be drawn from secondary sources like the World Competitiveness Report.[1]

SPOTLIGHT
China Targets U.S. Tech Startups in Investment Loophole

Chinese investors targeting startups have historically focused their investments in the information and communications technology sectors, the health, pharmaceuticals and biotechnology sectors. They are also targeting technologies such as 3-D printing, robotics and artificial intelligence. Recent investments have been into companies such as Grail, a Silicon Valley cancer detection startup. Some of the most active Chinese investors in the United States have been tech giants Alibaba Group Holding Ltd. and Tencent Holdings Ltd., which in recent years have showered the startup sector with dozens of investments, including video game makers, a cellphone developer and multiple autonomous car companies. However, tighter national security reviews have curbed Chinese deal-making in the United States. As of December 2018, lawmakers put the finishing touches on legislation to curb a range of Chinese investment by strengthening the Committee on Foreign Investment in the United States.

Based on
https://www.wsj.com/articles/china-targets-u-s-tech-startups-in
-investment-loophole-1531742441

10.2 Competitive Positioning: The First Mover Advantage

Expanding operations in key places in order to gain a competitive advantage is another reason companies choose to operate globally (Porter, 1990, 1998). A company may expand an operation abroad in order to gain **market share** in that area or to prevent another company from gaining an advantage over them. They may need to follow their competitors into markets in order to prevent them from gaining an advantage. Alternatively, if it is possible for a firm be the first to enter the market, possibly the company will gain the **first mover advantage**. In other words, firms invest in one country to gain a competitive position. With time, the competitiveness decreases when competitors try to match the strategy. Eventually, firms need to continue investing in other countries to maintain or regain competitiveness.

> *Examples:* EBay was the first to implement an active online consumer auction process. Xerox, invented and patented the photocopying technology and for 15 years dominated the photocopying industry. Apple was the first to introduce real touch screen tech; although now the control of this market is slowly eroding as more competitors enter the market.

10.3 Following Customers or Suppliers

It may be in a company's best interest to remain in close proximity to their strategic customers or suppliers. If a supplier chooses to open a division in a foreign market, it may prove worthwhile for the customer to open an operation there to take advantage of the reduced transportation costs and potential new market for the product. Another possibility is that the company may wish to follow the supplier to prevent a competitor from gaining an advantage by opening an operation close to the supplier's facility.

> *Example:* Wal-Mart has more than 10,000 Chinese suppliers. However, Wal-Mart is now becoming a major retail presence there as well. The company has already opened about 200 stores in 101 Chinese cities and hopes to roll out ever more big-box emporiums across the urban Chinese landscape (Chan & Unger, 2011).

10.4 Government Regulation

Companies often choose a location in order to avoid government regulations that increase costs or make operating in a location more difficult, costly, and risky. For example, cruise lines register their ships in Panama in order to avoid taxes and stringent U.S. employment rules, even though the majority of passengers on the cruise ships are American citizens.

Another case of avoiding regulation is a company choosing to manufacture a product in a given country in order to avoid paying duties that would be imposed if the product was manufactured outside of the country and then imported into the country. The company may be trying to avoid lengthy procedures associated with opening a business in a foreign market. In China, for example, lengthy paperwork is required in order to establish a wholly owned

SPOTLIGHT
The "Doing Business" Report

Every year, the World Bank issues their "Doing Business" report. The main findings of the 2019 report indicate that worldwide, 128 economies introduced substantial regulatory improvements making it easier to do business in all areas measured by Doing Business. The 10 top economies in the ease of doing business ranking share common features of regulatory efficiency and quality, including mandatory inspections during construction, automated tools used by distribution utilities to restore service during power outages, strong safeguards available to creditors in insolvency proceedings and automated specialized commercial courts (DoingBusiness, 2019).

subsidiary. Multiple layers of government need to approve the application before the business can begin operations. The application and approval procedure can take years to finalize. Therefore, a company may choose to form a joint venture or a strategic alliance instead of a wholly owned subsidiary in order to avoid such a lengthy start-up time. Some countries enact legislation to protect their domestic companies. India and China, for example, prohibit foreign companies from having 100% ownership.

The discussion above highlights the primary factors that influence the internationalization of a firm. In the globalization era, some firms internationalize in order to survive, while others expand overseas to continue to grow.

10.5 Additional Benefits to Internationalization

Risk diversification is another benefit of the internationalization of a firm. Risk diversification of investment has been studied from financial and strategic perspectives (Barney, 1997). Dependency on one location bears a location specific risk. Government regulations, economic downturn, and decline in demand are some of the examples of risk of operating in one country only. Operating in different countries distributes the risk among various locations because when the economy of a country is not going well, it is possible that other economies are experiencing economic growth. It must also be noted that geographic diversification involves incremental risk. The countries to which a firm expands may have higher risk than the home country, thus increasing the overall risk of the firm (Kwok & Reeb, 2000; Reeb, Kwok, & Baek, 1998).

Tax benefits are another advantage of international business operation. Transfer pricing and cost have been noted as major advantages for firms

> **SPOTLIGHT**
> **Why Tech Workers and Global Companies Are Choosing Canada**
>
> Canada's public and commercial sectors place a premium on growing entrepreneurial communities and connecting them with the best business and academic institutions. Toronto, Vancouver and Montreal are growing as hubs for startups. The country's open commercial atmosphere, geographical proximity, and cultural similarities, often entice U.S. companies to expand to Canada as their first international foray.
>
> *Based on*
>
> https://www.forbes.com/sites/forbestechcouncil/2018/07/02/why-tech-workers-and-global-companies-are-choosing-canada/#6cc3e2e759a0

operating internationally. Firms take advantage of tax rate differentials between various countries by allocating the cost to the country with a higher tax rate thus reducing the corporate taxable income as much as possible. This approach to value creation for stockholders has been questioned both legally and ethically. The Organization of Economic Cooperation and Development (OECD) provided extensive rules for international business, particularly for transfer pricing (OECD, 2014).

10.6 Internationalization Process Models

Once a company decides to go abroad, there are different methods to internationalize. The method they choose can be based upon the level of experience they have in the host country, the amount of risk they are willing to undertake, and the amount of control they wish to keep. As companies gain more experience, they may change the method they use. Other well-known internationalization theories, which are now considered as traditional approaches, are the Uppsala Model (Johanson & Vahlne, 1977), Vernon's Product Life Cycle theory (Vernon, 1966), Internationalization theory (Buckley & Casson, 1998, 2009), and the Eclectic paradigm theory by J.H. Dunning (Dunning, 1979, 2001).

10.6.1 Incremental Internationalization— The Uppsala Model

The **incremental internationalization** or **Uppsala model** proposed by Johanson and Vahlne explains how firms gradually intensify their activities

Figure 10.2 Internationalization stages.

in foreign markets. The key features of the model are that firms first gain experience in the domestic market before they move to foreign markets. Then firms start their foreign operations in culturally and/or geographically close countries, and move gradually to culturally and geographically more distant countries. In addition, the model posits that firms start their foreign operations by exporting and gradually move to using more intensive and demanding operation modes such as sales subsidiaries in the foreign country. The Uppsala model also proposes that foreign sales begin with occasional export orders that are followed by regular exports. Finally, the firm will not commit higher levels of resources to the market until it has acquired increasing levels of experiential knowledge and therefore the internationalization evolves incrementally at a relatively *slow pace* because of local market regulations and/or organizational learning. As companies gain more experience, they can move through the various stages of internationalization illustrated in Figure 10.2 (Johanson & Vahlne, 1977).

10.6.2 International Product Life Cycle (PLC) Theory

The **international PLC theory** states that the optimal location for the production of certain types of goods and services shifts over time as they pass through the stages of market **introduction, growth, maturity,** and **decline** as shown in Figure 10.3.

A company will begin exporting a product and later undertake foreign direct investment as the product moves through the life cycle (a country's export eventually becomes its import). A great majority of innovation and new technology that results in new products and production methods originates in developed countries. Because the product is not yet standardized, the production process tends to be relatively labor-intensive, and innovative customers tend to accept relatively high introductory prices. As demand grows, competitors enter the market. Foreign demand, competition, exports, and often direct investment activities also begin to accelerate. Worldwide demand begins to level off (maturity), although it may be growing in some countries and declining in others. At this stage, the production processes are relatively standardized and global price competition forces a

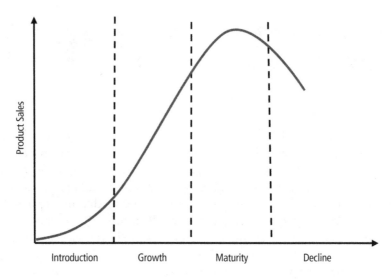

Figure 10.3 International product life cycle.

production site relocation to lower-cost developing countries. The product is then imported by the country where it was initially developed.

Exceptions to the typical pattern of the product life cycle theory include products with high transport costs, products that have very short life cycles, luxury goods and services, products that require specialized labor, products that can be differentiated from direct competitors, and products for which transportation costs are relatively high (Vernon, 1966).

Limitations of the Theory

The United States is no longer the dominant innovator of products in the world. New products spring up everywhere as the research and development activities are globalized. Companies today design new products and make product modifications at a very quick pace. Companies introduce products in many markets simultaneously to recoup a product's research and development costs before sales decline. The theory is challenged by the fact that more companies are operating in international markets from their inception. The Internet has made this type of business expansion easier, particularly for small and midsize companies. In addition, small companies are more often teaming up with companies in other markets to develop new products or production technologies. The theory does not explain either why companies choose Foreign Direct Investment (FDI) over other forms of market entry, yet the theory retains explanatory power when applied to technology-based products that are eventually mass-produced.

10.6.3 Market Imperfections and Internalization Theory

The **market imperfections theory** is a trade theory that arises from international markets where perfect competition does not exist. In a perfect market, prices are as low as possible and goods are easily available. Flaws in the efficient operation of an industry are **market imperfections**.

The **internalization theory** is an extension of the market imperfection theory that posits that when an imperfection in the market makes a transaction less efficient, a company will undertake foreign direct investment to internalize the transaction and remove the imperfection. In other words, the theory states that by investing in a foreign subsidiary rather than licensing, a company is able to send the knowledge across borders while maintaining it within the firm. In addition, foreign subsidiaries allow the company to capitalize on the company's technological advantages if they face concerns regarding intellectual property rights protection, licensing difficulties or any other imperfections such as tariffs (Buckley & Casson, 2009).

10.6.4 Eclectic Paradigm or OLI-Model

The **eclectic paradigm** is a further development of the internalization theory. The theory posits that firms undertake foreign direct investment when the features of a location combine with ownership and internalization advantages to make a location appealing for investment. When each advantage is present, a company will undertake FDI (Dunning, 2001).

> *Ownership advantages.* Specific competitive advantages of the company trying to expand abroad through foreign direct investment. The greater the competitive advantages (some special asset such as a powerful brand, technical knowledge, or management ability) of the investing firms, the more they are likely to engage in their foreign production.
> *Location advantages.* The advantage of locating a particular economic activity in a specific location because of the characteristics (natural or acquired) of the location.
> *Internalization advantages.* Firms may organize the creation and exploitation of their core competencies. An internalization advantage is the advantage that arises from internalizing a business activity rather than leaving it to a relatively inefficient market (Dunning, 1979, 2001).

10.7 Competitive Advantage and the Value Chain

Michael Porter developed the **value chain model** to describe the process by which businesses receive raw materials, add value to the raw materials through various processes to create a finished product, and then sell the finished product to customers. Companies conduct value-chain analysis by looking at every production step required to create a product and identifying ways to increase the efficiency of the chain. The overall goal is to deliver maximum value for the least possible total cost and create a competitive advantage (Porter, 1998).

A firm's value chain forms a part of a larger stream of activities. A **value system**, or an industry value chain, includes the suppliers that provide the inputs necessary to the firm along with their value chains. After the firm creates products, these products pass through the value chains of distributors (which also have their own value chains), all the way to the customers. All parts of these chains are included in the value system. Businesses aim at enhancing their margins and thus work to change input into an output, which is of a greater value (the difference between the two is the company's profit margin). The more value a company creates, the more profitable it is. The enhanced value is passed on to the customers, which further helps in consolidating a company's competitive edge. To achieve and sustain a competitive advantage, and to support that advantage with information technologies, a firm must understand every component of this value system (Porter, 1990).

The value-chain activities are categorized into primary activities and secondary activities. The **primary activities** are directly related to the creation of a good or service (i.e., Research & Development, Production, Operations, Inbound/Outbound logistics, Marketing and in some cases Customer Service), while the support, or **secondary activities** help in enhancing the efficiency of the primary activities in a value chain (e.g., Procurement, Human Resources, IT support, Company infrastructure, etc.). Figure 10.4 illustrates a generic value chain.

10.7.1 Example: Starbucks and the Value Chain Model

Primary Activities

- *Inbound Logistics.* This refers to the company's coffee buyers selecting the finest quality coffee beans from various producers around the world. These are transported to the storage sites, after which the beans are roasted and packaged. They are then sent to distribution centers, a few of which are company owned and some of which

Support or Secondary Activities

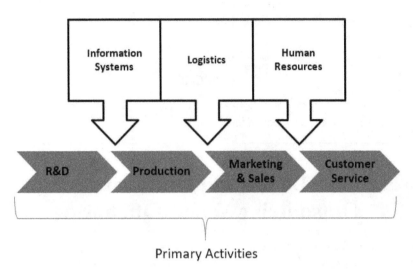

Figure 10.4 Generic Value Chain diagram.

are operated by other logistic companies. The company does not outsource procurement, ensuring high quality standards right from the point of selection of coffee beans.

- *Operations.* Starbucks operates in 65 countries, either in the form of direct company-owned stores or licensees.
- *Outbound Logistics.* There is very little or no presence of intermediaries in product selling. The majority of the products are sold in their own or in licensed stores only.
- *Marketing and Sales.* Starbucks invests more in superior quality products and high level of customer service than in aggressive marketing. However, marketing activities are done in-house during new products launches.
- *Service.* Starbucks aims at building customer loyalty through customer service.

Support Activities

- *Infrastructure.* This includes departments like management, finance, legal, etc., which are required to keep the company's stores operational.
- *Human Resource Management.* The committed workforce is considered a key attribute in the company's success and growth over the years. Starbucks employees are motivated through generous benefits and incentives.

- *Technology Development.* Starbucks is well-known for use of technology, not only for coffee-related processes (to ensure consistency in taste and quality along with cost savings) but to connect to its customers.

EXERCISE

Based on the description above and the generic value chain in Figure 10.4 draw a value chain diagram for Starbucks.

Debate the Merits of Outsourcing Versus Offshoring

Divide the class into two teams. Each team has 10 minutes to prepare, 5 minutes to present its arguments, and 5 minutes to refute the opposing team. Use these additional readings:

What is Offshoring? What is Outsourcing? How are they Different?
https://www.forbes.com/sites/jwebb/2017/07/28/what-is-offshoring -what-is-outsourcing-are-they-different/#5e3561022a2e

Hot Spot for Tech Outsourcing: the United States
https://www.nytimes.com/2017/07/30/technology/hot-spot-for -tech-outsourcing-the-united-states.html

Team A

Outsourcing and Offshoring helps US companies be more efficient. This benefit of outweighs the potential job losses.

Team B

The benefits of outsourcing and offshoring do not outweigh negative consequences such as workforce displacement.

10.8 Conclusion

In a globalizing world, the complexities of expansion to new foreign markets present challenges for managers. The internationalization motives are highly dependent on the strategy and the leadership of a business. Going abroad or internationalizing without careful consideration may be detrimental to overall performance, especially for smaller businesses. Therefore, understanding the motives and the process of internationalization is of utmost importance.

This chapter described the most common motives of internationalization. Several models of internationalization are also discussed. These models help managers undertake the first stages of internationalization decision-making. However, this is only the beginning. It takes a lot more to succeed overseas.

TBL Connection
China Leading the Way to Electric Cars

The auto industry is undergoing a revolution. "Internationalization, electrification, and intelligent connection have evolved from just ideas to reality," says Wang Chuanfu, president and chairman of BYD in a press release.

In addition to new versions of its existing models, BYD introduced its latest concept vehicle, the E-SEED, which stands for Electronic Sports Experience Environmental Device.

BMW is still searching for its electric car identity. Sales of the i3 are not setting the world on fire. BMW's i division has not generated the kind of sales traffic the company was hoping for. In Beijing, the company showed the iX3 concept, which is a battery electric version of the X3 SUV manufactured in South Carolina. The real news is that BMW intends to manufacture the iX3 in China. The German company has quietly been moving production of the conventional X3 from South Carolina to China and may have plans to export cars made there to other countries. This is a sign of the increasing influence China has over the automotive industry, especially with respect to EVs. It is the largest car market in the world, and it is certainly the biggest for all-electric cars at the moment. With the government aggressively pushing to clean up the country's greenhouse gas emissions while also loosening manufacturing restrictions on foreign automakers, China is an attractive location to set up shop.

At least, nine new electric car companies are gearing up for production in China, including Nio, Byton, BAIC, Zhidhou, Changjiang, and Kandi. Clearly if you look at the ferment that is brewing electric cars in China and compare it to the slow walk American manufacturers are doing, the center of gravity for the future of the industry has shifted from Detroit to Asia.

Not to be left out, GM is taking advantage of this year's Beijing auto show to take the wraps off its latest electric SUV concept, the Buick Enspire. Buick is a trade name that is falling out of favor in the United States, but it is one of the more respected brands in China.

> All conventional carmakers, and even unconventional companies like Tesla, need to keep a close eye on China. In the near future, Chinese companies could dominate the global new car market and push the electric vehicle segment forward in a way few could have predicted a few years ago.
>
> *Based on*
> https://cleantechnica.com/2018/04/26/china-leading-the-way-to-electric-car-future-byd-bmw-highlight-beijing-auto-show/
>
> 1. *Describe the internationalization process of electric cars. What are the determinants of the observed patterns?*
>
> 2. *Which of the internationalization models presented in this chapter best captures the internationalization process of the car industry, and more specifically of E-vehicles? Elaborate.*
>
> 3. *How would the shift to produce electric cars impact the "Triple Bottom Line" or an automotive company? Explain.*

Chapter Review

Key Terms

- Market seeking motive
- Resource seeking motive
- Strategic asset seeking motive
- Competitiveness
- Value Chain
- Host country
- Home country Incremental Internationalization/Uppsala Model
- Market imperfection/internationalization theory
- Eclectic paradigm/OLI framework
- International Product Life Cycle

Questions & Assignments

Questions

1. Describe the internationalization process of a company of your choice. What are the determinants and characteristics of the observed patterns?
2. Select a product or a company and determine which of the internationalization models presented in this chapter best captures the internationalization process of the company/product.

Assignments

1. Research and examine a firm that has applied one of the internationalization theories discussed in the chapter. How does the theory help explain the internationalization process of the selected firm?
2. Research a product that is a good example of the Product Life Cycle Theory. Clearly show all of the stages of the product life cycle for the product as it was produced in one country and is gone through its final stage.

Note

1. http://www3.weforum.org/docs/GCR2017-2018/05FullReport/TheGlobal CompetitivenessReport2017%E2%80%932018.pdf

Suggested Reading

How SMEs can internationalize
   https://www.forbes.com/sites/iese/2015/04/20/how-smes-can -internationalize/#24b5bc071eb8

A Shift in the Business Mindset: A Key Factor in the Process of Internationalization
   https://www.mastercardbiz.com/caribbean/2017/03/24/a-shift-in-the -business-mindset-a-key-factor-in-the-process-of-internationalization/

References

Barney, J. B. (1997). *Gaining and sustaining competitive advantage* (P. Education Ed.). Reading, MA: Addison-Wesley.

Buckley, P. J., & Casson, M. C. (1998). Analyzing foreign market entry strategies: Extending the internalization approach. *Journal of International Business Studies*, 539–561.

Buckley, P. J., & Casson, M. C. (2009). The internalisation theory of the multinational enterprise: A review of the progress of a research agenda after 30 years. *Journal of International Business Studies, 40*(9), 1563–1580.

Chan, A., & Unger, J. (2011). Wal-Mart's China connections. *The American Prospect*.

DoingBusiness. (2019). *2019 doing business report*. Retrieved from http://www.doingbusiness.org

Dunning, J. H. (1979). Explaining changing patterns of international production: In defence of the eclectic theory. *Oxford Bulletin of Economics and Statistics, 41*(4), 269–295.

Dunning, J. H. (2001). The eclectic (OLI) paradigm of international production: past, present and future. *International Journal of the Economics of Business, 8*(2), 173–190.

Johanson, J., & Vahlne, J.-E. (1977). The internationalization process of the firm—a model of knowledge development and increasing foreign market commitments. *Journal of International Business Studies, 8*(1), 23–32.

Kwok, C. C. Y., & Reeb, D. M. (2000). Internationalization and firm risk: An upstream-downstream hypothesis. *Journal of International Business Studies,* 611–629.

OECD. (2014). *Transfer pricing.* Retrieved from http://www.oecd.org/ctp/transfer -pricing/

Pan, Y., & Tse, D. K. (2000). The hierarchical model of market entry modes. *Journal of International Business Studies,* 535–554.

Porter, M. E. (1990). The competitive advantage of nations. *Harvard Business Review, 68*(2).

Porter, M. E. (1998). *Competing across locations: Enhancing competitive advantage through a global strategy.* Brighton, MA: Harvard Business School Press.

Reeb, D. M., Kwok, C. C. Y., & Baek, H. Y. (1998). Systematic risk of the multinational corporation. *Journal of International Business Studies,* 263–279.

Vernon, R. (1966). International investment and international trade in the product cycle. *The Quarterly Journal of Economics, 80*(2), 190–207.

Cross-Cultural Management

Opening Case

Airbnb and its Cultural Management Challenges

Airbnb is a platform sharing business model that allows for peer-to-peer transactions involving underutilized home space, cars, or other assets. Sharing platforms are an invention that emerged due to technological advances. They are rapidly disrupting the way many industries currently operate. Since its creation, Airbnb has successfully expanded to over 191 countries. Considering

Global Business, pages 225–244
Copyright © 2019 by Information Age Publishing
All rights of reproduction in any form reserved.

Figure 11.1 Airbnb. *Source:* https://www.flickr.com/photos/fotosebe/15793094042/ in/photolist-o53EbL-q4zJCS-pSEuf8-pSYsqb-bqRWL5-oW3RxY-vbUqqi-sjBNo9

the vast difference in social, economic, and regulatory environments across these countries, as well as the complicated and novel implications of sharing platforms, such success is exceptional and impressive. Managing and operating in a different country and culture and at the same time providing high quality services can be a great challenge.

Even Western cultures differ in their housing preferences. Americans, for instance, usually live in big houses and apartments with a lot of common space and open doors, while Germans tend to close their doors and have more private spaces. Furthermore, refrigerators and especially the freezers are smaller in a German apartment. This is an important cultural distinction of Germans, as it influences their attitudes towards home-sharing.

Mexico, a country known for its colorful culture and amazing food, is a popular attraction among frequent travelers. The arrival of Airbnb was a big controversy because a lot of money could be made by just turning an apartment into a temporary rental space. People who rent out simply receive the money through Airbnb, and can immediately cancel a reservation if a visitor misbehaves. Mexico's culture is accustomed to tourism, and, therefore, the locals safeguard their ability to rightfully profit from it.

Japan struggled with bringing together the people who are renting out Airbnb houses and apartments with the local neighbors who are not renting out to anyone. Due to the strictly distinct culture of Japan, strangers in the neighborhood were very upsetting to some residents. For instance, TV specials began to focus on the foreign guests. Furthermore, many guests were excessively messy and did not obey the residential rules of the area. The local neighborhoods' main argument against Airbnb is entirely based around the impact foreign guests have on strong cultured small Japanese neighborhoods and cities.

Based on

The German Way & More "Cultural Comparison 5"; https://www.german -way.com/history-and-culture/cultural-comparisons/cultural-comparisons- part-5/

Airbnb International Growth Strategy, July, 2016; http://www.mylotrade .com/airbnb-international-growth-strategy.html

1. *How can Airbnb successfully operate and be considerate of culture, given the challenges described above?*

11.0 Introduction

This chapter presents fundamental issues for successfully managing cross-culturally with a global mindset. Cultural differences should be appreciated because understanding such differences is instrumental in successfully managing global operations. The chapter also describes how a global manager can be effective in managing change in a global organization.

Globalization, as described earlier in the book, has been the most important phenomenon that has challenged the mindset, decision-making, and strategic direction of most companies' leadership. Globalization has been defined in a variety of ways throughout the last century, but one common trend amongst the definitions is **interdependency**. *The New York Times* columnist Thomas Friedman defines globalization, in his book *The Lexus and the Olive Tree,* as "the inexorable integration of markets, capitals, nation-states, and technologies in ways that allow individuals, groups, corporations, and countries to reach around the world farther, faster, deeper, and cheaper than ever before." (Friedman, 2000). This definition implies that managers need not just address globalization in every managerial decision, but also see the opportunities and challenges that arise with it.

The biggest challenge that a manager faces in the era of globalization is adapting to cultural differences. A manager with a global mindset and knowledge about cultural issues should be able to make efficient, appropriate, and ethical decisions given the opportunities and constraints. For example, the former chair and Chief Executive Officer (CEO) of PepsiCo, Indra Nooyi, and the former Coca-Cola CEO, Muhtar Kent, represent leaders with a global mindset and cross-cultural awareness. Both had significant cross-cultural interaction and exposure through their personal background and international assignments around the world. Therefore, because of their cultural background, exposures and experiences, they have a good global mindset.

A management style that matches the international business environment can reduce the cost of doing business. With a lower cost of doing international business, firms have an incentive to expand their operations. Global managers need to have a mindset that enables them to clearly link customers' interests with the company's strategic goals and objectives. This mindset enables a manager to engage cross-cultural employees in the success of the company skillfully and ethically, in addition to efficiently building an organizational structure that is capable of delivering the best output possible.

11.1 Factors Affecting Global Management

Lane et al. articulated that global managers need to have the capability to skillfully and effectively deal with the following four factors so they can execute a plan with some degree of predictability (Jones,1995; Lane, Maznevski, Dietz, & DiStefano, 2009).

- *Command Interdependency.* The globalized world has led companies, governments, and citizens of the world to be more interdependent.
- *Variety.* CEO's have to deal with a variety of issues, internally and externally (nationally and internationally). Therefore, having a diverse educational and experiential background is very useful.
- *Ambiguity.* Because so many factors are at play in operating in the global economy, there is a high degree of ambiguity and complexity. Thus, leadership should have the ability to identify essential factors that require focus and attention.
- *Fast flux.* So many things (i.e., public policies, political landscape, market conditions, competitors, labor market, etc.) are moving so rapidly and changing at a fast pace (24/7) that CEOs are required to make decisions under these circumstances.

The above factors highlight some of the key issues a global manager has to deal with systemically across different time zones and cultures. This job demands a prudent application of global human resource management because many factors such as hiring, promotion, salary increases, team building, job delegations, relocation strategies, and dealing with various stakeholders in a different culture are at play. Additionally, many exogenous and endogenous variables may shock an organization. The exogenous variables are external shocks that influence a company. Therefore, the company must react or respond to the shocks as they see it fit. These shocks could be unanticipated macroeconomic policy changes or a natural disaster, and managers cannot do much about them before they happen. However, endogenous variables such as pricing strategy, marketing channels, responding to market demand, product warranties, and distribution centers are planned internally and are usually within the control of the leadership team.

Successful leaders apply this system when formulating their strategic direction and in their daily activities. For example, Samuel J. Palmisano, IBM's CEO, was able to articulate clearly the goals and objectives of the company while adding values to them (Hempel, 2011). The same is true for Mr. Zhang, the CEO of Haier. The company was operating in China, but the CEO was applying American innovation, Japanese quality control methods, and Chinese collectivist culture (Haier.com, 2014). Other well-known CEOs such as the late Steve Jobs, founder and former CEO of the Apple Corporation, and Jeff Bezos, the CEO of Amazon have adopted strategies that led to the success of their companies in many countries. Steve Jobs fundamentally redefined the role of the telephone and significantly expanded its services and usability. Based on recent articles and books, his management style was less dependent on committees and had more emphasis on outcomes (Isaacson, 2015). Bezos came up with the idea of eliminating intermediaries and selling products cheaply and efficiently. Both of these leaders applied the above-mentioned concepts effectively and expanded their reach across the globe. However, in the long run, even these four factors noted above will also change. Interdependency creates a cultural convergence that to some degree reduces the variety and ambiguity. When variety and ambiguity are reduced, managing international business may become easier, which in turn might facilitate a higher degree of success.

Recent policies in countries such as the United Kingdom and the U.S. have led to nationalist movements and protectionism. This kind of backlash is due to a set of factors such as rapid expansion of globalization, environmental changes, and migration. Scholars such as Stiglitz already in 2008 warned about the potential backlash due to globalization expansion, which in his opinion, did not address the concerns of those who did not benefit from globalization. In addition, evolving social issues due to mass migrations are creating some frictions. These sets of political and social factors are leading to uncertainties, which makes the job of global managers even more challenging.

In many aspects, global managers are facing an imperfect world of cultural differences that brings in significant opportunities and hindrances. Organizations and their leaders need to carefully navigate this muddy river to be able to survive. One of the most difficult aspects of managing globally is being able to deal with cross-cultural issues ethically. Organizations frequently encounter ethical dilemmas that raise organization-wide questions regarding their stance on corruption, bribery, slavery, underage employment, racial and gender discrimination, human rights issues, environmental changes, and other aspects that could dramatically impact the organization. Some scholars (Asgary & Mitschow, 2002; Sethi, 2005) have proposed a series of voluntary codes of ethics that the leadership of multinational corporations should implement and follow. In his book, *Management Across Cultures*, Steers et al. note that organizations can approach this issue in two polarized ways. First, a global organization needs a clear ethical compass to guide their organizational actions. This approach tries to standardize ethical behaviors throughout all the different environments where the organization is operating. The second approach, used in some organizations is to not judge what is right or wrong. These organizations believe that right or wrong only exists in the eye of the beholder (Steers, Sanchez-Runde, & Nardon, 2010). Both views approach the issue of ethical values in different cultures somewhat differently. However, organizations need to have clear and transparent ethical guidelines and implementation policy. Otherwise, problems can arise from incongruence among decisions within the organization.

11.2 Culture and Global Management

Expanding to new international environments is increasing the pressure on organizations to understand and adapt to cultural differences. As discussed in an earlier chapter, in order for organizations to be successful in the global economy, they should consider all cultural aspects that directly and indirectly affect their outcomes in terms of their global strategy, business relationships, employees' performance, and daily operations. Leadership's ability to adapt to the different environments and expectations that cross-cultural management requires starts with correctly identifying the mix of cultures involved in business partnerships.

Leadership, employees, and negotiators who conduct cross-cultural activities should be very careful not to make mistakes due to the lack of cultural awareness. Mistakes can happen if the wrong type of humor is used while communicating, failing to understand the cultural hierarchy, or rushing to close a deal in a relationship-centered culture. Additionally, these kinds of mishaps can lead to marketing failures. These are unchartered territories for some newcomers and require training and preparation of engaged employees.

To fully understand the impact that culture has on organizational behavior, managers need to clearly understand the foreign cultures and their impact on the organization. The concept of culture is essential to understand the need for managers to analyze the cultural implications on the operation of the organization. It is imperative to note that the culture of an organization can be significantly influenced by the broader cultural characteristics of the society in which it operates. Furthermore, as Steers et al. explain, in addition to learning a country's culture, managers need to understand normative behaviors from organizational cultures to be able to successfully guide organizations.

Although some components of societal cultures may be static, other characteristics of culture evolve over time because of globalization. Also, since culture can evolve faster than physical or biological aspects in humans, it becomes the method used to survive and evolve as a community or civilization. Organizations have to be able to handle the adaptation that individuals go through on a daily basis, in their ever-changing environment, without affecting those aspects that make the local and organizational culture unique.

Assessing cultural impact is the first step for organizations to examine when managing in a cross-cultural environment. The second step is to understand the different levels or components that conform a culture. As described earlier, Hofstede presented in his 1980 Dimensions of Culture study three different levels of mental programming that explained how individuals behave in regular circumstances (Thomas & Peterson, 2017). These three levels (universal, cultural, personality) help managers understand their employees' behavior and their underlying causes. Hofstede's six dimensions of culture (Individualism vs. Collectivism, Power Distance, Uncertainty Avoidance, Masculinity vs. Femininity, Long vs. Short term Orientation, Indulgence vs. Restraint) can be used as a general guide to understand the reasons for cultural differences and their implications for successful operation of organizations.

SPOTLIGHT
How Culture Drives Behaviors

Julien S. Bourrelle argues that we see the world through cultural glasses. By changing the glasses, you can change the way you interpret the world. Watch the following 12-minute video for more information.

https://www.youtube.com/watch?v=l-Yy6poJ2zs

The importance of identifying the different levels of individual behavior for managers is that confusing one group with another can lead to cultural misinterpretation, which will impact organizational performance. Managers must be able to differentiate the types of behavior and their roots, before generalizing anything as cultural behavior. For example, if a firm's home country has a low power distance (e.g., USA, Germany or the Nordic countries) where upper level managers and middle level managers interact easily, operates in a high power distance (e.g., India or the Arab countries)

> ### SPOTLIGHT
> ### Leadership and Teamwork Around the Globe
>
> Hofstede's cultural dimensions and current research illustrate that effective leadership and teamwork might vary significantly around the globe. A study of more than 30,000 leaders in Australia, Belgium, China, Denmark, India, Netherlands, Norway, Sweden, UK, and the U.S., identified several differences between popular leadership styles in different regions. Leaders in emerging markets (India and China, specifically) focus significantly on managing performance and operational processes. They tend to be very hands-on. Due to both the cultural and economic environment, the success of leaders from emerging economies is often driven by their ability to hire and train individuals quickly. In such organizations, any change in management typically occurs through clear top-down leadership, which can be explained by high power distance that characterizes many emerging economies. Benelux and Nordic leaders, on the other hand, focus on the "collective good," long-term planning, values, and common vision. Interestingly, the US and UK leaders employ hybrid leadership models. The individualistic culture of the United States explains the focus on execution and accountability of individuals within the firm (Bersin, 2012).
>
> *Based on*
>
> https://www.forbes.com/sites/joshbersin/2012/10/31/are-expat-programs -dead/#3ce52bd82304

host country's culture, then there is a strong possibility of a culture clash between the business' parent company and the subsidiary. However, through the interaction between the headquarters and the subsidiary, there will be a convergence of cultures that eventually will create a new "business culture" unique to the firm headquarters and its subsidiary. Otherwise the venture will likely to fail. The extent to which the headquarters and the subsidiary create a business culture depends on the size of the firm and the size of the subsidiary. In many cases, large multinationals operating in a small country have a significant impact in the culture of their host country.

11.3 Styles of International Management

There are three types of cultural perspectives for individuals: **Ethnocentric**, **Polycentric** and **Geocentric**. These three approaches can influence an individual's behavior. These perspectives can also be implemented as managerial philosophies for companies when they operate in other countries or manage their subsidiaries overseas. These three philosophies can also be viewed as different styles of management for MNEs.

Ethnocentrism. A firm's belief that business practices and management techniques that have worked in their home country must also work abroad. Therefore, managers use a more centralized approach to run their subsidiaries in other countries. In such cases, it is common for the company to use expatriates to manage the subsidiary overseas. **Expatriates** are managers from the home country who are sent to another country to manage the foreign subsidiary.

Polycentrism. A business philosophy that suggests that each culture has its unique ways of doing business, and it is difficult to apply the home country policies across cultures. Under this philosophy, managers do not attempt to standardize business practices and management techniques across cultures. Therefore, they allow each country's subsidiary to run operations in their own way.

Geocentrism. Under this approach, many "best" business practices and management techniques are not culture bound. Such "best" practices and techniques may develop in any cultural setting. Thus, managers must look for best practices, regardless of the culture of origination. Managers who subscribe to this approach, promote mutual learning among all country units in the entire company.

Each of these approaches can be effective in some industries in some countries. There is not one correct approach or better management style.

Debate—Multinationals Should Use Expatriates to Manage Their Subsidiaries Overseas

Pros

- *Familiarity.* Expatriates understand the organizational culture of the home country and could transfer them to subsidiaries.
- *Human Capital.* Expatriates bring technical and business expertise from the parent to the subsidiary.
- *Experience.* Expatriates can apply management practices that were effective at home to a subsidiary overseas.
- *Standardization.* By hiring expatriates to run the foreign subsidiaries, the company could more effectively coordinate and control its uniform practices.

Cons

- *Adjustment.* Expatriates and their families sometimes face difficulties in adjusting to international assignments and foreign cultures.
- *False Comparison.* Expatriates have the tendency to believe that their way of managing at home can be applied to a foreign culture.
- *Expense.* It is very expensive to use expatriates to manage foreign subsidiaries.
- *Probability of Failure.* The failure rate of using expatriates is very high.

11.4 Global Mindset and Managerial Skills

Managers in multinational organizations face different challenges than traditional managers in domestic firms. Before identifying some of these challenges, it is important to evaluate the managerial styles and skill sets that managers in multinational organizations must have to overcome cross-cultural challenges. Managers' skill sets can be classified differently according to their degree of exposure to different cultures. It is difficult to encounter managers that do not find themselves impacted in the era of globalization, even if their organizations have been operating locally and are technically "domestic" companies.

Global managers are individuals engaged in cross-cultural management who have a global mindset and are capable of interpreting situations, conflicts, opportunities, and weaknesses from all angles. Managers must identify their limitations regarding cross-cultural challenges and try to address them beforehand to prevent conflicts within the organization and among partners.

SPOTLIGHT
Training Global Leaders

A study based on the input from 1,358 business leaders from more than 90 countries concluded that only 50% of the organizations surveyed make it a priority to develop leaders' global skills and competencies, and only a third described their development efforts as effective. The study also highlighted that it is much more effective to develop global leadership traits early in the career of future leaders through experiential learning, which transcends traditional on-the-job training.

Based on

https://www.td.org/insights/want-a-global-mindset-integrate-global-skills-into-training-for-first-level-leaders

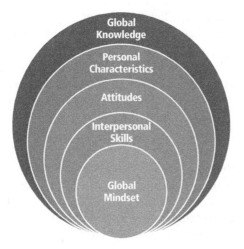

Figure 11.2   Global competencies.

Lane et al. frame the development of global competency as a stepwise process. The process can be explained as a 360-degree format, with a foundation of global knowledge and four levels of traits, attitudes, and orientations (see Figure 11.2). Open-minded individuals who are effective learners will be able to manage successfully in a global setting. A global leader should be nearly perfect in terms of the stated characteristics or be capable of acquiring advice from councils with expertise (Lane et al., 2009).

Lane et al. define **global mindset** as follows.

> ...the capacity to develop and interpret criteria for personal and business performance, that are independent from the assumptions of a single context; and to interpret those criteria appropriately in different contexts. (Lane et al., 2009, p. 2)

In the current worldwide economic situation, being culturally aware and inter-culturally competent is necessary for success in this highly competitive international market. Successful businesses from all over the world are competing for the top spots in international industries. Being business savvy and having a good track record at home is no longer enough to secure the best opportunities globally. A global mindset is what organizations need in order to be successful globally. They need to be capable of adjusting to different environments, and have the ability to work effectively with other international businesses. Scholars have identified two constructs that comprise a global mindset; these are cognitive complexity and cosmopolitanism. To have a global mindset, an individual or an organization must have the ability to perceive multiple aspects of complex issues from several perspectives, known as **cognitive complexity**. At the same time, individuals or organizations must have an openness to different cultural experiences, a willingness to explore, learn, and change, known as **cosmopolitanism**. Besides these competencies, there are four types of knowledge in which global mindsets operate. The four types of knowledge an organization should have include the knowledge about self (CEO), knowledge about others (other CEOs), knowledge about their own organization, and knowledge about other organizations.

The value of a global mindset lies in enabling the company to combine speed with accurate response. The benefit of a global mindset derives from the fact that, while the company has a grasp of the needs of the local market. The key word of global mindset is cultivation, and the shape of that mindset is our interpretation of the world around us.

How does an *individual* cultivate self-consciousness regarding their current market?

1. They ask managers or organizations to articulate their beliefs about the subject area.
2. They conduct a comparative analysis of how different people or companies appear to interpret the same reality.

Similarly, *companies* cultivate exposure and increase knowledge of diverse cultures and markets in two ways. Both approaches are essential for every company and complement each other.

1. They facilitate knowledge-building at the individual level. This approach focuses on building cognitive diversity in the mindsets of individuals (top executives and workers.)
2. Companies diversify the composition of the people making up the company. This approach focuses on assembling a diverse knowledge base across the organization's members; it may provide companies with lots of cultural background and ideas.

SPOTLIGHT
Huawei—Integrating East and West

The Chinese telecom giant Huawei employs more than 180,000 people around the world and serves more than 3 million customers, excluding the United States. Beyond its technology, the company is recognized for its goal of creating a culture where East meets West. The founder of the company, Ren Zhengfei, strongly believes that a company that wants to have a global reach needs to cultivate a global mindset amongst its employees. Based on the founder's philosophy, Huawei developed an employee performance system that measures "global experience." Global thinking is expected from all employees. Zhengfei explains, "the management teams in our research centers in China must be world-class and have a global perspective. They must not operate like a local team, because a Chinese style will lead to complacency." The company, however, does not leave Chinese values behind; even collectivism and individualism join forces at Huawei. Zhengfei said: "People should compete in solidarity and be united in competition." Such an approach suggests that Huawei's employees reach collective goals by focusing on individual pursuit of creativity and proactivity.

Based on

https://www.london.edu/faculty-and-research/lbsr/lessons-from-huawei-when-chinese-companies-go-global

---

SPOTLIGHT
Global Mindset and Senior Management

Many successful U.S. multinationals are managed by immigrants. Elon Musk, the co-founder and CEO of Tesla was born in South Africa. He originally came to the United States as a college student. Uber is led by Dara Khosrowshahi who immigrated to the United States during the Iranian revolution. The former CEO of PepsiCo, Indra Nooyi, is an immigrant from India. There are many reasons why those individuals succeeded in their careers. One could argue that beyond talent, intelligence, and dedication, they also have a global mindset due to their personal experience of living in several different cultures. Such a trait allows them to understand the complexities of global business and make business decisions accordingly.

Multicultural senior management teams generally have several strengths. A diverse leadership team is generally be well-equipped to address culture and diversity-related issues within and outside the corporation. Leaders from different backgrounds might also provide a competitive advantage to a corporation by providing creative insights about business and operations. The table below provides some examples of multinationals led by CEOs with multicultural experience.

MNE	CEO
Google	**Sundar Pichai**, CEO, from India
Oracle	**Safra Catz**, CEO, from Israel
Microsoft	**Satya Nadella**, CEO, from India
Uber	**Dara Khosrowshahi**, CEO, from Iran
PepsiCo	**Indra Nooyi**, Chairwomen and former CEO, from India
Tesla	**Elon Musk**, Founder and CEO, from South Africa

Based on
https://smallbusiness.chron.com/advantages-global-companies-gain
-deploying-multicultural-senior-management-teams-70784.html

11.5 Challenges of Operating Globally

When organizations engage in international business, it is certain that they will face the additional challenge of cultural differences. Identifying the types of issues or challenges organizations face demands that managers prepare themselves in advance of international assignments to be able to avoid conflicts. Scholars highlight that most of the challenges are interpersonal communication and performance rather than technical and organizational behavior. The fact is that people's cultures differ from organizational identities. Steers et al. identified some of the most important challenges, which are explained below.

Develop a learning strategy for professional development. Managers need to develop a strategy for professional development that would guide them throughout their career. When managers face cultural differences in their environments, it is important that managers have a strategy in the short run for how to resolve and act through adversity, as a part of a long-term goal.

1. *Basic knowledge of different cultures.* The differences between cultures cannot only bring up conflicts or challenges, but also opportunities and advantages for businesses to be successful. Managers in cross-cultural organizations need to understand the main differences between the cultures in a new working environment to fully address the needs of all parties involved in the organization. This process includes a self-assessment of the manager's own culture that will allow him/her to find the most important similarities and potential issues.
2. *Action strategies.* Managers need to know how and when to act to create an environment that would foster success and avoid conflict.

It is the manager's responsibility to know in advance how the differences in culture will affect interactions and communication among the key stakeholders. An absence of a plan of how to mitigate the cultural shock can create organizational conflicts that will negatively impact overall performance. On the other hand, if a manager develops plans of action according to the environment, it will be easier to identify the right moments for intervention, which will most likely reduce cultural barriers.

3. *Ethical and legal differences.* As noted before, knowing the differences in ethical values between cultures should minimize cultural shock experienced by managers. It is important for managers to know what is ethical and legal in the place of work in order to take appropriate actions. Multinational organizations can face difficult challenges when operating in two countries with different ethical values. Adapting and trying to respond legally and ethically is the correct approach. Adhering to the legal system of each country is one of the first steps in entering to that country's market. Of course, there are many gray areas between what is legal and ethical in each culture. If a manager is not careful in dealing with these issues appropriately it can become costly for the organization and the individual. Overall, organizations must assess these differences, and managers must become protectors of an ethical identity throughout the organization.

4. *Leadership roles vary between cultures.* Managing organizations and leading organizations means different things in different cultures. The expectations of a leader can drastically change depending on the place where the organization is operating. Managers need to understand the employees' expectations and try to meet that outlook in order to gain respect and avoid misunderstandings in the long run. Successful managers can turn the challenges to opportunities for the organization and themselves. Also, managers that have the capacity to use diversity in a cross-cultural setting add value to the organization.

11.6 Managing Change in Global Organization

Change in organizations is a continuous process because in the global arena, changes are taking place at the macro level, industry level, labor market, and in consumer preferences. Therefore, an organization has to respond to any or all of the above mentioned factors to stay in business. However, the word "change" has a broad definition. Three types of change are: crisis change, reactive change, and anticipatory change. First, some companies (i.e., GM,

Ford, and Chrysler) had to make drastic changes in 2009 in their strategy in their strategy, due to the global financial crisis, in order to survive because they were not prepared for unanticipated macroeconomic shocks in the marketplace and changes in the consumers' preferences in the global economy. This type is a **crisis change**. In these cases, organizations' survivability is at stake and significant changes are necessary.

The second type occurs when companies need to react to the consumers' complaints, quality control, and other changes in the market conditions, is defined as **reactive change**. These cases are not as severe as the first case, but requires serious and timely attention of the organization. For example, Toyota responded aggressively to a recall of defective airbags in 2010 and offered 24/7 services to its customers. If an organization does not respond to a new condition by making appropriate changes, then the situation can become too costly for the organization in terms of the bottom-line, market share, and reputation.

The third case is defined as **anticipatory change** in which a company anticipates changes in the market circumstances. For example, the demographic changes in the United States and internationally are demanding that institutions of higher education carefully assess their recruitment strategy. In these cases, organizations are proactive in assessing their status in the market place, and have formulated appropriate responses.

Evaluation of globalization has forced organizations to be on alert in addressing any one of the noted changes. Many organizations have a review process every three to five years to ensure growth of their business. Perhaps, a division called "change," with the responsibility of reviewing their strategy is needed. Those organizations that are continuously monitoring the

SPOTLIGHT
Amazon's Management of Continuous Global Change

Amazon went online in 1995 selling only books. By 2017, Amazon was selling more than 200 million products to customers all over the world, and even producing feature films, which have been awarded Oscars. Additionally, as of August 17, 2018, the stock price had increased from about $2 to $1882. Recently, Amazon has expanded its business line to food-stores (purchased Whole Foods) and medical drug services. For the past two decades, Amazon has been led by the founder Jeff Bezos.

Based on
https://www.tinypulse.com/blog/sk-case-studies-successful-change -management

1. *Analyze how Amazon is managing so many changes in such a short period.*

market might be more prepared to avoid big shocks and try to ensure the growth of their business. For example, KODAK, a well-known global company, was forced to go to bankrupt in January 2012. This example shows how a pioneering 19th century company failed because it did not appropriately analyze the changing marketplace and consumer demand.

11.7 Conclusion

This chapter highlights key issues that global managers have to be knowledgeable about when leading their organizations. The CEOs of many MNEs such as PepsiCo, IBM, and Haier have been very successful in functioning effectively in the global marketplace, while other big corporations such as KODAK have failed to adjust their strategies and paid the price. The economic environment has become increasingly global and thus cultures are converging for certain segments of society. An interesting aspect of this trend is that increasingly companies are hiring international CEOs. Organizations are now focusing on the qualities and skills of the workers instead of purely focusing on their nationalities. It is a challenge for a company to expand to another country while still keeping its original brand origin because they want to cater to other countries as well. Companies must adapt to the culture of the country they want to enter or expand to while maintaining some authenticity. Experience has shown that global companies gain advantages by adapting to the specific cultures where they choose to operate. Therefore, they should research the cultural norms, attitudes, and behaviors, so that they are less likely to experience a "cultural shock" and can fit into the new culture without much difficulty. This awareness will help global companies to satisfy their customers' needs, which will eventually lead to the company being more profitable.

TBL Connection
Netflix Managing Global Expansion-Profit

In January of 2016, Netflix, a subscription-based online streaming company, announced that it had expanded to over 130. By 2017, it was operating in over 190 countries. The achievement seemed remarkable, given that the company was operating only in the United States prior to 2010. Netflix's journey, however, has not been easy. The company had to secure content deals region by region and in some cases, country by country. In some countries, the company faced content restrictions. Indonesia's censorship agency, for instance, argued that a lot of Netflix's content was not be suitable for local audiences. Vietnamese and Malaysian regulators had similar concerns. While the company's Chief Content Officer, Ted Sarandos

---

believes that "great storytelling transcends borders," the company still chose to respond to local preferences. Original content is now produced in 17 markets and the company constantly analyzes customer data to identify its offerings for each market. Despite its success, Netflix, still needs to address some issues. Despite its global reach, Netflix, still needs to address issues regarding content, which is currently only available in about 20 languages. Furthermore, the company still has not been able to enter the Chinese market.

The story of Netflix is a clear illustration of the fact that country-specific knowledge is crucial for success. Company's leadership teams had to gain an understanding of cultural, regulatory, political environments of Netflix's new markets to develop relationships with key stakeholders. The company's approach had an impact on its profit, one of the elements on the triple bottom line. Over 2016, the profit has increased by 30.26%, reaching $8.831 billion. More than 60% of the company's profits are now generated by its international streaming division.

Based on

https://hbr.org/2018/10/how-netflix-expanded-to-190-countries-in-7-years

https://www.macrotrends.net/stocks/charts/NFLX/netflix/revenue

https://www.uni-erfurt.de/fileadmin/public-docs/Betriebswirtschaftslehre/
Teil_9_Netflix__Case_Study___Strat_Man_II_B_UEb_WS_17_18.pdf

1. *To what extent should Netflix adjust its content country-by-country?*
2. *Why is the company facing challenges entering the Chinese market?*

Chapter Review

Key Terms

- Interdependency
- Variety
- Ambiguity
- Fast Flux
- Global Mindset
- Cosmopolitanism
- Cognitive complexity
- Crisis change
- Reactive change
- Anticipatory change

Questions & Assignments

Questions

1. Identify the leadership approach of two companies, one that has been successful cross-culturally and one that has failed. Analyze and discuss the top five key personal characteristics and differences between these two leadership approaches. Were there other factors, besides personal characteristics, that caused leadership failure?
2. Review and discuss the concept of global mindset and its implications for organizational change.
3. Compare/contrast the influences of individualism or collectivism concepts on leadership.

Assignments

1. Develop a case study for a company whose leadership has been able to succeed in two countries with different cultural characteristics such as China and USA.
2. Select an MNE of your interest. What kind of crisis, reactive, and anticipatory changes might this enterprise have to deal with in the near future?
3. Take the Intercultural Effectiveness Scale (IES) survey from Aperian Global. Aperian charges a fee for the survey. Aperian websit: www.aperianglobal.com/modes-of-delivery/assessments-surveys/

Suggested Reading

Hewlett, S. (2016). *The attributes of an effective global leader.* Retrieved from https://hbr.org/2016/10/the-attributes-of-an-effective-global-leader

Shoji, K. (2019). *Changing times: Seiko eyes global luxury watch market as CEO takes iconic firm in a new direction.* Retrieved from https://www.japantimes.co.jp/news/2019/01/06/business/corporate-business/changing-times-seiko-eyes-global-luxury-watch-market-ceo-takes-iconic-firm-new-direction/

References

Asgary, N., & Mitschow, M. C. (2002). Toward a model for international business ethics. *Journal of Business Ethics, 36*(3), 239–246.

Bersin, J. (2012). It's not the CEO, it's the leadership strategy that matters. Forbes Magazine.

Friedman, T. L. (2000). *The Lexus and the olive tree: Understanding globalization:* Macmillan.

Haier.com. (2014). Haier Group Chairman & CEO, Zhang Ruimin, ranked among "The World's 50 Greatest Leaders." Retrieved from http://www.haier.com/uk/newspress/pressreleases/201404/t20140409_216131.shtml

Hempel, J. (2011). IBM's Sam Palmisano: A super second act. *Fortune Tech: Technology Blogs, News and Analysis.* Retrieved from http://fortune.com/2011/03/04/ibms-sam-palmisano-a-super-second-act/

Hofstede, G. (1984). *Culture's consequences: International differences in work-related values* (Vol. 5). SAGE.

Jones, R. J. B. (1995). *Globalisation and interdependence in the international political economy: rhetoric and reality.* London, England: Pinter.

Lane, H. W., Maznevski, M., Dietz, J., & DiStefano, J. J. (2012). *International management behavior: Leading with a global mindset* (6th ed.). London, England: Wiley.

Sethi, S. P. (2005). Investing in socially responsible companies is a must for public pension funds–because there is no better alternative. *Journal of Business Ethics, 56*(2), 99–129.

Son, Sabrina (Jun 12, 2017). *5 case studies about successful change management.* https://www.tinypulse.com/blog/sk-case-studies-successful-change-management

Steers, R. M., Sanchez-Runde, C. J., & Nardon, L. (2010). *Management across cultures: challenges and strategies:* Cambridge University Press.

Thomas, D. C., & Peterson, M. F. (2017). Cross-cultural management: Essential concepts. SAGE.

Vladimir Pucik, Katherine Xin, Donna Everatt, (2003). *Managing performance at Haier.* Retrieved from http://www.haieramerica.com/en

4

CURRENT ISSUES IN GLOBAL BUSINESS

12. Environmental Changes and Global Business

13. Disruptive Innovation and Global Business

14. Sustainability, Social Enterprise, and Impact Investment

CHAPTER 12

Environmental Changes and Global Business

LEARNING OBJECTIVES

- Understand the impact of **environmental changes** on global business
- Identify the **causes** of environmental changes
- Appreciate the **interconnections** between the environment and stakeholders
- Describe the aims and objectives of the **Rio, Kyoto**, and **Paris Agreements**
- Discuss climate change and its effects on businesses and the **global food supply**

Opening Case

Bentley University Sustainability Goals

Bentley University, one of the nation's leading business schools believes sustainability is everyone's business. Bentley is a private, not-for-profit higher education institution located in Waltham, Massachusetts. Its curriculum is a unique

Global Business, pages 247–266
Copyright © 2019 by Information Age Publishing
247

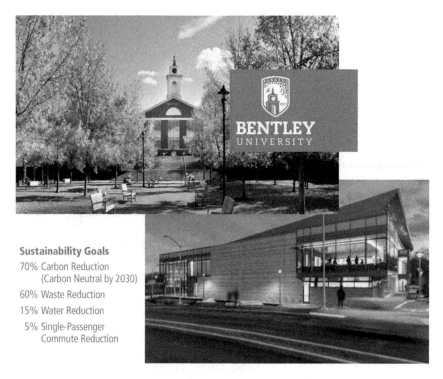

Sustainability Goals

70% Carbon Reduction
    (Carbon Neutral by 2030)
60% Waste Reduction
15% Water Reduction
5% Single-Passenger
    Commute Reduction

Figure 12.1   Bentley University. *Source:* Rebecca Bishop. Courtesy of Bentley University.

blend of business, technology, and liberal arts that utilizes an interdisciplinary approach to provide international leadership in business education and research. Students are encouraged to make connections between business and the environment while emphasizing the need for corporate social responsibility in increasingly transparent global markets. The university has become a champion for sustainability through educational, environmental, and social efforts, which created a wholly integrated and sustainable mind set community.

Presidents' Climate Commitment

Bentley University signed the Presidents' Carbon Commitment (PCC) in 2007 in order to address climate change. The university pledged to reduce their greenhouse gas emissions and achieve carbon neutrality by reducing emissions, increasing support for faculty and student research on sustainability issues, promoting extra-curricular sustainable activities and other actions. To achieve this goal, the university has made capital and operational commitments to the goals listed in the box.

The Bentley Arena is among the first collegiate ice arenas in the country to receive a LEED Platinum certification. It is also the first LEED certified building on Bentley's campus and has quickly become a symbol of the university's sustainability ambitions. Designed by Architectural Resources Cambridge and built by Suffolk Construction, this 76,000 square foot arena demonstrates how a space ubiquitously recognized as highly inefficient can be built sustainably.

Please see the case in the below link.

https://www.usgbc.org/sites/default/files/Bentley%20Case%20Study_October%202018.pdf

1. *Examine the feasibility of Bentley achieving its stated goal.*

2. *Describe and discuss feasibility for other higher education institutions planning similar goals.*

3. *Conduct a global comparison for higher education institutions in terms of their sustainability plan.*

4. *Draft a similar case study to this opening case for a for-profit organization and a not-for-profit organization.*

5. *From the profitability perspective discuss if these sustainability plans are financially viable?*

12.0 Introduction

In the past decades, environmental degradation has been identified as one of the main challenges humans face. Environmental degradation significantly impacts the quality of life for humans. Therefore businesses and governments need to be prepared to address such changes. The primary key issues are global warming, depletion of natural resources, and high population levels. Significant population growth and demand for goods and services in the last two centuries have been the most important changes that influence global warming. Therefore, controlling and reducing population growth should be seriously examined and public policies must address this issue.[1]

The repercussions of global warming will be felt by all nations, irrespective of their wealth and locations. Of course, the negative impact on developing countries is expected to be much higher than the impact on developed countries since they have more resources to mitigate the damage stemming from global warming. Global warming is also leading to political instabilities, migrations, draughts, hurricanes, and other harmful natural disasters. Many argue that the global society has been slow to recognize and react to these changes, and has been even slower and ineffective at taking corrective action.

Since the 1990s there have been twenty four **Conference of the Parties** (COP) sessions for the **United Nations Framework Convention on Climate Change** (UNFCCC). These conferences and gatherings attempt to converge on the reasons for global warming and develop action plans that are acceptable by most, if not the entire global community.

On December 12, 2015 at the 21st COP (COP 21) in Paris, over 190 countries agreed on an essential millstone to accelerate actions and investment required for a sustainable low carbon future. In the December 2018 meeting, COP 24, held in Katowice, Poland the objective was to focus on the implementation and acceleration of the COP 21 agreement. The main reason for convergence and agreement on global warming is the "tragedy of the commons" at its core. In other words, all stakeholders would benefit from preserving the common goods, but they do not agree to pay for its preservation and sustainability due to the fact that it is a common, shared resource.

12.1 The Tragedy of the Commons

The **United Nations Development Program** (UNDP) refers to **Global Commons** as the resources that are not within the authority of any country. These are resources such as the atmosphere, Antarctica, outer space, and the high seas. This means that these resources belong to all humanity, are the heritage of all, and are essential to all species on earth. Any group, company, and/or government that intentionally or unintentionally abuse these resources will impact species.[2]

Joseph Stiglitz defined the **Tragedy of the Commons** as follows: "When there is a common resource that can be used freely by all, each user fails to think about how his actions might harm others; each loses sight of the common good." (Stiglitz, 2006, p. 162). Most governments are moving toward setting up institutions to minimize the "tragedy of the commons" as the markets, when left unregulated, create negative externalities. These institutions are established in order to reduce the overuse of a public good through different methods such as privatizing the resources. The aim of a market system is to achieve a level of environmental goals through a supply and demand market. This system will work for some industries, but it has limitations and cannot achieve a global solution.

Governments have control over many essential natural resources that have positive or negative effects on global warming. For example, managing appropriate levels of fishing requires government agreements on rules, regulations, and enforcement. A market system does not work in this case. Global fishing companies around the world are extracting food resources from the oceans faster than they can be replenished. Not only this trend could destroy the aquatic ecosystem, but it also changes the genetic buildup of aquatic life. The average size of catch, across all species, is becoming smaller due to larger fish being removed from the reproductive cycle. This has led to a race to reach the areas with healthier and larger catch. This race in turn is a source of conflict between nations as they try to define their water boundaries to include these areas. In most cases, the wealthier and

SPOTLIGHT
Global Warming

According to Live Science (a science news website) global warming is defined as the "Gradual increase in the average temperature of the Earth's atmosphere and its oceans, a change that is believed to be permanently changing the Earth's climate." The ongoing debates among scientists, activists, and the general public are about what should be done to mitigate emissions, and how to implement possible solutions. Scientists, activists, and many governments are actively studying how to slow down global warming because they observe and forecast many negative impacts of global warning. However, there are global warming deniers who claim that global warming is not real and even call it a hoax. It is of utmost importance to examine the impact of global-warming on global business, especially its implications. Additionally, it is important to understand the different scientific perspectives on global-warming. For some of the latest scientific studies check the following links: https://www.hbo.com/vice; https://www.livescience.com/topics/global-warming.

The former U.S. Vice President Al Gore created a documentary regarding global-warming (https://www.youtube.com/watch?v=9lm2O6dzpUE).

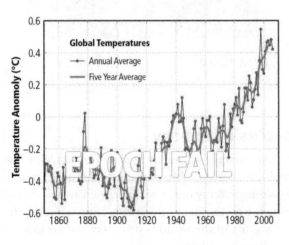

more powerful nations win this race at the expense of smaller nations who now face a food shortage. For example, one of the main reasons some of the Somalian fishermen have become pirates in coastal areas is due to the scarcity of fish nearby. Therefore, this situation has a significant impact on nations, fishing companies, restaurants, and other industries.

SPOTLIGHT
University Students Come and Go
in the Dense Air Pollution

The World Health Organization Global Conference on Air Pollution and Health (October 30–November 1, 2018) reported that "the combined effects of ambient (outdoor) and household air pollution cause about 7 million premature deaths every year, largely as a result of increased mortality from stroke, heart disease, chronic obstructive pulmonary disease, lung cancer and acute respiratory infections."

Based on

https://www.who.int/airpollution/en/

vtpoly/ CC BY-NC-ND 2.0

12.2 Sources of Energy

Jeffrey Sachs, the director of the Earth Institute, explains that the world's economy continues to grow, which means more energy is used.[3] For example, China's growing energy usage will increase the pace of carbon dioxide (CO_2) entering the atmosphere, which is a serious concern. In his opinion, the current trajectory of the world is very risky and reckless, and there are no significant changes in sight.

Figure 12.2, the total primary supply of sources of energy is shown. There is a significant growth over time from 1900 to 2016, which indicates a response to high demand. Due to the economic development in many parts of the world including China and India, the demand for energy has increased. All forms of energy supply have increased over time, including coal which is more harmful to the environment than some other sources of energy.

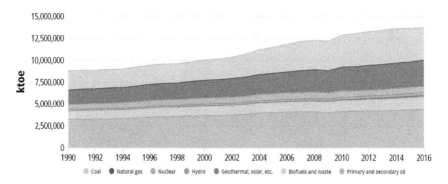

Figure 12.2 Primary Supplies of Sources of Energy: *Source:* IEA World Energy Balances 2018; https://webstore.iea.org/world-energy-balances-2018

12.3 Environmental Degradation: Causes and Solutions

Figure 12.3 illustrates some of the main causes of environmental degradation. The rise in urbanization and increased consumerism have been crucial in this process. This has led to an increase in emissions, power generation, and transportation. Figure 12.3 identifies eight sets of key factors that are at the heart of **environmental degradation**. In the process of this rapid urbanization and increased consumerism, very little attention has been paid to the negative impact. Now we have reached a critical stage in which we need to act to either by slowing down or by reversing the negative impact of environmental degradation. Therefore, nations, firms, and citizens need to significantly modify their rules and regulations, production processes, and consumption habits to reduce negative footprints in order to stop or reverse global warming.

In 1988, the United Nations created the Inter-governmental **Panel on Climate Change** (IPCC) of scientists to conduct research on climate change.[4] The panel brought together the world's leading experts to assess the scale of climate change and its impact. The IPCC published three studies between 1990 and 2001 and concluded that global warming was real and its effects were only getting worse. The following are some of the incontrovertible facts related to global warming:

1. Small changes in the global temperature have large effects;
2. The global temperature increased by 0.6 Celsius in the last century;
3. This rate of warming is unprecedented;
4. Sea levels have risen by 10–20 cm (4–8 inches) in the last century;

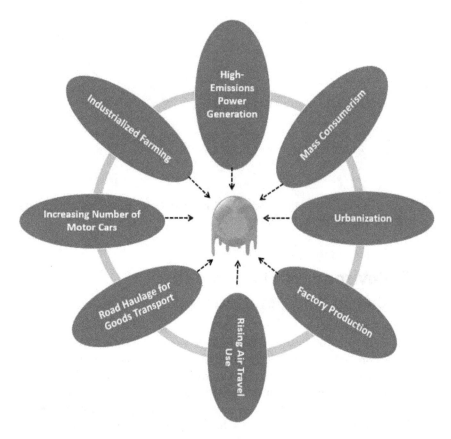

Figure 12.3 Causes of environmental degradation. (At the center of the figure is Natural Environment). *Source:* Morrison, 2017.

5. There has been a huge increase in the concentration of greenhouse gases;
6. The pace of change of the temperature could accelerate with even small increases in the level of greenhouse gases.

If we ignore these six facts, global warming will only increase and become a serious problem for future generations. A series of international meetings continues to study and address climate changes.

12.4 The Rio Earth Summit

In 1992, more than 100 heads of state gathered in Rio de Janeiro, Brazil to address some of these problems. While no emissions limit was set, the representatives of 153 countries (including the U.S.) decided to stabilize the levels of greenhouse gases in the environment in a manner that would "prevent dangerous anthropogenic interference with the climate system". This was in accordance with the United Nations Framework Convention on Climate Change. The charter was signed by all the countries involved and became the cornerstone in the international community's attempt to combat the most serious threat to our planet.

12.5 The Kyoto Protocol

A direct result of the **Rio Earth Summit** was the meeting in Kyoto, Japan during 1997. More than 150 countries converged in Kyoto as the final part of a series of meetings held to focus on the reduction of **greenhouse gas emissions** by industrialized nations. Their main aim was to devise a way of cutting emissions that was fair and efficient. In other words, they sought to minimize the economic cost of emissions and share the burden equitably among countries.

The **Kyoto protocol** made no immediate demand to developing nations, but called on developed nations to cut their emissions by specific amounts, based on their 1990 emissions, by 2012. Europe as a whole was given a target of 8%, Japan of 6%, and the United States of 7%. The Kyoto Protocol came into effect on Feb. 16, 2005. The reasoning behind this move was that developing countries could not be held responsible for the current levels of emission accumulation, which were mostly the result of the past actions of developed nations. The signees recognized that what they were enacting was not a perfect system, but that it was a significant start towards reducing emissions.

The agreement focused on reducing carbon dioxide, methane, nitrous oxide, hydrofluorocarbons, perfluorocarbons, and sulphur hexafluoride. Once a nation ratified the protocol they were required to work on reducing their output levels. The reductions in emissions were based on each country's baseline emissions, in the year 1990. If the countries were successfully reducing their emissions they were in compliance with the protocol, otherwise the country would have to buy carbon credits from other countries that were exceeding the reduction outlined for them.

The **carbon credits tradeable system** that was established placed a theoretical limit on the total amount of emissions that can be reached. By practically capping emissions, an international market of emissions exists so that nations with high emission levels can purchase the emission levels granted to nations that do not emit enough to necessitate the credits they have. The Kyoto Protocol established a market for trading these credits. The market is open to countries that ratified the Kyoto Protocol.

The Kyoto Protocol has three different mechanisms that allow nations to acquire the carbon credits (unfccc.int).[5]

1. Under Joint Implementation (JI) a developed country with relatively high costs of domestic greenhouse reduction would set up a project in another developed country.

2. Under the Clean Development Mechanism (CDM) a developed country can 'sponsor' a greenhouse gas reduction project in a developing country where the cost of greenhouse gas reduction project activities is usually much lower, but the atmospheric effect is globally equivalent. The developed country would be given credits for meeting its emission reduction targets, while the developing country would receive the capital investment and clean technology or beneficial change in land use.

3. Under International Emissions Trading (IET) countries can trade in the international carbon credit market to cover their shortfall in Assigned amount units. Countries with surplus units can sell them to countries that are exceeding their emission targets under Annex B of the Kyoto Protocol.[6]

These three mechanisms help developed nations with high emission levels find a place within the allocated cap to keep their required levels of emissions. These mechanisms have significant implications for international businesses and local businesses. Stiglitz (2006) stated that the Kyoto Protocol was a very nice guideline but was not successful due to the lack of sufficient enforcement mechanisms among member nations. However, the protocol did a great job at getting member nations to acknowledge there was a problem but failed to engage nations in actively reducing their emission levels.

12.6 Paris Agreement

As a follow up to the prior meetings and especially the Kyoto agreement, leadership from 175 countries gathered in Paris, in December 2015, and "reached a landmark agreement to combat climate change and to accelerate and intensify the actions and investments needed for a sustainable low carbon future."[7] For the first time, the **Paris Agreement** brought all nations into a "common cause to undertake ambitious efforts to combat climate change." In this agreement, allocating support to assist developing countries to combat climate change was a new course of action (Figure 12.4).

The central objective of the Paris agreement was to reinforce the global response to keep a global temperature rise well below 2 degrees Celsius. In other words, keep the temperature above pre-industrial levels in this century. Additionally, efforts to limit the temperature increase even further to 1.5 degrees Celsius were put in place. To achieve these primary objectives, countries agreed to collaborate and complement each other in this endeavor. The

Figure 12.4   Adoption of the Paris Agreement. *Source:* CC by 2.0, flickr/Creative Commons

Agreement also supports efforts to advance a transparency framework for action. This agreement has a significant impact on governments' policies, firm strategy, as well as on consumption and behavior patterns of consumers.

The objective of the 2015 agreement is twofold:[8]

1. To bind nations together into an effective global effort to reduce emissions rapidly enough to chart humanity's longer-term path out of the danger zone of climate change, while building adaptation capacity;
2. To stimulate faster and broader action now. To these ends, governments agreed to communicate their respective contributions towards the universal agreement well in advance of the meeting in Paris in 2015.

At the December 2018 UN Climate Change Conference in Poland, governments took essential decisions towards securing the implementation of the Paris 2015 Agreement as universal climate change. For the details of the agreement, please see https://unfccc.int/.

12.7 Business Implications of Climate Change

Saving the planet goes beyond just saving its climate. Energy production, food supply, and climate change are interconnected. Climate change is impacted by the world's energy needs, which in turn impact the world's food supply. The problems facing these global commodities and resources also need to be addressed. A regime's failure to provide citizens the basic needs for a good quality of life eventually leads to internal conflicts and potentially system changes. The Paris Agreement provides details about how to approach most of these issues.

12.7.1 Energy Market and Environment

Energy is the essential factor of production and is a necessity for modern societies. Our education, health, nutrition, transportation and communication systems all depend on it. In the last 150 years, we have heavily depended on fossil fuels as our primary source of energy. However, problems related to accessing fossil fuels, a decrease in the reserves, and the environmental damage caused by the acquisition and utilization has rendered it unsustainable. On the other hand, shifting away from fossil fuels can cause insufficiency in meeting current demands and there are huge costs associated with the structural changes that would need to be implemented for this shift to occur. In this context, the hope is that innovations in technology, especially renewable energy technology, will help decrease the costs of this shift.

An **energy crisis** can be defined as "a great strain in supply of energy sources in an economy." In the past few decades the global demand for energy has increased at an average rate of 1.6%. If countries continue on this path it is not implausible to conclude that a crisis will arise in the near future due to diminishing fossil fuels and increasing costs (Öztürk, Sözdemir, & Ülger, 2013). It is estimated that in the next 25–30 years, a major proportion of the increase in energy demands and use of fossil fuels will be attributed to developing nations.[9] The estimates state that from the global energy consumption only 14% will be used by OECD countries and 84% by non-OECD countries.[10] Thus, the majority of the increase in green-house gas emissions will be coming from non-OECD countries. Meeting current energy demands and assimilating current environmental costs are already proving to be a challenge for energy providers, and it is even more challenging in developing nations.

In the USA the shale gas revolution has gone a long way in easing the demand for energy in the country. European countries have begun to invest in fracking projects, even though these projects have potential negative externality effects. While there is some opposition to the fracking movement in the United States, it can be seen as a positive outcome. Figure 12.5 shows the annual energy outlook for 2005 with projections to 2025.

Recently the USA has been a net exporter of refined petroleum products and natural gas. Associated with these statistics is a vast degradation of the environment in areas where fracking occurs. These sources of energy have

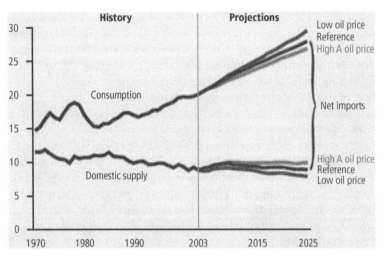

History: Energy Information Administration. Annual Energy Review 2003. DOE/ EIA-0384 (2003) (Washington, DC, September, 2004). Projections: Tables A11, C11, and D11. Note: Domestic supply includes domestic crude oil and natural gas plant liquids, other crude supply, other inputs, and refinery processing gain.

Figure 12.5 Petroleum Supply, Consumption, and Imports, 1970–2025 (million barrels per day). https://www.iea.org/statistics/

decreased prices, which benefit consumers financially in the short run. The scenario discussed here exemplifies the deadlock facing the energy crisis and the environment. Will the environment continue to be sacrificed to avoid the energy crisis? This question holds even more weight in today's world where the alternative of investing in renewable resources seems to be expensive. However, environmentalists, some governments, and activists are actively working on innovations to minimize harm to environment.

For most developing countries generating energy is even a bigger challenge. Many countries are still trying to provide electricity to all their citizens. Investing in green energy at a national level is too expensive. Money saved by using fossil fuels can instead be used towards other development projects. If they continue to use fossil fuels they will contribute to global warming. Any increase in their energy capacity built on fossil fuels will increase their emissions. If such countries were to face economic sanctions for polluting, as suggested by Joseph Stiglitz, the results for the people of the country could be harmful (Stiglitz, 2006).

Energy security is the "the relation between national security and achievement of natural resources for energy consumption". For an economy to function, it is very important to have a steady inflow of affordable energy. Energy can be seen as a strategic objective in a military sense. It can also be a strategic target in a military action by harming the enemy's energy infrastructure. There are some examples of these cases, especially in the Middle East, such as the conflict between Egypt, Israel, Britain, and France. The concentration of energy sources in certain areas and the military and civil interventions for controlling these areas have made the world energy supply sensitive and made the energy prices highly volatile. As the natural reserves of fossil fuels decrease and demand rises it will become more important for nations to obtain a supply, which is not only secure but is also not affected by high and inconsistent price fluctuations.

Energy security is an important goal of energy policy within the framework of sustainable energy development. The development of sustainable energy includes the diversification of energy supplies, energy autonomy, low levels of energy imports, efficient use of energy in the industry, the quality of energy supply, the suitable cost in energy supply, sufficient investment financing, and renewable contribution. The energy should be both adequate and sustainable for social, economic and military needs. Therefore, energy security is a basic prerequisite for sustainable development and that is good for global business.

The dominance of **fossil fuels** on energy production has caused serious problems globally and a few wars. Some of these problems related to current energy use are climate change caused by greenhouse gas emission, the breakdown of the ozone layer with the consequent increase in ultraviolet light levels, acid rains, the decrease in biodiversity, the increase in soil erosion, the contamination caused by industrial waste, and lifestyles.

However, the cost of building and operating **renewable energy** power plants, in terms of dollars per unit of electricity produced, can be higher than that of natural gas or coal plants (see Figure 12.6). Thus, this has been a major reason for the slow growth in the use of such technologies. Many renewable resources are only available on remote areas, which requires building transmission lines in order to deliver power to major areas. This process can be quite expensive and it is another major reason for the slow

Figure 12.6 Solar and wind technology. *Source:* flickr/Creative Commons.

SPOTLIGHT
TED Talk

Harald Haas is the pioneer behind a new technology that can communicate as well as illuminate. Harald and his team have pioneered a new technology that transmits data using light, bridging the digital divide.

https://www.ted.com/talks/harald_haas_a_breakthrough_new_kind_of _wireless_internet

adoption. Recent innovations in solar and wind technology combined with some government incentives are leading to the generation of renewable energy and increased competition among sources of energy. Environmentalist, scientists, and philanthropist are playing an active role in this domain and are changing the market system. For example, many households and businesses have installed solar panels. Also, around the world many private and public organizations are creating solar farms to generate electricity, which is environmentally friendly and helps improve quality of life in far places where it was not feasible before.

Below are some of the policies aimed at expanding renewable energy generation that have direct business implications.[11]

- *Tax credits* such as the Renewable Electricity Production encourage increased usage of eligible renewable sources.
- *Renewable Portfolio Standards* force electricity providers to supply a certain portion of their overall output through renewable sources.
- *Renewable Energy Certificates and Credits (RECs)*. Building these certificates/credits into the Renewable Portfolio Standards allows electricity providers to sell renewable energy certificates/credits.

12.8 Climate Change, the Energy Crisis, and Global Food Supply

Understanding the overall effect of **climate change** and **carbon dioxide increase** on our food supply is rather difficult. Climate change could make it more difficult to grow crops, raise animals, and catch fish in the same ways and same places as we have done in the past. Warmer water temperatures are likely to cause the habitat ranges of many fish and shellfish species to shift, which could disrupt ecosystems. The effects of climate change also need to be considered along with other evolving factors that affect agricultural production, such as changes in farming practices and technology.

The primary raw material of modern agriculture is fossil fuel. Advancement in agricultural technology has reduced the relative share of labor input in the production process for crops. Most modern agricultural practices use energy inputs in the form of fertilizers and pesticides, especially in developed countries. However, in most developing countries the agricultural process tends to be more rudimentary and with lower use of energy.

The **crop yield** is highly dependent on specific climate factors. For example, an increase in the average temperature and carbon dioxide levels can be beneficial for some crops, other factors such as the nutrient levels, soil moisture, and water availability also need to be considered. Shifts in weather patterns such as reduced precipitation or a short but heavy monsoon season will also reduce crop yield. Such changes will not only affect irrigation but will also have a large impact on soil quality. If these factors are not at an optimum level due to a drought or soil nutrients are washed away the crop yield will suffer. If the atmospheric temperature exceeds this optimal temperature, the yield will decrease. There are many regions of the world such as the Middle-East, many parts of Africa, the United States, and other locations where climate change has caused significant environmental damage that has led to migrations to urban areas.

Climate Change Effects on Global Food Supply

Agriculture. The success of a crop yield is highly dependent on specific climate factors. Therefore, an increase in the average temperature and carbon dioxide will lead to lower yield.

Livestock. Livestock are under a direct threat from heat waves, which are expected to increase due to global warming.

Fisheries. Many marine species have certain temperature ranges at which they can survive and the warming of seawater will have big negative impact on their reproduction.

Based on

https://19january2017snapshot.epa.gov/climate-impacts/climate-impacts
-agriculture-and-food-supply_.html

In sum, there is a connection between climate change, extreme weather, and health. The facts are given, but there must be more action by policymakers, private sectors, and consumers. Anything to reduce or eliminate the release of heat-trapping gases to the atmosphere will help slow the rate of warming. The TBL Connection case below is a good example of a private sector company addressing the negative impact of sediment and nutrients they generated.

Debate—Environmental Changes (EC) & Global Business (ECGB)

Pros (ECGB)

- It will impact most business operations globally.
- ECGB must be studied in higher education institutions.
- Public policies shall be developed to address the impact of EC on the quality of life.
- EC have and can potentially lead to wars, poverty, hunger, and migration.
- Governments shall have an active role in supporting the creation of renewable and clean energy to sustain human life.

Cons

- It will have very little impact on a small number of firms and industries.
- There is no need for higher education institutions to engage; firms will address any issues related to EC.
- No need for any public polices; the market will address it.
- EC have no direct impact on war, poverty, hunger, and migration.
- Governments shall not have any role in supporting the creation of renewable and clean energy.

12.9 Conclusion

This chapter, discussed the consequences of environmental changes on all aspects of human life and on the global business environment. The causes of environmental changes were also discussed. A summary of the actions stockholders could take to minimize the negative impact of climate change, and possibly reverse the course of global warming were provided. Global businesses, governments, and consumers need to seriously consider their footprint on the environment and proactively initiate practical solutions to clean the environment and apply environmentally friendly methods of development and lifestyle. Finally, initiating public policies that lead to population control shall be seriously examined.

TBL Connection—Land O'Lakes

Land O'Lakes SUSTAIN offers new precision technology to help Minnesota farmers protect water resources. The precision conservation-planning tool developed by Agren Inc., and Land O'Lakes, Inc., allows a conservation planner to custom-design crop field buffers to trap sediment and nutrients as water flows off a field. The Ag BufferBuilder tool uses site-specific soil information, 40 years of daily climate data and precise topography mapped by lasers to model the flow of water and sediment from a crop field. This technology identifies where a concentrated flow of water will be so farmers can strategically place buffers where they are needed. Farmers can install a variable-width buffer that achieves the same, or better, water quality protection using significantly less acreage than a 50-foot buffer.

Based on

https://www.precisionag.com/service-providers/tools-smart-equipment/
land-olakes-sustain-offers-new-precision-technology-to-help-minnesota
-farmers-protect-water-resources/

Chapter Review

Key Terms

- Climate Change
- Environment
- Renewable energy
- Stakeholders
- Rio Summit
- Kyoto Protocol
- Paris Agreement
- Energy crisis
- Energy security
- Global food supply
- Crop yield

Questions & Assignments

Questions

1. Describe some of the causes of environmental changes.
2. Discuss the impact of each stakeholder on the environment.
3. Analyze the interconnections between the environment and stakeholders.
4. Describe the role of global business in protecting the environment.
5. Discuss the successes and failures of the Rio and Kyoto agreements.

Assignments

1. Write a case study about the main objectives of the Paris Agreement for a developed country and a developing one.
2. Write a case study about two companies, one that proactively engages in addressing the negative impacts of climate change, and another one that does it reactively.
3. Analyze the relationship between oil from the Middle-East, wars, and climate. You could analyze this assignment by discussing the background of the First Gulf War in 1990 (Also known as the Kuwait War).
4. Draft a case and examine how environmental changes affect the global food supply.
5. Suggest five actions you could take to save the environment. Explain.

Notes

1. http://www.un.org/popin/icpd/conference/bkg/wppa.html
2. http://www.undp.org/content/undp/en/home.html–2015
3. Global Warming Effects: Jeffrey Sachs, Michael Mann: Video." Bloomberg.com. Bloomberg, n.d.
4. IPCC Third Assessment Report–Climate Change 2001–Complete online versions | GRID-Arendal–Publications–Other. https://rmets.onlinelibrary.wiley.com/doi/abs/10.1256/004316502320517344
5. https://unfccc.int/
6. https://unfccc.int/process/the-kyoto-protocol/mechanisms
7. https://unfccc.int/process-and-meetings/the-paris-agreement/what-is-the-paris-agreement
8. https://unfccc.int/process/conferences/the-big-picture/milestones/outcomes-of-the-warsaw-conference.
9. https://www.weforum.org/agenda/2017/10/fossil-fuels-will-dominate-energy-in-2040/
10. https://www.eia.gov/todayinenergy/detail.php?id=32912
11. https://www.eia.gov/energyexplained/?page=renewable_home

Suggested Reading

Global Warning, NASA report, https://climate.nasa.gov/causes/

Climate Change Threatens National Security Says Pentagon, https://unfccc.int/news/climate-change-threatens-national-security-says-pentagon

Montiel, Ivan; Antolin-Lopez, Raquel; Gallo, Peter Jack (2018). Emotions and Sustainability: A Literary Genre-Based Framework for Environmental

Sustainability Management Education. *Academy of Management Learning & Education, 17*(2), 155–183.

Wall-Tweedie, Joanna; Nguyen, Sheila N. (2018). Is the Grass Greener on the Other Side? A Review of the Asia-Pacific Sport Industry's Environmental Sustainability Practices. *Journal of Business Ethics, 152*(3), 741–761.

Sachs, Jeffrey, Columbia University Mailman School of Public Health https://sip

Global Warming Effects: Jeffrey Sachs, Michael Mann: Video." Bloomberg.com. Bloomberg.

Stiglitz, J. (2006). *Making globalization work.* New York, NY: Norton. https://unfccc .int/news/

References

Morrison, J. (2017). *The Global Business Environment: Challenges and Responsibilities* (4th ed.): Palgrave Macmillan.

Öztürk, S., Sözdemir, A., & Ülger, Ö. (2013). The real crisis waiting for the world: Oil problem and energy security. *International Journal of Energy Economics and Policy, 3*(S), 74-79.

Stiglitz, J. E. (2006). *Making globalization work.* New York, NY: Norton.

CHAPTER 13

Disruptive Innovation and International Business

LEARNING OBJECTIVES

- Describe the **disruptive innovation** and **disruptive technology** concepts
- Identify the **impacts** of technology on international business
- Describe the concept of **international business process outsourcing**
- Discuss how **green-technology** helps companies achieve a triple-bottom line

Opening Case

Pulling Carbon from the Air to Avert a Climate Catastrophe

At a major climate meeting in Poland, nearly 200 countries tried to reach a deal to dramatically reduce carbon emissions. However, a recent U.N. report

Global Business, pages 267–284
Copyright © 2019 by Information Age Publishing
All rights of reproduction in any form reserved.

found that reducing carbon emissions alone might not be enough to avoid dangerous impacts of global warming. In fact, it might be necessary to pull massive amounts of carbon dioxide out of the atmosphere.

According to the company Carbon Engineering, the process of capturing CO_2 starts with an "air contactor," which looks like an oversized semitrailer with a huge fan on top. In front, there is a black grill with a solution containing potassium hydroxide flowing down, so it sounds like a waterfall. Once the solution comes in contact with air, it captures and retains carbon dioxide in the form of micro pellets, which can later be injected into the soil.

This is another type of technology to address climate change. Nevertheless, there's no business model for such technology yet, thus the company is looking for profits to help its technology expand.

Excerpt from

https://www.npr.org/2018/12/10/673742751/how-1-company-pulls-carbon-from-the-air-aiming-to-avert-a-climate-catastrophe?utm_source=twitter.com&utm_medium=social&utm_campaign=npr&utm_term=nprnews&utm_content=2040

1. *Explore a possible business model for the technology described in the case.*

2. *Describe and discuss the challenges associated with carbon capturing technology.*

3. *What other types of carbon capturing technology are currently available in the market? Are they profitable? Investigate and elaborate.*

Figure 13.1 Peabody Energy. *Source:* Peabody Energy, Inc. https://commons.wikimedia.org/w/index.php?curid=34320064

13.0 Introduction

One of the driving factors for the expansion of international business activities, besides trade and foreign investment, has been the emergence of **Information and Communication Technology** (ICT). The emergence of ICT increased transparency, decreased the cost of information flow across boundaries, and increased the volume and speed of information flow (Samii, 2004). This trend has allowed Multinational Enterprises (MNEs) to benefit from locational advantages by networking activities and locations.

Information and Communication Technology flattened the international competitive environment, making it more balanced, which resulted in the rise of **emerging market multinational** (EMNEs) as major competitors for firms from developed economies. Access to market information, technologies, finance, and a competitive environment were instrumental in this respect (Friedman, 2006).

In a sense, information technology has disrupted the normal patterns of international business. While changes in the institutional environment, such as the establishment of the World Trade Organization, have facilitated international trade and investment, ICT has created structural changes in the pattern of trade and investment.

13.2 Disruptive Technology

What is disruptive technology? The concept of **Disruptive Technology** was first coined by Clayton Christensen in 1995 (Bower & Christensen, 1995). Later in his book *The Innovator's Dilemma* (Christensen, 1997) expanded the concept of disruptive technology to disruptive innovation. **Disruptive innovations** are those technologically based innovations that fundamentally change the structure of an industry. Innovators use technology to identify a niche segment of the market that established firms are not interested in because of low margins. However, with new technology, the neglected segment becomes a profitable low-cost business model for a new entrant into the industry. Over time, the segment improves and grows to the point of being an established competitor using a low-cost and a low-price strategy to force the incumbents to recognize them.

The main elements of disruptive innovation are the following:

a. Incumbents improve along the trajectory of sustainable innovation
b. Disruptive innovators exceed the market and customer requirements
c. Disruptive innovators have the capability to respond to disruptive threats, and
d. The incumbents stumble as a result of the disruption (King & Baatartogtokh, 2015).

The specific characteristics that make disruptive innovation successful include simplicity, convenience, accessibility, and affordability. These characteristics make the new industry segment more competitive against established segments of the industry that are high cost and complex.

13.2.1 Differentiating Sustainable Innovation and Disruptive Innovation

Sustainable innovations are those that improve the quality and performance of an existing product. Such technologies improve the competitive position of a firm within a certain industry. The continuous introduction of technology gives the existing firm an advantage in relation to its competitors. For established firms to sustain competitive advantage they must continuously use technology-based innovation to improve product quality.

On the other hand, the disruptive technology concept focuses on technologies that transform the industry. Disruptive technology aims at the low end of the market that established firms have not covered or that they do not have any interest in because of the low rate of return. Through new technology, innovators can develop the low end of the market.

In sum, while sustainable technology can improve the current product quality and is introduced by the incumbent firms to sustain their competitive advantage, the disruptive technology changes the structure of an industry by introducing more affordable products and services to the market. The existing literature on innovation suggests that innovation lies on a spectrum with disruptive innovations on one end of the spectrum and sustainable innovations on the other end (Cowden & Alhorr, 2013).

The incumbents and their customers normally view a disruptive innovation as an inferior product and reject it. Additionally, since in the early stage of the industry life cycle, the uncertainty and complexity are high, the established firms may not embrace the innovation or in the extreme case resist it. Moreover, established firms move along a path that focuses on incremental innovation and not disruption (**Path dependency theory of innovation**).[1] Therefore, established firms usually do not build barriers to entry against the new disruptive innovators.

Disruptive innovation should also be viewed from the value chain analysis perspective. For example, the concept of **build to order** was a disruptive business model adopted by Dell Computer back in the early 1990s. Dell came up with a system that reduced the inventory cost of operation. By focusing on a niche market initially, the new firms, in this case Dell did not incite competition from incumbent firms with higher financial resources, stronger name recognition, and greater network.

The question is how established firms compete against new firms entering the industry through innovative and disruptive technology. The options include; changing the process and values of the organization, creating an independent organization, acquiring a different organization (Christensen & Raynor, 2013). However, for MNEs, the process is different and the source is internal through their subsidiaries (Cowden & Alhorr, 2013).

The capabilities of a firm include the ability to identify, integrate, develop and configure their own competencies and resources to innovate (Teece, 1997). However, path dependency capabilities create obstacles to change to radically new technologically driven innovation. This is called a **capability misfit**. A capability misfit has a direct relation with disruptive innovation (Habtay & Holemen, 2012).

The theory of disruptive innovation has received considerable attention both from scholars and from business executives. Indeed, the theory is considered as one of the most important to contribute to the understanding of how innovation and technology affect business and industries. The Economist has called the concept of disruptive innovation "one of the most influential modern business ideas" (Economist, A third industrial revolution, December 2018).

Nonetheless, there are still questions about the empirical work on which the theory was based. The empirical analysis showed that only 9% of firms meet all four elements of the disruptive innovation theory (King & Baatartogtokh, 2015).

13.2.2 Disruptive Innovation in International Business

The dependence of MNEs on their subsidiary networks makes them resistant to disruptive innovation. At the same time, such dependence provides an opportunity for transferring disruptive innovations across locations. The networks are both external and internal to the organization. While feedback from customers does not necessarily lead to disruptive innovation in each market, it can potentially provide disruptive innovation across a region. The learning potential among subsidiaries can lead to information that with technological usage could lead to disruption in other markets. According to Cowden and Alhorr (2013), for MNEs that pursue disruptive innovation, the following applies:

1. More disruptive innovation will be discovered through the firm's internal network rather than through open networks.
2. More disruptive innovations will be discovered in subsidiaries than in the parent company.

3. More disruptive innovations will be discovered in subsidiaries that pursue local market initiatives.
4. For subsidiaries that pursue local market initiatives, more disruptive innovation will be discovered in those located in emerging markets.

The above propositions still need empirical proof. However, they point to interesting aspects regarding the relationship between the parent company and a subsidiary in terms of the development of knowledge and technology sharing. The propositions also allude to the establishment of channels and a corporate culture that would improve the flow of information from the headquarters to network of subsidiaries, and vice-versa, from the subsidiaries to the headquarters.

13.2.3 Technology Innovating in International Business

Disruptive innovation, as explained earlier, is an **industry-based theory**. The theory explains how new technologically driven innovation changes the structure of an industry. However, the theory can be applied to other circumstances. For example, in international business there has been a number of important developments that were brought about by innovation in information and communication technology. One such development has been the emergence and growth of International Business Process Outsourcing.

SPOTLIGHT
Amazon

Jeff Bezos established amazon.com as an online bookstore in 1994. Later it diversified into an online platform offering videos, music, audio books, computer games, and eventually selling a full range of consumer products online.

Amazon has become a multinational company that has disrupted the traditional brick and mortar retailing by pioneering e-commerce. With revenues of over $177 billion dollars in 2017, and innovation as a core competency, Amazon has moved to other technology areas including cloud computing and artificial intelligence.

Amazon has also considered delivery of packages using drones, which if successful would change the way mail and packages are delivered.

Based on

https://en.wikipedia.org/wiki/History_of_Amazon

International Business scholars have argued that the internalization of activities creates value added for firms and particularly for firms involved in international operations since it reduces the transaction cost of operation. The internalization argument is based on the **transaction cost theory**. Through internalization a firm can reduce transaction costs. It is argued that organizations use a range of intermediate inputs and generate a range of intermediate outputs. It is the market for these intermediate inputs and outputs that may be internalized (Buckley & Casson, 2009) However, technological development has created the potential for cost reduction through outsourcing and partnership.

The **information technology revolution** brought three important dimensions into the global business environment and operations.

1. It led to an increase in transparency regarding market structures, business environments, and institutional factors.
2. It has resulted in a decrease in the cost of information acquisition.
3. It has resulted in an increase in speed and volume of information flows both internally and externally. In fact, the expectation is that information exchange should be instantaneous and **just-in-time** (M. Samii & Karush, 2004).

While information and communication technology has had major advantages, it has also some *disadvantages*. The two most important drawbacks are:

1. *Unreliable Information.* Although the various search engines currently available have helped in disseminating information, it is still a complex process to find how reliable and dependable the information obtained online is. In many cases misinformation is circulated either purposely (i.e., inflation of data by various countries) or unconsciously (i.e., misinterpretation of information).
2. *Expectation of Quick and Immediate Responses.* The expectation of fast replies could lead to reactionary responses without much thought or analysis.

Notwithstanding these shortcomings, the ICT has revolutionized international business activities.

13.3 International Business Process Outsourcing

Another important impact of ICT has been the rise in global business process outsourcing. **Outsourcing** refers to the procurement of selected value-adding activities, including the production of intermediate goods of finished products, from external independent suppliers (Cavusgil, Knight, & Riesenberger, 2011). **Business process outsourcing** specifically relates to the outsourcing of business services such as accounting, customer services, data maintenance, and payroll among others. There are important considerations regarding outsourcing decisions:

1. *Core Competency.* The **core competency concept** introduced by Prahalad and Hamel claimed that core competencies are the collective learning in the organization, and especially the know-how to coordinate diverse production skills and integrate multiple streams of technology (Prahalad & Hamel, 1999). Firms should focus their resources and capabilities on a set of core competencies, which result in unique benefits for customers and outsource activities for which the firm does not have a strategic need nor special capabilities. Effective core competencies are a skill and knowledge set (not a product), flexible, long term platforms that are capable of adaptation or evolution, limited in number, and a unique source of leverage in the value chain. Additionally, competencies occur in areas that a company can dominate, are important to customers in the long run, are embedded in the organization's system, and create key strategic barriers (Quinn & Hilmer, 1994).

2. *Cost.* Outsourcing can also reduce the cost of the firm's operation. In the operational areas that provide support for other functional and operational aspects the firm may not have economies of scale or specialization, therefore, despite the benefits of internalization, it may have a cost disadvantage. In such a situation, outsourcing an activity to external firms that specialize in these activities can reduce the cost. Moreover, using internal sourcing implies that the firm is using captive supplies whereas through outsourcing, it can ask for competitive bids with a lower price.

3. *Gain in Flexibility.* Outsourcing provides flexibility for the firm by adjusting the contract depending on the needs. Such adjustment could be driven either by changes in customer or operational requirements or changes in the scale of the operation.

Nevertheless, most of discussion has been focused on local outsourcing both for control and communication purposes. However, technological innovation that makes communication fast and cheap across geographic regions has made businesses more cost effective by outsourcing internationally. The emergence of Bangalore in India is a testimony of the importance of innovation and technology in this region. This has created opportunities for firms to reduce cost and deliver activities on a timely basis to their customers in their home country. At the same time, it has benefited the host country by creating local employment, and through spillover effects on other industries and regions.

An advantage of disruptive innovation is that it is based on a relatively simple technology platform. It generally faces lower market entry barriers, and in many cases, it relies on open network and collaboration. This helps ideas to be implemented quickly. In the early stages, there is a distinct advantage for entrepreneurs and a major disadvantage for large multinational enterprises that are very bureaucratic.

13.4 Emerging Technologies and International Business Activities

Technology development and innovation is a dynamic process. New technologies will reshape the future of business and particularly international business. For example, technology can redefine the traditional division of labor. A study by the McKinsey Global Institute (McKinsey, May 2013) identified twelve potential technologies that can potentially change the future of international trade and international business. These technologies are listed below:

- Mobile Internet
- Automation of Knowledge
- The Internet of Things (IOT)
- Cloud Technology
- Advanced Robotics
- Autonomous and Near-Autonomous Vehicles
- Next Generation Genomics
- Energy Storage
- 3D Printing
- Advanced Materials
- Advanced Oil and Gas Exploration and Recovery
- Renewable Resources

13.4.1 Distance Will Matter Even Less

ICT has made distance less relevant. Cairncross argues that the death of distance loosened the grip of geography but it has not destroyed importance of distance (Cairncross, 2001). The use of email, file transfers, and more recently, social media have changed the way business is done. Although in international business institutional factors such government regulation, culture, and local competition remain important in setting geographic boundaries, information and communication technology has diminished the relevance of distance.

Emerging technologies, particularly the internet of things, and cloud technology further reduce the importance of distance. The **Internet of Things**, which is a low-cost network that monitors, collects data, and optimizes processes between various devices, is not affected by the location of various devices, and can expedite cross-border commerce. These days, subsidiaries located across the globe are integrated with other international locations for sales, warehouses, and production units across in a complex system. All this is done automatically in a way that minimizes time and cost. The cost savings in terms of human cost, inventory maintenance, and avoiding delays in customs clearance are substantial.

13.5 Green Energy

Advances in oil and gas exploration technologies, partly in response to higher oil prices, has changed the structure of the oil market and the pattern of oil trading. For example, the United States had been a major importer of oil, but in 2018, became a net oil exporter. This is partly due to technological developments, such as horizontal drilling and fracking. These new technologies helped increase supply of oil and thus lowered oil prices. More importantly, they have reduced the dependency on oil from high-risk regions of world. However, the dependency on hydrocarbons and fracking are criticized due to the potential adverse and harmful effects on the environment.

One advantage of high oil prices has been the emergence of **renewable energy** such as solar and wind energy. Renewable energy not only provides a long term and sustainable source of energy, but they are also environmentally friendly and non-polluting.

Solar and wind energy will become important components of the future energy mix. Their share in the future energy mix, however, depends on the profitability of the energy industry, government subsidies, the price of oil, and the rate of technological innovation to lower the cost for consumers.

Solar Energy. Solar energy is either generated by household solar panels or by solar farms. The residential solar panels help the environment, and are also cost effective in the long run. Over time, the electricity cost increases due to increases in the cost of oil. However, after the initial capital investment, the cost of energy from installed solar panels remains negligible.

Solar farms have become the commercial way of providing green and clean energy. Normally, the construction of solar farms takes approximately four months from start to finish. A typical solar farm requires 36 acres of land with only one third being covered by solar panels.

Wind Energy. Wind energy is created by using wind turbines. There are mainly three types of wind turbines; the large-scale ones create over 100 Kilowatts, small turbines for household or farms, and offshore turbines, which create considerably more energy than onshore ones. The functionality of a turbine depends on the wind speed. The criticism of wind farms (and solar farms) is that they are not aesthetically pleasing, and several communities oppose their establishment in their communities.

Solar and wind energy also provide a great opportunity for firms to provide alternative sources of energy part of their strategy. According to McKinsey, "The incremental impact of solar and wind technology, after netting the cost of government subsidies, could potentially be $165 billion to $275 billion a year by 2025."[2] This potential should not be overlooked.

Finally, technologies that lead to energy saving are important in reducing the dependency on hydrocarbons and their adverse influence on the environment. The development of electrical vehicles is an example of a potential technology that will be important for a more sustainable energy mix.

13.6 Cloud Technology

Cloud computing is the practice of using networks of remote servers on the internet to manage and store data (see Figure 13.2). Some of the benefits of cloud computing are cost, speed, global scale, productivity, performance, and reliability. Cloud computing provides three different but related services:

1. Software as a Service;
2. Platform as a Service; and
3. Infrastructure as a Service (e.g., renting IT infrastructure) (Elmonem, Nasr, & Geith, 2016).

Cloud computing has restructured the cost configuration of software. Rather than purchasing software, with cloud computing, software is obtained through **subscription**. The ability to have "per user" rates relieves institutions from license management, overhead, and potential piracy. **Piracy** is one of the major concerns of software companies, particularly

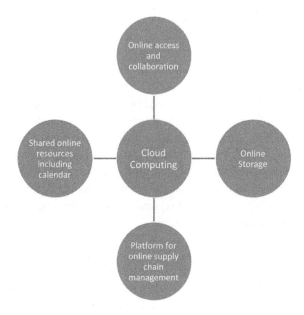

Figure 13.2   Cloud computing.

internationally, because Intellectual Property Rights (IPR) protection is typically lacking.

Cloud computing is an on-demand platform that provides the opportunity for **scalability** for multinational firms that require IT service availability for their offshore units. The **connectivity** capability and ability to share information across the globe is also important since it helps to enhance productivity within the firm, and more importantly with the firm's suppliers, customers, and partners. While the internet has reduced the distance, cloud computing provides simultaneous communication and information sharing across globe. A project set on a cloud offers the opportunity for various team members to work on an assignment where each team's input is included and recorded for others to see. Another example is the use in global supply chain management inventory structures on a cloud so that each unit in a different country sees what part is needed, where in the world the part is, and how long it takes to deliver it.

Just as cloud computing has helped sharing *information* across globe; **3-D printing** has helped spread the creation and sharing of *objects*. Economists have called cloud computing the "third industrial revolution"[3] and claim that some manufacturing related to 3-D printing will return to rich countries. They argue that as the cost of producing goods by 3-D printing decreases below wages and other production costs in emerging economies, production will return to developed economies. In this scenario, the wage rate differential becomes less relevant, and by producing products through 3D printing, the foreign country risk is considerably reduced.

13.7 Artificial Intelligence (AI)

Machine learning is a branch of artificial intelligence. In this case, a machine relies on data to determine patterns and make decisions with minimal human involvement. What has led to machine learning is the growing volume of information, data, and the reduced cost of data storage. Machine learning is used in product development, marketing, and decision-making. For example, interactive toys recognize questions and can answer them through an internet connection. Perhaps the most popular such gadget is Alexa marketed by Amazon. It plays music, gives information about the weather, keeps a daily schedule, turns lights on-off, connects to a house thermostat, and many other activities.[4]

In a more macroeconomic dimension, AI affects the type and quality of economic growth. This has the following implications for international trade.

1. It improves productivity;
2. It provides investment in technology; and
3. It incentivizes better technological innovation

Nevertheless, at the same time AI expands automation and speeds up job losses for low skilled and blue-collar workers (Bughin, J. 2018)

AI is already impacting **global value chains** (GVC). AI not only improves the predictability for demand of various products, but it also helps to determine inventory levels and networking of each facility in different locations

---

SPOTLIGHT
GE Power

In their attempt to deliver energy into the 21st century, GE Power uses big data, machine learning and the Internet of Things (IoT) technology to build an "internet of energy." Advanced analytics and machine learning enable predictive maintenance and power, operations and business optimization to help GE Power work toward its vision of a "digital power plant."

Based on

https://www.forbes.com/sites/bernardmarr/2018/04/30/27-incredible -examples-of-ai-and-machine-learning-in-practice/#7d9bacb87502 across globe. Cost cutting through just-in-time and warehouse management are also specific benefits.

AI will also affect the **global division of labor**. Machine learning will shift economic growth towards the knowledge economy and reduce demand for low skill workers. This not only will happen in developed economies but globally. Historically, it is argued that the main benefit of international trade is the reduction in the wage differential between developed and developing economies with automation and reduction in demand for low skilled workers jobs will be returning to developed economies that have capital and technology to invest in machine learning (Meltzer, Decemeber 13, 2018).

13.8 The Digital Divide

While technology and AI has the potential to contribute significantly to the economic growth of countries and significantly increase the profitability of MNEs, it also has the potential to create a gap in the income and the economic condition of the haves and have-nots. The term **digital divide** refers to the gap in access to communication and information technology. The gap is noticeable between countries and even within countries. This information technology gap leads to the economic gap between the two groups.

In a study by the McKinsey Global Institute, countries were divided into four categories:

1. *Active Global Leaders*—United States and China
2. *Economies with Strong Competitive Strength*—Korea, and Sweden
3. *Economies with Moderate Foundation*—Italy and Brazil
4. *Economies that Need to Strengthen Foundation*—Pakistan and Zambia

The study also finds that AI can significantly enable growth in advanced economies, such as Sweden (*Notes from the AI frontier modeling the AI impact on the world economy*, 2018).

Debate—Impact of Technology

Pros

- *Economic Growth.* IT helps individual countries grow economically.
- *Efficiency.* IT can help optimize the use of a firm's factors of production.
- *Job Creation.* The technology industry has created a number of high paying jobs.
- *Environmentally Friendly.* IT has contributed to the development of clean energy and energy saving industries.

Cons

- *Increases Inequality.* IT has helped increase the digital divide due to the absence of adequate infrastructure and low levels of technical education.
- *Upsets the Division of Labor.* Automation may have negative effects on the division of labor.
- *Loss of Jobs.* Loss of low-skill jobs to machines.
- *Environmentally Harmful.* IT may have a negative environmental impact, as in the case of fracking or horizontal drilling.

13.8 Conclusion

Technology has had a profound effect on international business, the environment, and more generally in our way of life. This chapter explored only a few of the technological developments and their impacts and by no means claims to be comprehensive. Yet, the potential of disruptive impacts that innovation can have on changing the way business is conducted is always there. Technology provides opportunities but also challenges for the future.

TBL Connection

Renewable energy, especially solar and wind power will play an important role in the future energy mix and make a major contribution to the overall world economic growth. McKinsey estimated that the "Solar and wind power could represent 15 to 16 percent of global electricity generation in 2025." The incremental economic impact of this growth could be $165 billion to $275 billion annually by 2025. Of this, $145 billion to $155 billion could be the direct value added to the world economy from this power, less the cost of subsidies. The remaining $20 billion to $120 billion per year reflects the possible value of the reduction in CO_2 emissions" (McKinsey, May 2013).

Several international companies have taken advantage of this opportunity. One such a company is Vogt solar. Vogt Solar is a company involved in building solar farms the UK. The solar farms typically generate around five MWp enough clean energy to power approximately 1,200 homes, with a CO_2 saving of around 500 g/kWh or CO_2 saving of 55,000 tons over the 25-year lifetime.

To learn more, visit:

https://vogtsolar.co.uk/de/home/why-solar/solar-farms/

Chapter Review

Key Terms

- Information and Communication Technology (ICT)
- Disruptive Innovation
- Capability Misfit
- Transaction Cost Theory
- Business Process Outsourcing
- Core Competency Concept
- Internet of Things
- Renewable Energy
- Solar Energy
- Wind Energy
- Cloud Computing
- Machine Learning
- Artificial Intelligence
- Digital Divide

Questions & Assignments

Questions

1. What is disruptive innovation and how is it different from innovation?
2. In the recent past ICT has had a profound impact on the way business is done internationally. Give an example of the effect of ICT on international business.
3. What are some of the positive impacts of new technologies on the environment? Provide examples.
4. What is the digital divide, and why does it have to be addressed with regards to economic development?

Assignments

1. Determine the potential impact of Artificial Intelligence, AI, on international business particularly in various activities of multinational firm along the value chain.
2. There are many efforts toward the elimination of the digital divide. Using resources such as online tools or your local library, describe at least three efforts (such as a fundraising event) in this direction.

Notes

1. Path dependency theory argues that past preference for product and services can are important in the determination of the future pattern of demand,

even if new products and service are available. That is the future behavior is determined by the past preferences that resists the new products or technology (JH Lim, 2011)

2. McKinsey, 2013: *Disruptive technologies: Advances that will transform life, business, and the global economy*
3. *The Economist.* "A third industrial Revolution," December 2012
4. For an interesting discussion of AI in international Business please see https://www.mckinsey.com/featured-insights/artificial-intelligence/notes -from-the-ai-frontier-modeling-the-impact-of-ai-on-the-world-economy

Suggested Reading

McKinsey. (May 2013). *Disruptive technologies: Advances that will transform life, business, and the global economy.*

Christensen, C. M. (1997). *The Innovator's Dilemma.* New York, NY: Harper Collins.

Christensen, C. M., & Raynor, M. (2013). *The innovator's solution: Creating and sustaining successful growth.* Harvard Business Review Press.

References

Bower, J. L., & Christensen, C. M. (1995). Disruptive Technologies: Catching the Wave. *Harvard Business Review*(January–February), 43–53.

Buckley, P. J., & Casson, M. C. (2009). The internalisation theory of the multinational enterprise: A review of the progress of a research agenda after 30 years. *Journal of International Business Studies, 40*(9), 1563–1580.

Cairncross, F. (2001). The Death of Distance: How the Communications Revolution Is Changing. Cambridge, MA: *Harvard Business School Publishing.*

Cavusgil, S. T., Knight, G., & Riesenberger, J. (2011). *International Business: The New Realities* (3rd edition ed.). Boston, MA: Pearson.

Christensen, C. M. (1997). *The Innovator's Dilemma.* New York, NY: Harper Collins Publishing.

Christensen, C. M., & Raynor, M. (2013). *The innovator's solution: Creating and sustaining successful growth*: Harvard Business Review Press.

Cowden, B. J., & Alhorr, H. S. (2013). Disruptive innovation in multinational enterprises. *Multinational Business Review, 21*(4), 358–371.

Elmonem, M. A. A., Nasr, E. S., & Geith, M. H. (2016). Benefits and challenges of cloud ERP systems–A systematic literature review. *Future Computing and Informatics Journal, 1*(1–2), 1–9.

Friedman, T. L. (2006). *The world is flat: The globalized world in the twenty-first century*: London, England: Penguin.

Habtay, S. R., & Holemen, M. (2012). From disruptive technology to disruptive business model innovation: In need for an integrated conceptual framework. *Creativity and Innovation Management.*

JH Lim, T. S., TS Wirjanto. (2011). path dependency of dynamic information techology capapbilitiy: An imperical investigtion. *Journal of Management,* 45–84.

King, A. A., & Baatartogtokh, B. (2015). How useful is the theory of disruptive innovation? *MIT Sloan Management Review, 57*(1), 77.

McKinsey. (May 2013). *Disruptie technologies: Advances that will transform life, business, and the global economy.* Retrieved from

Meltzer, J. (Decemeber 13 2018). *The impact of artificial intelligence on international Trade.* Retrieved from

Notes from the AI frontier modeling the AI impact on the world economy. (2018). Retrieved from

Prahalad, C. K., & Hamel, G. (1999). The core competence of the corporation *Knowledge and strategy* (pp. 41–59): Elsevier.

Quinn, J. B., & Hilmer, F. G. (1994). Strategic outsourcing. *MIT Sloan Management Review, 35*(4), 43.

Samii, M., & Karush, G. (2004). *International Business and Information Technology: Interaction and transformation in the global economy.* Psychology Press.

Samii, M. a. K., G. (2004). *International Business and Information Technology.* New York, NY: Routlege.

Teece, D., Pisano, G., Shuen, A. (1997). Dynamic capabilities and strategic management. *Strategic Management Journal,* 509–533.

CHAPTER 14

Sustainability, Social Enterprise, and Impact Investment

LEARNING OBJECTIVES

- Describe the history and the concept of **sustainable development**
- Understand the advantages and challenges of **sustainability assessment frameworks**
- Identify common **sustainability assessment indices**
- Define **Social Enterprise** and **Impact Investing**

Opening Case

Divine Chocolate: Cocoa Fair Trade

Divine Chocolate Limited is a unique chocolate producer. The company is an international social enterprise that is 44% owned by farmer cooperatives in

Global Business, pages 285–301
Copyright © 2019 by Information Age Publishing

Figure 14.1   Divine Easter Eggs. *Source:* https://www.flickr.com/photos/wheatfields/2310153414/in/photolist-5bXnzq-XPryAJ-4w998h-7b2zeF

Kuapa Kokoo, Ghana. Kuapa Kokoo stands for "good cocoa growers" and its mission is to empower farmers in their work, increase women's participation in all the activities of the cooperatives, and develop environmentally friendly and sustainable processes for the cultivation of cocoa. Beyond passing 44% of its profits to the cooperatives' members, the organization pays the Fairtrade premium of $2,000 per ton of cocoa. Farmers then democratically decide how to spend the Fairtrade premiums. The proceeds have been previously used for skills and training initiatives, community improvements including water wells, schools, and clinics, as well as bonuses for farmers.

The first ever Divine Chocolate bar was sold in United Kingdom's confectionary market in 1998. In 2007, a sister company was set up in the United States. Today, customers can purchase delicious Divine Chocolate online. For its continued growth and impact, Divine Chocolate won several awards including the Guardian's Sustainable Business Award for Social Impact Innovation in 2015.

For more information, visit the company's website: http://www.divinechocolate.com/us/about-us

Based on

https://www.theguardian.com/sustainable-business/2015/apr/30/cocoa-farmers-spread-the-taste-for-divine-chocolate; http://www.divinechocolate.com/us/

https://www.britishcouncil.org/society/social-enterprise/news-events/news
-international-social-enterprise-champions

1. *What characteristics make Divine Chocolate a social enterprise?*

2. *Investigate and describe the requirements to obtain a "Fair Trade" designation.*

14.0 Introduction

The demand for businesses to conduct their operations in a sustainable manner is continuously increasing. Nowadays companies are expected to support and advance the interests of their stakeholders. This trend has resulted in the development of concepts such as business ethics, corporate social responsibility (CSR), discussed earlier, and also concepts such as sustainability and social enterprise. The opening case of the chapter showcases a company with a mission to empower farmers, and develop environmentally-friendly means for the cultivation of cocoa. In the era of global transparency consumers are informed and reward companies that are sustainable, ethical and socially responsible.

This chapter discusses sustainable development, the Global Reporting Initiative (GRI) framework, social enterprise, Social Return on Investment (SROI), and impact investing concepts and their influence on businesses.

Corporations deal with a wide variety of sustainability issues in their operations, directly or indirectly. Advances in technology have allowed for more efficient equipment, machines, buildings, and other devices which need less energy to keep running. Technology has also allowed for safer processing of industrial waste that can be toxic to the environment.

14.1 Sustainable Development

Similarly, to the concept of corporate social responsibility, the concept of sustainable development is present in discussions about economic development and the environment. That, however, has not always been the case. In 1972, Donella Meadows, Dennis Meadows, Jørgen Randers, and William Behrens III (1972) published their well-known book titled *Limits to Growth* in which they demonstrated that population and economic growth increase exponentially but are limited by the resources available. When this concept was presented, the idea of sustainable development was unknown. However, in retrospect, what the authors described in their book was the early alarm that initiated the drive for sustainable development (Meadows, Meadows, Randers, & Behrens Iii, 1972; Meadows, Randers, & Meadows, 2004).

It was only after the 1972 United Nations Conference on the Human Environment in Stockholm, when the terms **environmentally sound development** or **eco-development** began to be used more frequently and sustainability gained popularity. Although back in the 70s these concepts were not accurately defined, it was obvious that the type of development implied by the term **eco-development** and sustainable development were different from the type of development discussed until then (Daly, 1997).

In the early 1980s, the first major breakthrough in conceptual insight came from the formulation of the *World Conservation Strategy* by the International Union for Conservation of Nature (IUCN),[1] the World Wildlife Fund (WWF), and the United Nations Environment Program.[2]

The debate provided a platform that allowed for the addition of a range of issues such as efficiency, distribution of equity, conservation, resource management and inter-generational responsibility that had not been included before.

In the late 1980s the term "sustainable development" began to gain wide acceptance after its appearance in a document called *Our Common Future,* also known as the *Brundtland Report* published in 1987 by the Brundtland Commission (or the World Commission on Environment and Development, WCED). This report is considered to be the milestone that started the process of re-thinking the established ways of living and governing by introducing the idea that sustainable development can be achieved through governance and society's involvement (Sachs, 2006; Stiglitz, 2006). In addition, some economic, social, and political prerequisites for sustainable development were identified. The report also provided the most commonly accepted definition of **sustainable development**—"development that meets the needs of the present without compromising the ability of future generations to meet their own needs" (Brundtland, 1987; Trzyna, 1995).

The strength of the sustainable development concept is that it reflects a change in the vision of how the economic activities of human beings relate to a finite environment. A condition of sustainable development is that the regeneration of raw materials and the absorption of waste are kept at ecologically sustainable levels. In other words, the regeneration and waste absorption of resources should be in equilibrium. This shift of thought involves the replacement of the standard economic quantitative measures of expansion such as economic growth with qualitative societal and environmental norms as the way to move forward. However, this shift is resisted by most economic and political institutions which are founded on traditional quantitative growth (Brundtland, 1987; Moran, Wackernagel, Kitzes, Goldfinger, & Boutaud, 2008; Trzyna, 1995).

> ## SPOTLIGHT
> ## The UN General Assembly
>
> The UN General Assembly's Second Committee (Economic and Financial) meets every year to debate issues related to the 2030 Agenda. For example, in 2017 member states stressed the importance of strong educational systems that promote sustainable development; enhanced cooperation in support of the most vulnerable countries; ratification and expedited implementation of the Paris Agreement on climate change; and localization of the Sustainable Development Goals (SDGs) at grassroots levels. In 2018, the discussion focused on disaster risk reduction, the rights of future people, desertification, biological diversity, harmony with nature, renewable energy, sand and dust storms, and radiation threats.
>
> *Based on*
>
> https://sdg.iisd.org/news/second-committee-concludes-sustainable -development-debate/
>
> https://sdg.iisd.org/sdgs/

At the macro level, sustainable development commonly relates to the concept of the **triple bottom line** (TBL) (Pope, Annandale, & Morrison-Saunders, 2004):

1. Economic growth (Profit)
2. Social equity (People)
3. Protection of the Environment (Planet)

The basis of the **economic component** is the principle that the well-being of a society has to be maximized and poverty has to be eradicated through the efficient use of natural resources (Redclift, 1987). The **social component** deals with the relationship of the society with the economy and the environment. Such relationship is very broad and includes issues such as the welfare of people, the access to basic health and education services, minimum standards of security, and respect for human rights. It also refers to the development of various cultures, diversity, and pluralism. The issue of equitable distribution of benefits and access to resources is an essential component of both the economic and social dimensions of sustainable development.

It is better to tackle the economic and social sustainability components separately. The definition and main characteristics of each sustainability

TABLE 14.1 Comparison of Social and Economic Sustainability	
Social Sustainability	Economic Sustainability
Definition	
Achieved by systematic community participation and strong civil society.	Achieved by maintenance of capital.
Characteristics	
Social cohesion, cultural identity, diversity, etc. constitute a part of social capital. This human capital requires maintenance and replenishment. Investments in the education, health and nutrition of individuals are now accepted as part of economic development.	Seeks the maintenance of capital. Economists prefer to value things in monetary terms, therefore valuing correctly natural capital, intangible, intergenerational, and common-access resources such as air is crucial in order to measure economic sustainability.

Source: Adapted from (Goodland & Daly, 1996)

dimension are contrasted in the summary presented in Table 14.1. There is some overlap between the two dimensions.

The concept of sustainable development has also shifted the perspective of how governments should make policies. Governments have the complex task of finding the appropriate balance between the competing demands on natural and social resources, without slowing down economic progress. Since the economic, social and environmental aspects of any actions are interconnected, they must be considered in an integral manner. It is especially important not to consider only one of these dimensions at a time to avoid errors in judgment and unsustainable outcomes. For example, the focus on profit margins only has historically led to social and environmental damages that in the long-term end up costing society. Similarly, taking care of the environment and the ability to provide social services depends a great deal on economic resources. The interconnected and interdependent nature of sustainable development also requires thinking beyond geographical and institutional borders in order to coordinate strategies and make good decisions (Strange & Bayley, 2008).

14.2 Sustainability Assessment

Sustainability assessment is often described as the process in which the implications of an initiative on sustainability are evaluated (Spangenberg, Omann, & Hinterberger, 2002). This generic definition includes a broad range of different processes.

Sustainability assessment is increasingly viewed as an important tool to aid evaluation of progress toward sustainability. However, this is a new and

---

SPOTLIGHT
Strategic Environmental Assessment (SEA) at the EPA

The Strategic Environmental Assessment is the process by which environmental considerations are required to be fully integrated into the preparation of plans and programs prior to their final adoption. The objectives of SEA are to provide for a high level of protection of the environment and to promote sustainable development.

Based on

http://www.epa.ie/monitoringassessment/assessment/sea/

---

evolving concept and there are few examples of effective sustainability assessment processes implemented so far.

Many of the existing assessment frameworks are examples of integrated assessments directly derived from the **Strategic Environmental Assessment** (SEA), the **Sustainability Impact Assessment** (SIA), and the **Environmental Impact Assessment** (EIA) frameworks that incorporate economic, environmental, and social considerations. This approach is also known as a "Triple Bottom Line" (TBL) approach to sustainability that we discussed above. These integrated assessment processes usually either try to find ways to minimize unsustainability, or attempt to achieve TBL objectives (Gasparatos et al., 2007; Jansen, 2003; Pope, Annandale, & Morrison-Saunders, 2004).

There is an ongoing debate about sustainability assessments. The major conclusions regarding sustainability assessment frameworks can be summarized as follows:

1. Sustainability assessment must assess the sustainability of an initiative in addition to assessing the final outcome.
2. Societal goals should be conceptually clear.

However, according to some scholars, the consensus about sustainability assessments is that any sound assessment should include the following (Gasparatos, El-Haram, & Horner, 2007, 2009):

- Integrate economic, environmental, social, and institutional issues as well as their interconnections.
- Consider the consequences of current actions far into the future.
- Recognize the uncertainty regarding the results of current actions.
- Engage the public.
- Incorporate intra- and inter- generational considerations.

The challenge of making sustainable development operational is the ability to evaluate and manage at a macro level the complex interrelationships among economic, social, and environmental objectives. At the United Nations Conference on Environment and Development in 1992, documents that outlined a plan and the principles to achieve sustainable development were put forward. These documents are known as the Agenda and the **Rio Declaration**. The Agenda and the Declaration had a wide range of initiatives that brought the sustainability concept closer to be an operational guide for assessing sustainability (Agenda 21, 1993; Dernbach, 1998).

In order to measure the progress toward sustainable development, it is necessary to identify operational indicators that provide manageable and accurate information on economic, environmental, and social conditions. Since the early 90s many indicators have been developed. The **Compendium of Sustainable Development Indicators** lists more than 500 sustainable indicators (Parris & Kates, 2003).

Debate—Banning Plastic Bags

Should the government ban the use of plastic bags?

Pros

- Plastic bags pollute the environment
- Plastic bags do not degrade easily
- Plastic bags are harmful to human health wildlife and marine life.
- It is not easy to recycle plastic bags

Cons

- Many items are bad for the environment; why focus on plastic bags so much?
- Banning plastic bags adds costs to businesses
- Paper bags could be worse for the environment than plastic bags
- Banning plastic bags increases the cost to consumers

14.3 Sustainable Development Indices

Böhringer and Jochem (2007) reviewed eleven sustainable development indices and studied their consistency and meaningfulness. They concluded that the indicators listed in Table 14.2 are concise and transparent, but that they do not appropriately use fundamental scientific requirements such as the technical aggregation method, the normalization of variables and their

TABLE 14.2	Sustainable Development Indices	
Acronym	Sustainable Development Indicator	Website/Source
EF	Ecological Footprint	https://www.footprintnetwork.org/our-work/ecological-footprint/
HDI	Human Development Index	http://hdr.undp.org/en/content/human-development-index-hdi
ESI	Environmental Sustainability Index	http://sedac.ciesin.columbia.edu/data/collection/esi/
EPI	Environmental Performance Index	https://epi.envirocenter.yale.edu/
EVI	Environmental Vulnerability Index	http://www.vulnerabilityindex.net/
EDP	Environmental Adjusted Domestic Product	https://unstats.un.org/unsd/environmentgl/gesform.asp?getitem=467
LPI	Living Planet Index	http://www.livingplanetindex.org/home/index

weighting, as well as the commensurability of input variables (Böhringer & Jochem, 2007).

The general conclusion is that sustainability indicators and indices can be powerful tools, but only if they are used appropriately. Even though the methods used for assessing the consistency and transparency of these indicators is relatively objective, a certain subjective **bias** is bound to exist. Composite indicators may give ambiguous and unreliable information if they are poorly constructed or misinterpreted. The lack of a clear understanding of how the indicators are developed and what information they convey is critical for policy-making decisions using such indicators. The incorrect interpretation of indexes and indicators may result in flawed policy decisions that could lead to the increase of economic disparities, promote environmental damage, and even decrease the possibilities for long-term sustainability(Golusin & Munitlak Ivanovic, 2009; Mayer, 2008; Siche, Agostinho, Ortega, & Romeiro, 2008; Singh, Murty, Gupta, & Dikshit, 2009).

Exercise. *Should indexes be used when assessing sustainable development of a country? Explain and illustrate with an example.*

14.4 Sustainable Development Goals

The **2030 Agenda for Sustainable Development**,[3] adopted by all United Nations Member States in 2015, established **17 Sustainable Development Goals** (SDGs). The common aim of these goals is to improve health and education, reduce inequality, and spur economic growth, all while tackling climate change and working to preserve our oceans and forests. Member States recognized that this is an urgent call for action and that to achieve the goals a global partnership is necessary. The Sustainable Development Goals are:

1. No Poverty.
2. Zero Hunger.
3. Good Health and Well-Being.
4. Quality Education.
5. Gender Equality.
6. Clean Water and Sanitation.
7. Affordable and Clean Energy.
8. Decent Work and Economic Growth.
9. Industry, Innovation and Infrastructure.
10. Reduced Inequality.
11. Sustainable Cities and Communities.
12. Responsible Consumption/Production.
13. Climate Action.
14. Life Below Water.
15. Life on Land.
16. Peace and Justice Strong Institutions.
17. Partnerships to Achieve the Goal.

14.5 Social Enterprise

The recognition that businesses have responsibilities beyond making profit and providing goods and services has resulted in the development of the social enterprise concept. **Social enterprises** can be defined as "organizations that address a basic unmet need or solve a social problem through a market-driven approach" (Social Enterprise Alliance, 2019).[4] Social enterprises can be both non-profit and for-profit, if the actions of the organization significantly contribute to addressing a social issue.

The **Social Enterprise Alliance** recognizes three models of social enterprises. Some social enterprises are opportunity employers; those are organizations that provide jobs for people who face significant barriers to mainstream employment. Other social enterprises contribute to social change by providing transformative products and services. Finally, donate back social enterprises donate a portion of their profits to social projects or nonprofits that address social issues. Table 14.3 highlights companies with each social enterprise model.

TABLE 14.3 Social Enterprise Examples		
Opportunity Employer	Transformative Product or Service	Donate Back
Akola Jewelry	Benetech / Kiva	Everly
Akola Jewelry is a jewelry company that provides jobs to women in Uganda who work with raw materials for jewelry, as well as women with criminal records in Dallas, TX, who assemble it and work in distribution centers.	Based in Palo Alto, Benetech develops technology that improves lives of people around the world. The company tackles problems such as education, human rights, environment, and poverty. Kiva, a non-profit organization uses a blend of technology, systems, and culture "to connect people through lending to alleviate poverty."	Everly is a contemporary clothing company that partnered with Global Hope Network International to help a village in Myanmar. Through the program, villagers are empowered to find solutions to issues in several key areas including wellness education, and family income generation.
https://akolaproject.org/	https://benetech.org/ https://www.kiva.org/	http://everlyclothing.com/

14.6 Impact Investing

The trend towards social conscientiousness has influenced investing approaches, as well as business missions and operations; the field of impact/ sustainable investing has been growing rapidly. **Impact investments** can be defined as the following: "investments made into companies, organizations, and funds with the intention to generate social and environmental alongside financial return" (Global Impact Investing Network).[5]

In a way, impact investing is an equivalent of social entrepreneurship in the world of finance (Asgary & McNulty, 2017). Just like social entrepreneurs, impact investors look for more than simply economic return. The growth of impact investing provides major opportunities for financing social projects. Various innovative ways of mobilizing funds for social issues have been developed in the field. Some examples include Social Impact Bonds (SIBs), ethical funds, and public-private partnerships.

14.7 Measuring Impact

The rise of **social entrepreneurship** affects investing and incentivizes corporate social responsibility and sustainability centered business models. In turn, this has created a need for frameworks and tools to measure the social impact of businesses (Asgary and Maccari, 2019).

The **Global Reporting Initiative** (GRI)[6] is a network-based organization that pioneered the world's most widely used sustainability reporting framework (GRI, 2014). The core goal of the Global Reporting Initiative framework is that the disclosure of a company's economic, environmental and social performance becomes a widely accepted standard practice.

The GRI provides a reporting framework that outlines the principles and performance indicators that organizations should use to measure and report their economic, environmental, and social performance. A **sustainability report** based on the GRI framework is expected to provide a relatively accurate picture of the sustainability performance of the reporting organization. In addition, the report is supposed to be somewhat balanced because it includes both the positive and the negative contributions of the organization.

The sustainability reports created based on this framework are required to disclose the outcomes and results that occur within the reporting period. Usually that reporting period is a year. Since different companies and organizations follow the same framework and the reports cover a particular period, these reports can be very useful in benchmarking and assessing the sustainability performance with respect to voluntary initiatives, performance standards, norms, codes, and laws. In addition, the organization's performance can be tracked over time as well as compared with other organizations and companies in a similar category.

One of the advantages of the GRI reporting framework is that it applies to any size company and it is independent of the location and the sector of the company. In other words, small companies can use the framework, as well as companies with geographically dispersed operations.

14.7.1 GRI Reporting Framework Dimensions

Economic Dimension. The economic dimension of the framework accounts for a company's impact on the economic systems at local, national, and global levels, as well as the impact on economic conditions of its stakeholders. Some of the economic indicators in this dimension include the flow of capital. Financial performance is crucial to understand the sustainability contribution of an organization to the larger economic system.

Environmental Dimension. The environmental sustainability of a firm is determined by the firm's impacts on the natural systems where the company operates. These include living and non-living ecosystems. Environmental indicators used in the framework are related to the performance of the inputs relative to the outputs. In addition, it includes measures that indicate the level of environmental compliance with laws and regulations of the company, as well as indictors that measure the impacts of the company's products and services on biodiversity.

Social Dimension. The indicators used to determine the company's sustainability performance in the social dimension measure aspects related to labor practices, education, product responsibility, and human rights.

To encourage the use of the GRI framework to address environmental sustainability concerns, we need to create a positive loop that connects a firm's environmental sustainability to the performance of the firm. If this positive relationship is developed, the firm will improve its performance and practice an environmentally friendly behavior at the same time. One way to develop this positive relationship is to encourage buyers to consider the environmental aspect of the firm as criteria to choose a product.

Another tool used to measure impact of organizations is the **Social Return on Investment** (SROI); it similarly considers social, economic, and environmental impact of the organization. It can also be applied to evaluate or plan individual projects of a given organization. The major challenge associated with the tool is that there is no standard way to conduct the SROI analysis and there is no single organization that is responsible for conducting it. The approach, however, is growing in popularity, which illustrates the need for its continuous improvement.

14.8 Conclusion

Increasingly small, medium, large and multinational are interested in incorporating sustainable practices into their value chain and business model. While this trend may mean that the maximization of profit is not the main goal, businesses are comfortable investing in practices that in the long run will have a positive impact on the environment and society at large. A main driver of this behavior are the Millennials and Generation Z who according to research are generations more concerned about the negative impact a business may have on the environment. Subsequently, multinationals are incorporating sustainable growth and social issues in their strategies.

TBL Connection
The Millennial Marketplace and
Propagating the Triple Bottom Line

Millennials now represent the world's most important consumer category. It is forecasted that about 70% of millennials are willing to spend more on brands that embrace sustainability, social responsibility, or a cause they care about.

A bottom line that focuses on more than just profit allows a company to make smart long-term decisions rather than dedicate every resource to increasing a number. Because of this, the triple bottom line can provide businesses with a certain amount of sustainability. As more businesses choose to pursue goals beyond maximizing profit, the Benefit Corporation, or "B Corp," has arisen to standardize the process of incorporating a triple bottom line and tracking social and environmental impact. Becoming a certified B Corp involves assessments, the completion of a disclosure questionnaire and background checks, as well as the possibility of an annual site review to confirm the accuracy of certain responses.

B Lab is a nonprofit that certifies potential B Corps after ensuring they meet the standards. Since B Lab was formed in 2006, more than 2,000 businesses, including clothing giant Patagonia, have been B Corp certified.

While millennials and Generation Z seem to be spearheading the movement, the triple bottom line is more than just a generational fad. Acknowledging that there's more to business than profit allows a company to accept social and environmental responsibility for its actions and puts it on track to creating a more sustainable future for everyone. For more information, visit https://bcorporation.net/about-b-lab.

Based on

https://www.forbes.com/sites/deeppatel/2017/07/28/the-millennial
-marketplace-and-the-propagation-of-the-triple-bottom-line/
#1580d098d04a

1. *If a business is turning a healthy profit, provide examples of ways the business can consider incorporating a TBL. Illustrate with examples.*

2. *What is the process of becoming a B Corp certified company?*

Chapter Review

Key Terms

- Eco-Development
- Brundtland Report
- Sustainable Development
- Sustainability Assessment
- Sustainability Indices
- Social Enterprise
- Impact Investment
- Global Reporting Initiative

Questions & Assignments

Questions

1. Analyze social enterprise effectiveness. Explain and illustrate with an example.
2. Briefly describe the concept of economic sustainability. What challenges and opportunities are created for MNEs by the growing trend of supporting economic sustainability?

Assignments

1. Work with a partner and develop an idea for a social enterprise. Which model does your social enterprise follow? Is it a for-profit or a non-profit? Pitch your idea to the class.
2. Suppose a consumer product corporation works with a credit card company to allow 5% of the price of its products, if charged by the credit card, to go to a non-profit foundation that helps low income families in the region where purchases were made. Analyze the impact of such a policy on all stakeholders.

Notes

1. IUCN. (1980). World Conservation Strategy: Living Resource Conservation for Sustainable Development. Retrieved from https://portals.iucn.org/library/efiles/html/WCS-004/cover.html
2. UNEP. (1992). Rio Declaration–Rio Declaration on Environment and Development–United Nations Environment Programme (UNEP).
3. https://sustainabledevelopment.un.org/post2015/transformingourworld
4. https://socialenterprise.us/
5. https://www.globalreporting.org/Pages/default.aspx
6. GRI–https://www.globalreporting.org/Pages/default.aspx

Suggested Reading

GRI Standards. Downloadable versions are available with registration. Registration is free
   https://www.globalreporting.org/standards/gri-standards-download-center
UN Sustainable Development Goals
   https://www.un.org/sustainabledevelopment/sustainable-development
   -goals/
The Coca Cola Company Sustainability Report 2017/2018
   https://www.coca-colacompany.com/content/dam/journey/us/en/private/
   fileassets/pdf/2018/2017-Sustainability-Report-The-Coca-Cola-Company.pdf
Sachs, J. (2015). *The age of sustainable development*. New York, NY: Columbia University Press.
Yunus, M., & Jolis, A. (1998). *Banker to the poor: The autobiography of Muhammad Yunus, founder of the Grameen Bank*. London, England: Aurum Press.
https://socialenterprise.us/about/social-enterprise/
https://thegiin.org/impact-investing/

References

Asgary Nader and Maccari Emerson (2019). Entrepreneurship and Innovation: Opportunities and Challenges, Routledge.

Agenda 21, E. (1993). *The United Nations Programme of Action from Rio de Janeiro*. New York, NY: UN Department of Public Information.

Asgary, N. H., & McNulty, R. E. (2017). Contributions and challenges in the struggle to end poverty: the case of Kiva. *Information Technology for Development, 23*(2), 367–387.

Böhringer, C., & Jochem, P. E. P. (2007). Measuring the immeasurable—A survey of sustainability indices. *Ecological Economics, 63*(1), 1–8. doi:10.1016/j.ecolecon.2007.03.008

Brundtland, G. (1987). Our common future: Report of the 1987 World Commission on Environment and Development: Oxford: Oxford University Press.

Daly, H. (1997). *Beyond growth: the economics of sustainable development.* Beacon Pr.

Dernbach, J. (1998). Sustainable Development as a Framework for National Governance. *Case Western Reserve Law Review, 49*(1), 1.

Gasparatos, A., El-Haram, M., & Horner, M. (2007). A critical review of reductionist approaches for assessing the progress towards sustainability. *Environmental Impact Assessment Review, 28*(4–5), 286–311. doi:10.1016/j.eiar.2007.09.002

Gasparatos, A., El-Haram, M., & Horner, M. (2009). The argument against a reductionist approach for measuring sustainable development performance and the need for methodological pluralism. *Accounting Forum, 33*(3), 245–256. doi:10.1016/j.accfor.2008.07.006

Golusin, M., & Munitlak Ivanovic, O. (2009). Definition, characteristics and state of the indicators of sustainable development in countries of Southeastern Europe. *Agriculture, Ecosystems & Environment, 130*(1–2), 67–74. doi:10.1016/j.agee.2008.11.018

Goodland, R., & Daly, H. (1996). Environmental Sustainability: Universal and Non-Negotiable. *Ecological Applications, 6*(4), 1002–1017.

Jansen, L. (2003). The challenge of sustainable development. *Journal of Cleaner Production, 11*(3), 231–245.

Mayer, A. L. (2008). Strengths and weaknesses of common sustainability indices for multidimensional systems. *Environment International, 34*(2), 277–291. doi:10.1016/j.envint.2007.09.004

Meadows, D. H., Meadows, D. L., Randers, J., & Behrens Iii, W. W. (1972). *The Limits to Growth: A Report for the Club of Rome's Project on the Predicament of Mankind.* New York, NY: Universe Books.

Meadows, D. H., Randers, J., & Meadows, D. L. (2004). *The limits to growth: the 30-year update.* Chelsea Green.

Moran, D. D., Wackernagel, M., Kitzes, J. A., Goldfinger, S. H., & Boutaud, A. (2008). Measuring sustainable development—Nation by nation. *Ecological Economics, 64*(3), 470–474. doi:10.1016/j.ecolecon.2007.08.017

Parris, T. M., & Kates, R. W. (2003). Characterizing and Measuring Sustainable Development. *Annual Review of Environment and Resources, 28,* 559–586.

Pope, J., Annandale, D., & Morrison-Saunders, A. (2004). Conceptualising sustainability assessment. *Environmental Impact Assessment Review, 24*(6), 595–616.

Redclift, M. (1987). *Sustainable development: Exploring the contradictions:* Routledge.

Sachs, J. (2006). *The end of poverty: Economic possibilities for our time.* New York, NY: Penguin Press.

Siche, J. R., Agostinho, F., Ortega, E., & Romeiro, A. (2008). Sustainability of nations by indices: Comparative study between environmental sustainability index, ecological footprint and the emergy performance indices. *Ecological Economics, 66*(4), 628–637. doi:10.1016/j.ecolecon.2007.10.023

Singh, R. K., Murty, H. R., Gupta, S. K., & Dikshit, A. K. (2009). An overview of sustainability assessment methodologies. *Ecological Indicators, 9*(2), 189–212. doi:10.1016/j.ecolind.2008.05.011

Spangenberg, J. H., Omann, I., & Hinterberger, F. (2002). Sustainable growth criteria Minimum benchmarks and scenarios for employment and the environment. *Ecological Economics, 42*(3), 429–443.

Stiglitz, J. E. (2006). *Making globalization work.* New York, NY: WW Norton & Company.

Strange, T., & Bayley, A. (2008). *Sustainable development: linking economy, society, environment OECD Insights*

Trzyna, T. (1995). *A sustainable world: defining and measuring sustainable development:* International Center for the Environment and Public Policy for the World Conservation Union (IUCN).

About the Authors

Nader H. Asgary, PhD
Professor of Management and Economics at Bentley University, Waltham MA

Professional Background: Professor of Management and Economics at Bentley University and founder and President of the CYRUS Institute of Knowledge (CIK). He also served as the Associate Provost for International Relations at Bentley, where he significantly expanded global reach of the university. He has led several successful entrepreneurship and leadership-based development projects in Nicaragua, Brazil, Iran, the United States, and etc. His extensive publication record coupled with his ample teaching and practical experiences in both public and private sectors enriches this textbook.

Dr. Asgary has published in numerous national and international journals, such as *Economic Inquiry, Journal of Business Ethics, Tourism Economics, Middle East Journal of Management,* and *Journal of Higher Education Policy and*

Global Business, pages 303–306
Copyright © 2019 by Information Age Publishing

Management and has participated in many international and national conference presentations and has been a guest speaker. He has taught courses in international business, global leadership, economics, and finance at the undergraduate and graduate levels and has been PhD students' advisor and the recipient of many educator awards.

CIK is a think-tank that focuses on research in business development, sustainability, and economic development. Some of CIK's (http://cyrusik .org/) activities include annual international conferences, executive training, and research/consulting services. As the president of CIK, he has created an intellectual and networking environment for scholars, practitioners, philanthropists to share their ideas and contribute to the advance of knowledge and make a difference.

Dina Frutos-Bencze, PhD
Associate Professor of International Business at Saint Anselm College in Manchester, NH.

Professional Background: Dr. Frutos-Bencze has corporate professional experience as Human Resources Manager and Training and Development Manager in Europe and the United States. In addition, Dr. Frutos-Bencze was the Associate Dean of Online Business Programs at Southern New Hampshire University-COCE, in Manchester, NH.

Dr. Frutos-Bencze has published several peer reviewed articles and chapters in journals such as *Critical Perspectives on International Business,* the *International Trade Journal,* and the *International Journal of Business and Emerging Markets.* Her most recent research has been about internationalization of family business groups, and monetary policy impact on renewable energy production in Latin America.

Dr. Frutos-Bencze is fluent in English, Spanish and Czech. Dr. Frutos-Bencze received her MS in Chemistry at the University of New Mexico, MBA at Oxford Brookes, UK, and her PhD in International Business at Southern New Hampshire University.

Massood V. Samii, PhD
Professor of International Business and the Director of the Institute
for International Business at Southern New Hampshire University,
Manchester, NH

Professional Background: Previously he was the chair of the department, director of PhD program, and interim dean of School of Business. He was also
senior lecturer on Construction finance at MIT's Department of Civil and Environmental Engineering from 1992 to 2007. Formerly, he was with the Ken-
nedy School of Government at Harvard University, where he did research on
global energy and oil markets. He served OPEC Secretariat in Vienna Austria
between 1979 and 1987 as a senior economist and the head of the finance
section. During his tenure at OPEC, he was involved in a numerous projects
including OPEC Long Term Strategy, and Oil Pricing Strategy.

Dr. Samii has directed numerous projects for the U.S. Department of
Education. In 2004, he was recognized by the Governor of State of New
Hampshire and the New Hampshire International Trade Association (NHI-
TA) for outstanding contribution to the State's International Business and
Trade. He was a member of the Advisory Board of Governor Office of Inter-
national Commerce (OIC) and of the Texas A & M International University
PhD program. In addition, he has done numerous executive training and
consulting internationally. He was on editorial board of *Journal of Emerging
Markets,* and *International Trade Journal.*

Dr. Samii has lectured and published widely on issues of energy, economic
development, risk analysis, and international business. His articles have ap-
peared in the journals of *Energy Policy, Energy and Development, OPEC Review,
Petroleum Management,* the *International Trade Journal,* and *Thunderbird International Business.* He was an official observer representative to the IMF Interim
Committee, World Bank Development Committee, and UNCTAD Trade and
Development Committee. His book titled *International Business and Information Technology* was published by Routledge. His area of research includes Risk
Analysis and Management for Foreign Direct Investment, International Busi-
ness Strategy, Dynamic Strategy, and International Oil Market.

Hossein Varamini, PhD
Turnbull-Jamieson Chair and Professor of Finance and International Business at Elizabethtown College.

Professional Background: Dr. Varamini joined Elizabethtown College in the fall of 2000 as the Director of the International Business Program after holding a similar position at a different institution for over ten years. His primary teaching areas are corporate finance, international financial management and international business. He has published numerous articles in peer-reviewed academic journals such as the *Journal of Economics, Journal of Finance Issues, American Journal of Business, Journal of East-West Business, Journal of Global Business* and *Journal of International Business and Economy.*

Dr. Varamini is a member of the Academy of International Business and has served as a reviewer for several academic journals. He has received numerous awards for excellence in teaching and scholarly achievements. He has presented his scholarly work extensively at national and international conferences.

CPSIA information can be obtained
at www.ICGtesting.com
Printed in the USA
BVHW041826130820
R11072700001B/R110727PG585986BVX6B/1